POWER, PROTECTION AND MAGIC IN THAILAND

THE COSMOS OF A SOUTHERN POLICEMAN

POWER, PROTECTION AND MAGIC IN THAILAND

THE COSMOS OF A SOUTHERN POLICEMAN

CRAIG J. REYNOLDS

PRESS

ASIAN STUDIES SERIES MONOGRAPH 12

For Chris Baker and Pasuk Phongpaichit
In memory of Pinyo Srichumlong (1934–2009)

Published by ANU Press
The Australian National University
Acton ACT 2601, Australia
Email: anupress@anu.edu.au

Available to download for free at press.anu.edu.au

ISBN (print): 9781760463168
ISBN (online): 9781760463175

WorldCat (print): 1123205971
WorldCat (online): 1123205860

DOI: 10.22459/PPMT.2019

Cover design and layout by ANU Press
Cover photograph: Khun Phan at age 102, by Chanthip Phantarakrajchadech

Contents

Plates

Transcription of Thai

The transcription of Thai follows the system prescribed by the Royal Institute of Thailand with the following exceptions:

j (*jo jan*) instead of *ch*.

Wat Khao Or instead of Wat Khao O.

Khun Phan's descendants spell the family name as Phantarakrajchadech (Phantharakratchadet).

Jatukham-Ramathep, the transcription used here, is the way most central Thai speakers pronounce the name. Southern Thai speakers who are less influenced by central Thai culture often drop a vowel in the second term: Jatukham-Ramthep.

Glossary

jon	outlaw, bandit; from Pali *jora*
kloe	friend, mate, buddy, usually of same sex; cohort of people formed in early years welcomed into families as kin; *kloe* groups can be 20–30 individuals; *kloe* is originally from the southern dialect but is common in central Thai
kok	group, faction, party; gang in the context of banditry and criminality; from Chinese *kuo*
metthamahaniyom	attraction/repulsion, the magnetic forces, for example, of an amulet after it has been consecrated; personal quality useful to investors, gangsters and political leaders at all levels
mongkhon	auspiciousness, often based on prognostications determined by a horoscope; from Pali *maṅgala*
monthon	provincial circle; groups of provinces created between 1893 and 1899
nak leng	tough guy of generous spirit and dignified bearing, especially but not exclusively in rural areas; local political leader with these characteristics; gambler (nineteenth century)
paritta	Buddhist recitations from Pali texts that keep a person safe from evil spells, betrayal, fire, poison and weapons (knives, guns)
phra	curved knife or machete used in cultivation or for clearing jungle; a weapon favoured by rural outlaws before firearms became widely available

pokkhrong	to rule, govern; from *pok* shield; possibly from Khmer *prok*; *khrong* to cloak or cover, sometimes to possess
prathetsarat	autonomous kingdom or state, sometimes translated as dependency, dominion, colony
saiyasat	magical knowledge of putatively Brahmanic origin, sometimes referred to as magical animism or esoteric Buddhism; formulas (*dhāraṇī* and *mantra*) associated with this knowledge
saksi	dignity, dignified bearing, especially as applied to *nak leng*
śastra	see *sat*
sat	a corpus of knowledge, body of learning, a science, suffix designating an academic or scientific field— for example, economics, geology, geography, history, medicine and so on; from Sanskrit *śastra*
sen	string, line, route; classifier for noodle; a connection with an important or influential person in high places (*mi sen*)
suea	tiger; epithet for outlaw, bandit, *nak leng*
Tai	term for language family and ethnic groups, including Thai
takrut	small cylinder containing a thin rolled sheet of tin or other pliable material inscribed with magical symbols (*yantra*), worn around the neck, from the waist or inserted under the skin
weikza	magician, wizard or sorcerer (Burmese); from Pali *vijja* ('possessed of wisdom'), cf. Thai *wicha*

Acknowledgements

I have dedicated this book to three people. Chris Baker and Pasuk Phongpaichit, friends for many decades, have made huge contributions to Thailand's cultural and political life through their research projects, books and journal articles, newspaper columns, op-ed pieces in the international press and public presentations. Chris, a Cambridge-trained historian who enjoyed a reputation as a specialist on Tamil India before he moved to Thailand and Thai studies, and Pasuk, a political economist who ventures forth fearlessly where few dare to tread, share their expertise and ideas with each other on everything from the black economy to literature and history. Their prize-winning English translation and exegesis of *Khun Chang Khun Phaen*, a folk epic that may be likened to the Japanese *Tale of Genji* and the Vietnamese *Tale of Kieu*, is a monumental work of scholarship. For years to come, scholars will be reading their translation and making their way happily through the forest of footnotes to learn of Siam's past and how the Thai elite codified the folk epic, preserving some themes but suppressing the parts for which it did not care. I salute Chris Baker and Pasuk Phongpaichit.

The other dedicatee, Pinyo Srichamlong (1934–2009), was a dear friend I met years ago in Krabi. We were both outsiders. I was an American Peace Corps volunteer assigned to the local boys' school as an English teacher; he had been exiled to the then remote province by the Ministry of Education for reasons I never understood. A native of Nakhon Si Thammarat and a proud graduate of Suan Kulap School, where he came second in his class, Pinyo was an author of short stories and novels and a poet of uncommon talent from an early age, who won competitions on Thai TV for his improvised verse (*klon sot*). He described himself truthfully as a 'champ', and a tribute at his passing called him a *nak leng* of the genre. He was steeped in the Thai literary canon and, on his visits to my bungalow behind the school, would regale me with tales of Siamese kings of yore and their literary accomplishments. He spoke often of his poet-hero Sunthorn Phu. I imagined that Pinyo had been transported by a time machine from an earlier century where he composed poems in the court of a Siamese prince. He was what the Australian language calls a larrikin, a maverick with little regard for convention. I would arrive at school on Monday mornings to hear the teachers' disapproving reports of Pinyo's embarrassing exploits in the market over the weekend.

Pinyo's historical novel, written when he was a young man, dramatised the life of Khun Phrai, a courtier in the early seventeenth century who was born into a modest family and worked his way up to minor noble rank in the palace only to be cheated and abused. He fled to take up the outlaw life. To community acclaim, he freed people held in bondage, joined a gang of pirates and returned to civilisation to successfully defeat his enemies. When challenged to defend the veracity of his seventeenth-century account, the novelist demurred and quoted Napoleon: 'What is history, but a fable agreed upon?' (Pinyo 1994: 7–10; Phanida 1997: 111). Pinyo was witty and lots of fun, but his own life was no romance. He had problems with money, was always in trouble with his bosses and his larrikin behaviour deprived him of the literary awards he expected and deserved. His daughter, Sriyapha Srichumlong, has been a loving custodian of his legacy.

This project is the most collaborative I have ever undertaken, and I have many people to thank for their help. Nasan and Chanthip Phantarakrajchadech took time to talk about their father and shared not only information about his life, but also an understanding of the world in which he lived. Samphan Kongsamut, Khun Phan's most prolific biographer, also spent many hours telling me about his interviews with the southern policeman.

Patrick Jory, Kasem Jandam, Jirawat Saengthong, Suwit Maprasong and Wannasan Noonsuk introduced me to the mid south and its society that they know so well. It would take many pages to explain what 'Sem, a poet and international scholar of birds' nests, has taught me about the region where he was born. Davisakd Puaksom, also from the mid south, took me on an unforgettable journey with his students through northern provinces, where we visited monasteries and the Nam Phi iron mine. In Uttaradit, where the southern policeman acquired his Red Sword, we planned to visit a spirit medium at Mueang Laplae who channels the eighteenth-century warrior Phraya Phichai, but we just missed her. She had departed to conduct a séance near the Bangkok airport.

Nick Cheesman, Patrick Jory, Maurizio Peleggi, Peter Zinoman, Jim Ockey, Ronit Ricci, Maria Myutel and David Chandler read drafts of chapters and enthusiastically shared their reactions. Over the years, I have had productive conversations about the project with Davisakd Puaksom, Chalong Soontravanich, Thongchai Likhitphonsawan, Charnvit Kasetsiri, Sujit Wongthes, Varunee Otsatharom, Villa Vilaithong, Suphot Jaengraew, Atthachak Satayanurak, Saichol Satayanurak, Paritta Chalermpow-Koanantakool, Roger Hillman, Samson Lim, Thak Chaloemtiarana, Chatthip Nartsupha, Jakkrit Sangkhamanee, Tamthai Dilokvidyarat and Poonnatree Jiaviriyaboonya. In the course of my research, colleagues suggested what I should read and gave me books, journal articles and newspaper clippings to make sure I read the material. Lindsay Falvey sent me, out of the blue, a book about bullfighting in the mid south.

Conversations with these colleagues and friends often brought to the surface ideas and connections I had not thought of, and I shamelessly picked these up and made them my own in what I was writing. Some people simply asked sharp questions, forcing me to consider something I had ignored. Even now, I can remember scraps of conversation that gave me insights into the southern policeman's world. Archaeologists at Sujit's Ruen Inn dinner table suggested that I should read Mana Khunweechuay's remarkable environmental and political study that set me on the right path. Simon Creak once expressed in a concise sentence what I was trying to say in the whole book. I must acknowledge the last communication I had with the late Benedict Anderson: a lengthy, good-natured and typically provocative challenge to my ideas that has never left my mind since I received it in 2011. Among the many people who saw value in the project and offered encouragement were Sulak Sivaraksa, Tej Bunnag, Ronit Ricci, Chris Baker, Pasuk Phongpaichit, Tyrell Haberkorn and the late Ian Proudfoot. Suzanne Davey and Ahmad Farshid provided invaluable assistance that made it possible to go forward at a critical time. Warm thanks to all the Gazys for good fellowship in their busy home.

My colleague at The Australian National University, Chintana Sandlands, who was born into a police family in Nakhon Si Thammarat, answered endless questions and in so doing passed on her insights into what made Khun Phan an effective policeman. I could not have completed the book in its present form without convenient access to the National Library of Australia in Canberra and its magnificent Thai-language holdings. The former head of the Thai section, Saowapha Viravong, and her successor, Chenwilai (Jane) Hodgins, as well as Vacharin McFadden and Suthida

Whyte helped in inestimable ways. In 2012, I benefited from a Harold White Fellowship at the National Library of Australia that allowed me privileged access to the Thai collection and the expertise of library staff.

Early in the project, Sue Rider suggested I could embed audio-video clips in the book as an auxiliary medium to tell the southern policeman's story, and Nicholas Farrelly, who was enthusiastic about this idea from the outset, was instrumental in bringing it to fruition. In late 2017, I spent two days in Nakhon Si Thammarat with Khun Tanavit and his HD Team Production crew filming monasteries, monuments, statues, parks, the Songkhla lakes, the Khrua Thale restaurant and the surrounding countryside. Kasem Jandam and Piyachat Suongtee, who accompanied us, were able to open doors with their native proficiency in the southern Thai dialect and, in one place where we were filming, were able to get us out of a sticky situation. I thank Alex Nichols in the College of Asia and the Pacific marketing unit for her cooperation and Peter Mahon for studio filming. Oliver Friedmann devoted many hours to crafting the audio-video clips that accompany each chapter. He worked through a busy schedule in difficult circumstances, and I appreciate his energetic and expert contribution to the publication.

Financial support for field research came initially from an Australian Research Council Discovery Grant with Andrew Walker (2008–10), and later from the School of Culture, History and Language, College of Asia and the Pacific, at The Australian National University. Karina Pelling in CartoGIS Services at the college designed the maps, and Jan Borrie copyedited the typescript. Three reviewers of the final draft made comments that helped me improve it, and Jim Fox and Emily Hazlewood with her team at ANU Press guided the book to publication.

'He doesn't argue, he tells'—a statement once made by an art critic about painting—was a dictum I took to heart while formulating my ideas and expressing them in words. The statement is quite contrary to the instructions supervisors in the humanities and social sciences give to their thesis students, who are urged to present an argument. As Sue Rider, my spouse, knows all too well, this project has taken a long time to complete. A lover of live radio, podcasts and interviews with academics who can speak to a wider audience, she has urged me to write in a way that is accessible to non-specialists and to put myself into the policeman's story wherever it seemed appropriate. I have tried to heed her advice and abjure scholasticism. Our sons, Simon and Oliver, will finally be able to find out why the southern Thai policeman was so important to their father.

Map 1 Thailand

Source: ANU CartoGIS.

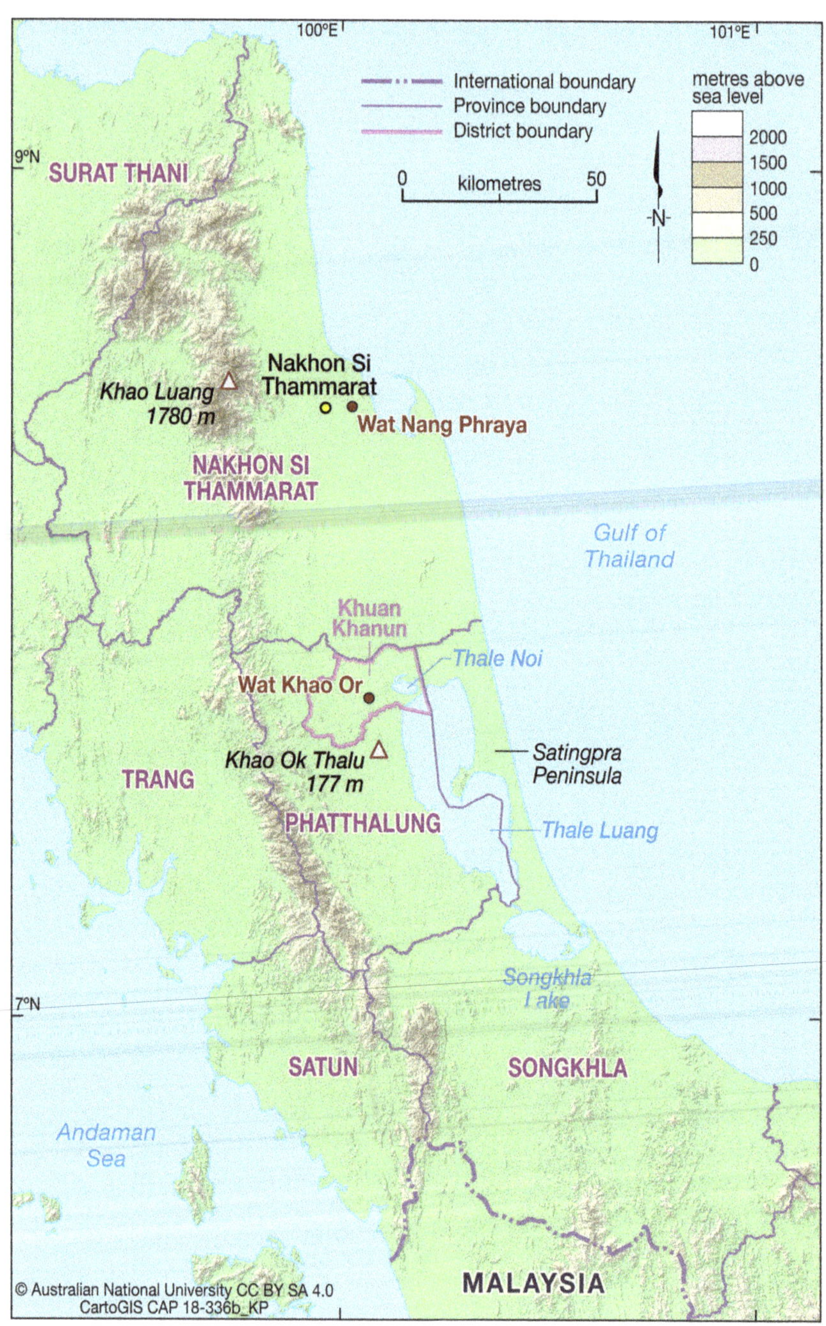

Map 2 Thailand's mid south

Source: ANU CartoGIS.

Map 3 Thailand's mid south from Crawford 1967 [1828], courtesy of Christopher Joll

Source: ANU CartoGIS.

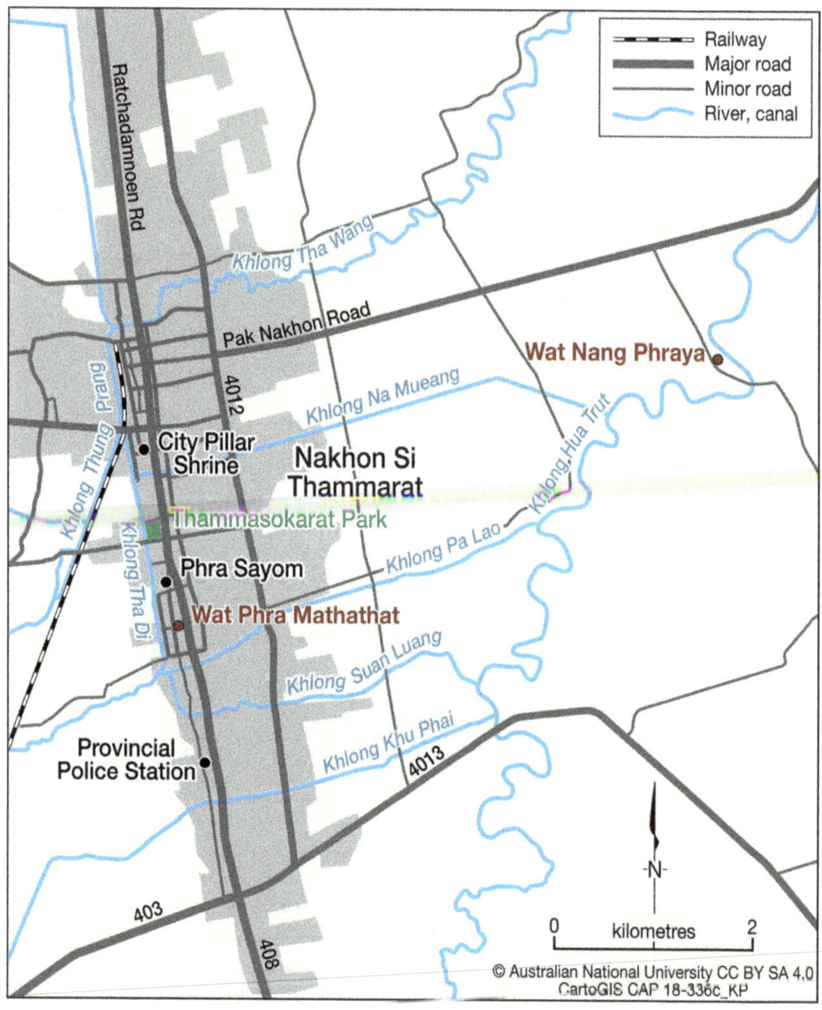

Map 4 Nakhon Si Thammarat town
Source: ANU CartoGIS.

1

Introduction

Video content for this chapter is available online:
press.anu.edu.au/publications/series/asian-studies/
power-protection-and-magic-thailand#media

Thai friends, knowing of my longstanding interest in Buddhism and offbeat topics, told me in 2007 of an amulet, originally produced in southern Thailand, which had been causing excitement in the markets and the media. Discussions about the object brought wry smiles because of the large sums people were willing to spend on it. Academics were holding forth at public seminars and on television, offering their opinions about the amulet's iconography and debating the significance of its inflated value. The boom–bubble–bust phenomenon sounded like a cargo cult, Thai-style.

Associated with the amulet's origins was a policeman from peninsular Thailand. In his heyday, when many parts of the country were still remote and undeveloped, he was known to have used rather too much lethal force in going about his business. When I first heard about the policeman, I was looking for a change of direction in my work—a research project that would reward me for effort expended to understand its complexities. The southern policeman's story intrigued me, and I wondered where I could begin to find out more about him.

Villa Vilaithong, who was a research student at the time, thought I should read *The Khao Or Masters of the Science of Struggle and Buddhist Incantations: The Shaolin of Phatthalung*, which had just been published and related the history of a cave monastery sunk into a limestone hill that rises from the plains in Thailand's mid south (Ran 2007). In residence at the monastery over many decades were senior teachers who cultivated the dark arts—what the Thai language calls *saiyasat*: arcane knowledge and practices useful to warriors and fighters of all persuasions, on both sides of the law. For the Thai expeditionary troops sent to fight in Vietnam in the late 1960s, *saiyasat* was defensive magic they considered necessary for their survival (Ruth 2012: 131–3). The Khao Or monastery had been Buddhist for a long time, but its history was replete with Brahmanic teachings and practices outside the ken of normative Buddhist activities. The campy reference in the book's title to the Shaolin monastery in China's Henan Province alluded to monks skilled in martial arts and meditation. Upon visiting the monastery later, I concluded that the idea of warrior monks was more of a marketing gimmick to promote the book than an accurate descriptor of the custodians of secret knowledge.

Deadly force as well as the rituals and knowledge to conjure it, possess it and use it effectively were themes that stood out as I turned the pages of *The Khao Or Masters* about the cave monastery and its monks. The central figure in the story is Butr Phantharak (1898–2006), the policeman from the mid south who retired in 1964 as a major general in the national police force.

At the beginning of his career, Butr Phantharak had submitted himself to rituals in the cave monastery to toughen himself physically and spiritually, and he became a lifelong exponent of the knowledge handed down to him by the monastery's master teachers. The last Thai absolute monarch ennobled him with the rank of *khun* and, by the end of his life, he had become known popularly as Khun Phan.

I decided to find out more about the legendary policeman, banditry in the mid south and magical thinking, so I travelled to Nakhon Si Thammarat, where a former student, Patrick Jory, had been teaching at a local university. Patrick had plenty of local lore to share about the policeman's deadly methods. He also told me about an amulet known as the Jatukham-Ramathep, a fount of auspiciousness that poured forth good fortune and wealth. It had been struck in Nakhon in the 1980s, and the policeman had presided at some of the key ceremonies. The amulet was named after two deities guarding the inner chamber of the Great Relic stupa at Wat Mahathat in Nakhon.

Plate 1 Dutr Phantharak as a young constable
Source: Chintapati (2007: 1).

One day I was driven past a museum of the policeman's artefacts that turned out to be the home of one of his relatives. Seeing the householder standing outside enjoying a Thai sweet, I walked up with a friend for an introduction; the householder invited us inside, where I found myself standing next to a small bronze statue of the policeman. I had to ask if it was lifesize, because he was not a very imposing figure. I was to learn later that his modest height and a life-threatening childhood illness played their part as he equipped himself with the grit and guile that made him such a feared law enforcement officer.

By the end of the week, I was interviewing one of the policeman's sons, Nasan, a retired bank manager, and after a trip to the cave monastery in the neighbouring province of Phatthalung, I began to collect materials and reacquaint myself with the history of the mid south where I once lived. The prospect of an extended study at first seemed dim. By the time I fell upon the topic, the policeman had already passed away and few of his peers in the police force were still alive. Outlaw adversaries survived him, and several notable ones had been ordained as monks, but I was unable to meet them. I presumed from the outset that the police archives would be closed to an academic researcher, let alone a foreign one, but biographical material was plentiful thanks to the tenacity of the southern-born writer and publisher Samphan Kongsamut, whose biographies of the policeman have gone through several editions. The policeman loved to boast about his exploits and Samphan's interviews with Khun Phan yielded detailed stories about his crime suppression in the provincial police force. Samphan was not the only southerner to write about Khun Phan. Southern writers, teachers and academics also had much to say about the mid south's environmental history, political economy and ancient heritage. My visit to the mid south took place only a year after the policeman's death, and authors were scrambling to publish their accounts of his life and the story of the amulet. Thai books of regional interest have limited print runs; once they sold out, they would disappear from the market. Their availability in the bookstores as I began my research was a bonanza for me.

The way I was coming to understand the policeman's world was haphazard, guided less by research planning than by instinct and the growing conviction that the instantiations of religion and power in the mid south—so central to the policeman's world—held significance beyond the region. The topic became increasingly compelling as I began to see connections between the policeman's life and arcane religious practices, national and local history and protection of the sovereign body. The elements to create the necessary *frisson* that would sustain my curiosity were coming together, and questions about the policeman and his world gradually coalesced around three lines of inquiry that underlie the discussion in the following chapters. In the most general terms, these are magical thinking and risk, history writing and the mid south and policing and the sovereign body.

Magical thinking and risk

The first line of inquiry that occurred to me after I read the absorbing account in *The Khao Or Masters of the Science of Struggle and Buddhist Incantations* has to do with how Butr Phantharak handled the risks inherent in his line of work and how he coped with fear and uncertainty. His beliefs and practices, which I loosely refer to as the dark arts favoured by warriors and fighters, were aimed at protecting himself from danger. This magical thinking is encoded in applied sciences of prognostication and protection that offer guidance on timing and shape everyday decision-making in Thailand, not only for police, but also for soldiers, criminals, businesspeople, politicians, agriculturalists, university students and householders. The policeman could protect the realm only if he could protect himself; to that end, he became a specialist in this knowledge, which he began to acquire when he was an adolescent. Equipped with this knowledge, he behaved at times like a folk Brahman, a shaman. The applied sciences of prognostication and protection are not unique to the Thai world but exist in variant forms elsewhere in Southeast Asia. Ancestor worship, healing rituals, homage paid by villagers to mountain spirits, astrology and rituals that promise to make the body invulnerable are common in the region's cultural landscapes and date from prehistoric times. Transcultural religions such as Buddhism, Islam and Christianity took root and thrived in these landscapes (Ileto 1999: 194).

Khun Phan was an agent of the emerging nation-state and—with other novice policemen recruited to the force—its armour of coercion as it expanded from the central plains and pushed into principalities and petit kingdoms in the countryside, replacing local lords and chiefs with appointed officials. In the early 1930s, at the beginning of his career, Khun Phan lost no time in visiting the cave monastery in Phatthalung to partake of its special knowledge. More than once in his lifetime he was renewed with a ritual bath to fortify himself spiritually, mentally and physically. He aimed to attain a degree of invulnerability. He would become 'a man with a tough hide' (*khon tai nang niew*), as the Thai saying goes, impervious to blades and bullets. For him, these beliefs and practices were a resource, a mother lode of potentialities on which he could draw to keep himself safe in life-threatening situations as he went about his duties. In rituals conducted by these same master teachers and their disciples, some of Khun Phan's outlaw adversaries had also been initiated into the dark arts. Warriors need protection and arming themselves with invulnerability techniques is as important as carrying a gun or wielding a knife. Given the lethal measures he employed to apprehend outlaws and criminals, the policeman needed invulnerability to protect his body just as he would rely on his police badge to warrant his actions as an agent of the state. He did not act with impunity (Haberkorn 2018: 4–5). Police procedures and directives made him accountable for his actions and he was disciplined more than once for exceeding his orders. His authority was provisional, subject to community, political and institutional constraints. The search for invulnerability to protect his body and his dedication to protect the sovereign body converged in his character throughout his police career.

Butr Phantharak, who later became Police Major General Khun Phantarakratchadet, was credited with 62 'kills' by gunshot either by his own hand or at the hands of police under his command (Wira 2001: 185–7). Some of the details in the accounts of these events are grisly and not for the faint-hearted. Tattooed on the knuckles of his hand were the consonants of the Thai word for executioner (*phetchanakhat*): if he fired a bullet at an outlaw, death was certain; if he threw a punch and it landed on his opponent, that person would be driven insane.[1] Whether grasping a pistol or fighting bare-fisted, his hands were offensive weapons, and he killed his first adversary by squeezing the life out of the man. Magic was another weapon at his disposal. As his career progressed, he became adept in the knowledge imparted to him at the cave monastery by the master teachers who were wizards by another name. An age-old relationship connected the policeman's willingness to take a human life and his knowledge of magical objects and powers. Marcel Mauss pointed out that, in many societies, executioners use spells and charms to capture thieves and catch demons. Magicians are executioners; executioners are

---

1   Nasan Phantarakrajchadech, Interview with the author, Nakhon Si Thammarat, 27 September 2009.

magicians (Mauss 2010: 37). By the same token, their social roles are interchangeable. In Melanesia, the chief of the clan possesses spiritual force (*mana*), and by means of this interchangeability, magicians can exercise political authority. The policeman was known in his hometown and the surrounding districts for his knowledge of the magical arts as much as for his lethal methods in catching criminals.

Policemen and the rural masculine types with whom they associated in the first half of the twentieth century were risk-takers. Encounters between desperate men fighting for their lives could lead to injury and death. The scars on Khun Phan's body were traces of the violent skirmishes in his past when he played with danger in the pursuit of thieves, kidnappers and outlaws. His willingness, even eagerness, to place himself in physical danger hints at something deeper than dedication to his job. Risk has its own charm and carries a valence of desire; the word charm in English derives from the Latin *carmen*, meaning incantation, and indicates attraction (Svendsen 2008: 73). Risk and fear can excite erotic desire.

Policemen—and for that matter the bandits they pursued—can be foolhardy by inviting themselves closer to the action for the thrill of it. They need to hedge against risk, and they do this by anticipating what may lie ahead. By means of ritual and semiotic wizardry, human action can be coordinated with the dynamics of an external order: the movements of the planets, the hidden forces of nature, the metaphysical laws of the universe and the powers latent in the conjunction of time and place. A word associated with the calculation of a propitious time to do something means beat or rhythm (*jangwa*). Time contains rhythmic beats that must be identified and obeyed, and timing is the key to successful human action. Wearing amulets, inserting talismans under the skin, inscribing the body with tattoos, divining, calculating horoscopes and ritual cursing were all methods of warding off adversity and misfortune. The practical sciences of prognostication—divination, numerology, astrology, palmistry, the interpretation of dreams and omens and deciphering signs on the body such as moles—are deployed to face up to risks, uncertainties and unpredictability in life (Reynolds 2015). Time and place need to be auspicious (*mongkhon*)—a keyword in the culture that has an Indic etymology (Pali, *mangala*).

Arming oneself for possible injury or death is the physical side of protection. The mental and emotional side involves keeping fear in check with self-belief. The sciences of prognostication offer practical reasons to be confident about making decisions as well as clues to auspicious places or times to perform a particular action. Magical thinking is an outlook on the world that has long been an interpretative problem for anthropological theory. Reason struggles against unreason in trying to understand other cultures, and one is tempted to present the beliefs and practices of these cultures as superstitious, confused or wrong (Shweder 1984: 29). Richard Shweder's research concerned judgements about personality, but his conclusions suggested ways to understand the magical thinking evident in Khun Phan's career. The policeman drew on a repertory of magical practices that emboldened his self-belief. These magical practices and his mastery of occult knowledge also equipped him with ways to bluff his adversaries. If he could frighten, outwit or deceive an adversary, he need not risk injury or death.

Episodes in his career show that he was as much a performer of magical thinking as he was a believer in it. He once captured a murderer by fooling the man into thinking that the dead could speak. He instructed the family of the deceased to prepare the corpse of their kinsman in a space enclosed by a sacred thread. On the appointed day, Khun Phan arrived in the white attire of a religious practitioner and leaned over the corpse to ask in a whisper for it to identify the murderer, who was watching the ritual from the sidelines in a crowd of curious villagers. 'I know who it is, I know who it is,' shouted Khun Phan, and the terrified murderer ran from the crowd into the arms of the police.[2]

Beliefs and practices that constitute the empowering body of knowledge of *saiysasat* are found in the religious systems of other Tai peoples, including the Shan, and they are also found in other mainland Buddhist cultures. For many decades, anthropologists working in Myanmar have studied cults of the *weikza*. Sometimes translated as magician, wizard or sorcerer, the term derives from the Pali *vijja* ('possessed of wisdom'). In modern standard Thai, *wicha/vijja* has come to mean a body of knowledge, and it is the word for school curricula or academic disciplines. It is also the word for magical arts. The *weikza* in Myanmar are intermediaries who channel esoteric empowerment. They deal in metal-based alchemy, death-enactment rituals, longevity practices, astrology and the use of dreams and visions (Crosby 2014: xxii). Through their behaviour, meditation skills and expertise in the magical arts, they

---

2   Bunsong Chamnankit, Interview with the author, 24 September 2009.

aim to live until the next Buddha, the Maitreya, appears in this world. The *weikza* cults are popular with Burmese people, but they dwell on the margins of the Buddhist practices and beliefs sanctioned by institutional authority. It is not that these practices have no foundation in Buddhism. Steven Collins, after asking 'what kind of Buddhism is that?', points out that many Pali texts are concerned with alchemy, esoteric drawing (*yantra*), spells (*mantra*) and medicine (Collins 2014: 225). Beyond the saving knowledge of the Buddha's teachings, all methods available must be deployed to conquer demons and the evil they incarnate and cause.

Religion and magic have been put through the critical wringer by scholars in anthropology and religious studies; the boundary between the two is constantly shifting and subject to challenge. The Burmese characterise the *weikza* phenomenon 'as being different from and superior to common rationality' (Rozenberg 2015: 44–8, 63). Invulnerability techniques—in which the Thai policeman became a specialist—might also be characterised as superior to common rationality. The workings of these techniques are deemed effective even if they cannot be divined. The techniques may be effective because they cannot be divined.

The policeman grew up amid a tangle of religions—animism, Brahmanism, Buddhism—found in everyday practice in Thailand that has challenged the hierarchical impulses of Thailand's ruling elites as well as the analytic skills of anthropologists. When King Chulalongkorn's administrators, many of them his brothers and sons, travelled to the far reaches of the kingdom to implement administrative reforms in the late nineteenth century, they discovered unfamiliar beliefs and practices they regarded as superstitions. The magical thinking that shocked these Bangkok officials was as empirical and logical as science; it just worked from a different set of assumptions and principles that the modernising elite feared.

History writing and the mid south

Khun Phan was born in a district of Nakhon Si Thammarat, the most populous of the four southern provincial circles (known as *monthon*), which were created by the new administrative system in the late nineteenth century (Porphant 2017: 231). His first postings were in Songkhla and Phatthalung, and he had tours of duty in other provinces on the Malay Peninsula, including provinces in the deep south: Songkhla, Yala, Narathiwat and Satun. He also served in the central plains, the lower north and in Bangkok, where he had a stint in the Department of Immigration. When he was little more than 30 years of age, he was in one of the last groups of government officials to be ennobled by the absolute monarch. Wherever he was posted, he spoke central Thai language with local people, but his mother tongue was southern Thai, and he felt most at home in the mid south of his birth. After he retired from active duty in the early 1960s with the rank of major general, he became a dignitary called upon to preside at local festivals and rituals. His popularity was exploited by the Democrat Party, which enlisted him in 1969 to run for a seat in parliament. He won the seat, but the army conducted a coup in 1971 and the parliament was abolished. His brief foray into national politics ended when he lost an election after 1973 as a candidate in M.R. Kukrit Pramoj's Social Action Party. In 1987, he was a key figure in the identification and consecration of an amulet struck to raise funds for the renovation of Nakhon's city pillar. After his cremation in early 2007, the value of the amulet inflated wildly until the bubble burst, and hopeful investors in the asset lost their money.

Khun Phan's career in the police force, his working methods and his expertise in martial arts were similar to how soldiers and police elsewhere in the country conduct themselves and augment their authority by drawing on religious beliefs and practices. He was one of many agents of law enforcement and administration who fanned out across the country as the Thai state extended its infrastructure to remote regions. He served no fewer than 12 national police chiefs; during and after World War II, he worked closely with some of them. At first sight, the environmental and geographical distinctiveness of the lakes district on the Malay Peninsula, which lies across ancient trade routes that brought Buddhist and Hindu artefacts, monks and priests to the mid south, would seem to render him a unique figure. Yet his story has broader implications for Thailand's modern history, so the second line of inquiry raises questions about the relationship between the mid south and the royal centres to the north. Was the policeman's story local, regional or national? The challenge was to write about him as both a southerner and a generic figure in Thai police history, who aided and abetted the making of the Thai nation-state.

Khun Phan belonged to an early cohort in the fledgling police force as the Thai state filled in the map mandated by treaties with France and Great Britain in the first decade of the twentieth century. His secondary education at a prestigious monastery school in Bangkok, his attendance at the police academy in Nakhon Pathom and his postings in the capital and other provinces, where he acquired his reputation for tough policing, familiarised him with beliefs and practices that were morphing into a national culture. Elements of this national culture included traditional martial arts, knowledge of the classic poem *Khun Chang Khun Phaen* and Buddhist and Brahmanic beliefs and ceremonies. Officers and civil servants born and raised in Bangkok might be posted to the provinces, where they served out their tour of duty pining to return to the cosmopolitan capital of their birth. Khun Phan, by contrast, was a provincial man appointed to duties wherever he was needed and who returned to the mid south at every opportunity. His final appointment, until he retired in 1964, was chief of the provincial circle at Nakhon Si Thammarat. These loops into the capital and out, and his postings elsewhere in the country and back to the south, were communicative. He mediated an exchange of cultural and social information between the centre and the south. Butr Phantharak, a local boy born in a tiny remote Nakhon village, made good in a national institution.

In the first millennium, the policeman's Nakhon was a commercial hub connecting Chinese ports with the Indian Subcontinent, Sri Lanka, the Middle East and the Western Orient. In the seventeenth and eighteenth centuries, Nakhon Si Thammarat was designated an independent principality in recognition of its hegemony over 12 satellites—smaller centres (*mueang*) that included some Malay centres in the deep south. That number—matching the 12 signs of the zodiac and the Chinese 12-year animal cycle—gave Nakhon's ruling lords a sense of overlordship in a mini-kingdom. Empire would be too grand a term for their ambition. Nakhon had its own chronicle, as did the nearby satellite states of Phatthalung and Songkhla, which occupied an environmental niche around the lagoons and brackish lakes of the mid south. Nakhon's local rulers chafed under the overlordship of Ayutthaya and, later, Bangkok, and rebelled many times against demands for manpower to bring smaller vassals to heal or to defend against Burmese invaders. When the Kingdom of Ayutthaya broke apart after the Burmese invasions in the eighteenth century, an army from Thonburi was needed to crush the rebellion in Nakhon and force it to submit (Davisakd 2008: 75). Not until the government restructure of the late nineteenth century was Nakhon finally subordinated, its local rulers replaced and, over the years, reduced in status as the new provincial framework was gradually implanted.

Thai historical writing has been dominated by preoccupations with royal centres and with Bangkok, the seat of the national government and the royal base of the Chakri dynasty since the late eighteenth century. As the reign of the ninth Chakri lengthened to 70 years (1946–2016), monarchy and heroic kingship crowded out other historical topics, particularly for the twentieth century, as political historians puzzled over the fall of the absolute monarchy in 1932 and tried to explain why the event had never yielded constitutional, multiparty democracy free from interference by the monarchy and the army. At critical junctures in the twentieth century, military leadership—always autocratic, often repressive and sometimes supported by the Crown—intervened to stymie the development of a more liberal political system. The unholy alliance of military and monarchy has also affected the study of the country's past by overvaluing royal accomplishment, creating myths about the kings and undervaluing regional histories.

From time to time, the power of the gun has been used to fasten this myth in place by means of the lese-majesty statute that constrains public comment by politicians, academics, public intellectuals and writers. Lese-majesty is a libel law that criminalises speech defamatory of the incumbent monarch and the institution of the monarchy (Streckfuss 2010: 105–6; 2011: 21–5). Over the half-century to 2009, lese-majesty cases grew from a mere handful to 164, 82 of which were adjudicated (Streckfuss 2011: 34). Long ago it became impossible within the country to hold the institution of the monarchy up to serious scrutiny in Thai language. Generations of Thai students have grown up not knowing any criticism of the king (Jory 2011: 555). Even comment about kings from premodern times has raised the charge of defaming 'the supreme institution'. In October 2017, the public intellectual Sulak Sivaraksa was accused of lese-majesty for questioning the accuracy of an elephant duel between King Naresuan and a Burmese ruler in the late sixteenth century. A few months later, prosecutors decided not to pursue the case, and the charges were dropped (Katz 2018).

Outside the country it is a different story. So dominant is the royal national ideology—buttressed by reverential sentiment for King Bhumibol, the ninth Bangkok king, who died in October 2016—that critical history in foreign languages has, since the military coup of September 2006, become narrowly focused on attacking the royal national narrative. What Hong Lysa observed more than a dozen years ago is still the case today: '[E]very self-respecting historical study in the English language, particularly those on the fifth reign, has since the late 1970s framed itself as a critique of the dominant royalist narrative' (Hong 2007: 189). With the assistance of a large palace establishment and collaborators in public institutions and the private sector, King Bhumibol, the revered and activist monarch who reigned for seven decades, restored the reputation of the monarchy after its nadir in the 1930s, when absolutism ended and the seventh Bangkok king abdicated. The king's deft use of the media and his influence in state institutions and public life lifted the reputation of all monarchs to the point where authoritarian regimes have been able to deploy the lese-majesty statute to sanction public statements about Thai kings past as well as the incumbent. Benedict Anderson's statement that royalism 'persists in a curiously antique form in contemporary Siam' has long been out-of-date. King Bhumibol's reign had another four decades to run from the time Anderson wrote and the monarchy only became stronger and the military more dependent on it (Anderson 2014: 27).

Thongchai Winichakul, in a series of publications, has dissected the royal nationalist ideology that underpins the historiographical myth and proposed that historians themselves have come to believe the myth and accept it as truth with all its distortions and errors (Thongchai 2011: 21–2).[3] His 2016 collection of Thai essays, *The Real Face of Royal Nationalism as it Affects Thai History*, promised to expose the truth behind the myth by borrowing from Jit Poumisak's 1957 radical history, *The Real Face of Thai Feudalism Today* (Reynolds 1994; Thongchai 2016). The myth stands on two legs. First, although Siam/Thailand was pressured by the Western imperial powers who imposed extraterritorial treaties that placed Asian subjects under foreign courts, the kingdom was never colonised. In the Paknam incident of 1893, French gunboats moored near the Grand Palace in Bangkok, and Great Britain and France soon moved to secure the borders of their colonies in eastern Burma, northern Malaya and western Cambodia by seizing vassal states that had paid tribute to the Siamese suzerain. As Shane Strate, who studied with Thongchai, has put it, these 'emasculating encounters' humiliated Siam and rendered it a disabled victim (Strate 2015: 6). Critics of the myth that 'Siam was never colonised' have proposed various terms to describe Siam/Thailand's real colonial condition: neocolony, indirect colony, semi-colony and cryptocolony —a suppressed, disguised form of colonialism (Thongchai 2011: 29). These labels that counter the royal nationalist ideology animate

---

3   The earliest statement by Thongchai on the idea of royal nationalist history was Thongchai (2001).

discussions in foreign classrooms, but in the vernacular it is unimaginable that the kingdom in the late nineteenth and twentieth centuries could have been colonised, even though the extraterritorial treaties fragmented Siamese sovereignty and placed some of it in the hands of Western imperial powers.

In the frame of nationalist ideology, it is impossible to 'think' of Siam/ Thailand as colonised directly, indirectly or even partially because Thai monarchs saved the country from this ignominy by skilful diplomacy. Heroic kingship is the second leg of royal nationalist ideology that underpins the myth. Through the centuries, Siam/Thailand's monarchs fought wars against foreign aggressors to liberate the Thai people and keep them independent. Court historians in the early twentieth century turned the royal chronicles into moral stories of national independence; at the same time, the histories of autonomous kingdoms and formal vassals came into the possessive care of the centralising government in Bangkok (Thongchai 2011: 36, 38). In the process of saving the country from Western colonialism, according to this critique, the Thai monarchs created a colonising state that subordinated smaller centres and brought them under Bangkok's unitary rule: 'Reform', says Thongchai, 'is merely a euphemism for Siam's imperial conquests' (Thongchai 2011: 30). And he is not alone in advancing the idea that Siam was a coloniser. *Subject Siam*, the title of Tamara Loos's 2006 study of the Siamese court's treatment of the southern Malay territories on both sides of the Siam–Malaya border, captures with clever wordplay the double identity of Siam as a subject of Western imperial will and as a subject active in its own expansion.

From the late nineteenth century, the emerging Siamese nation-state swallowed up independent principalities such as Nakhon Si Thammarat in the south and the kingdoms of Chiang Mai and Nan in the north. Chiang Mai enjoyed its own tradition of kingship that was intact as late as 1860, until British imperial power and the Siamese monarch collaborated to end the autonomy of the north. The princes of Chiang Mai and Lamphun came into conflict with the British Government over timber rights by granting concessions to British and Burmese concessionaires who then claimed extraterritorial rights. The issue was resolved by the Anglo-Thai Treaty in 1874 that allowed the Bangkok Government to adjudicate disputes in the north (Chaiyan 1994: 19). Annexation by the Siamese Government was swift. In less than 15 years, the Bangkok Government and the British Government were acting jointly as colonial powers in the north. Whereas in 1860 the Siamese foreign minister admitted to the

British consul in Bangkok that Chiang Mai was a sovereign state with its own laws—different from Siam—by 1874, the king in Bangkok could declare that Chiang Mai was a dependency that belonged 'to us' (Iijima 2008: 43, 46). The theme of internal colonialism—the state's push into territory populated by non-Thai peoples and governed by local lords—has never had traction in Thai historical writing. In the royal nationalist myth, it is anathema to think of Siam under the Chakri monarchs colonising territories in the same manner as, say, the settler societies of the New World that pushed through frontiers in South Africa, America and Australia to dispossess indigenous peoples of their lands.

What follows from Thongchai's stringent critique is that a transition to alternative frames or plots—at least in forms acceptable for school textbooks and research funding by Thai Government institutions—has been halted in its tracks by the myth. A people's history or a history of the peasantry or urban labouring classes inspired by Marxist approaches has never materialised. The long, continuous story of republicanism in the kingdom's political history is forever deprived of oxygen, unable to respire in an atmosphere full of royal birthdays, death days and annual celebrations of the dynasty's achievements (Jory 2015: 115). Thai historical writing has been slow to throw off the shackles of chronicle history, the story of royal accomplishment. While 'chronicle' (*phongsawadan*) is no longer the word for history as it was in the late nineteenth century, a mentality of chronicle history survives today in a history that privileges royal deeds. Even the country's fledgling electoral democracy is a royal project. By resolving the political crisis in 1973 that shook the country and brought down a military junta, King Bhumibol managed to reinvent the monarchy as a symbol of democracy (Jory 2011: 539).

It is as though the 'birth of Thai history', in the title of Thongchai's manifesto, has been the death of Thai history as we see it today. Yet this polemic, while it is not off the mark in important respects, has its own distortions and omissions. The master paradigm has an elitist feel and it targets the popular imagination informed by TV dramas, novels and films rather than by what academic historians write. To be sure, there are many kinds of academic history, and some history carries the imprimatur of official history that may be researched and written by formally trained historians. Many academic historians who publish in the vernacular work around the legal and institutional constraints created by the lese-majesty statute and write with nuance as they chip away at the royal nationalist narrative. Not every history book sold in Bangkok is about a Thai king, nor is it a vanity biography of a businessperson or a police or army officer.

Historians have foraged for topics that lie outside the frame of the royal national narrative and do not explicitly threaten it, leading to the proliferation of social histories such as studies of sport and recreation, Bangkok's night life and demimonde, tourism, regional banditry, rebellion of the poor in a Bangkok Chinese community and public health and sanitation.[4] The mentalities and class biases of elite thinkers have been brought into sharper relief (Saichol 2014). As Thailand became more urbanised and consumer-oriented, notions of public space and private space have been radically transformed, leaving modern people with a kind of social amnesia. A Thai historian studying sanitaryware explains how city dwellers today have no memory of how people of yore once defecated in family groups in the fields and forests, chatting with one another while doing so (Monruethai 2002: 335–52). Much of this research is publicly available in MA theses submitted to Thai universities, and many of these studies have been published as monographs. Thongchai gives little credit to this body of scholarship on the grounds that 'historians themselves believe the myths [about royal nationalist ideology], taking them as truthful knowledge' (Thongchai 2011: 21). Yet innovative works manage to slip into the marketplace, such as the study of the ninth king's 'royal projects' that was cleverly marketed with a photo of King Bhumibol on the cover dressed in his ceremonial robes for his 50th anniversary on the throne in 1996. An anecdote made the rounds that customers bought the book for their personal collections about the royal family unaware that the critique inside the book's covers exposed the social engineering and propaganda behind the royal projects (Chanida 2007).

A few of Thongchai's citations are in the vernacular; the majority are in English. His view is from a geostationary satellite hovering high above Thailand that takes no account of how historians based in Thailand have flourished within the strictures of royal-nationalist ideology. The task of dismantling royalist and court-centred narratives and creating new narratives—a challenge thrown down in lively academic debates following the watershed event of 14 October 1973—is not advanced by restating the problem in slightly different language. The problem remains the

---

4   Innovative works include Patravadi (2006); Wirayut Sisuwannakit (2006); Davisakd (2007); Sitthithep (2012); Wirayut Pisamli (2014); Walailak University (2017).

same—namely, how to pry chronicles and archives away from royalist and nationalist myth-making preoccupations (Reynolds and Hong 1983: 96). Although Thailand was under military rule for most of the 1980s, new vistas on the past opened up that promised to inspire fresh historical interpretations.

Young scholars who had returned from their studies abroad to spearhead the professionalisation of the Thai academy were now in their most productive years. Among these scholars was Nidhi Eoseewong (b. 1940), a historian based in Chiang Mai, whose provocative study of literary art in early Bangkok was first published in 1982. Nidhi demythologised the ruling class and exposed its ordinariness as a bourgeoisie created by commerce. Princes and nobles had become merchants and traders. Elitist literary traditions were loosened, and lively popular motifs made their way into more flexible and adaptable literary art. Aristocrats no longer compared themselves to gods; 'springs of realism' and 'humanistic thinking' appeared in their creations (Nidhi 2005: 119, 131). Even the life of the Buddha came to be written in a more down-to-earth way. During the reign of the fifth Bangkok king (1868–1910), the sacred was reintroduced and the liveliness and intellectual creativity of early Bangkok gradually turned into a pretentious, derivative literature that became 'a lifeless corpse' that students were forced to study (Nidhi 2005: 146). Nidhi's history was not so much national or even dynastic, as the story of a class. His approach, informed by the Marxian preoccupations of the previous decade, had an economistic edge: the bourgeois class was created by its materialist needs and tastes.

Another returned student inspired by the vitality of the mid-1970s was Chatthip Nartsupha (b. 1941), an economic historian who looked to the village and the countryside for historical insights and a historical narrative separate from the dynastic. Chatthip's best-known and most influential book was *The Thai Village Economy in the Past*, first published in 1984 and later translated into English (Chatthip 1999; Reynolds 2013: 2, 7–9). For Chatthip, the village was able to stand up against the dual powers of the state and capitalism owing to its self-reliance and its capacity for sustainability. During the second phase of his work, which began around 1990, he saw the village as an institutional site for rebuilding and renewal through the concept of community culture. His ideas of the village's capacity to self-strengthen and defend itself against the inequalities of capitalist development drew criticism from both anthropologists and economists who faulted him for misunderstanding the modern village that was not, and never had been, a standalone autonomous institution. Thongchai, who faulted Chatthip for contributing to a pernicious form of cultural nationalism, saw him as an example of Thailand's intelligentsia who supported a 'leftist-royalist anti-democratic alliance' (Thongchai 2008: 589). In Thai academic circles, this bruising rhetoric is not for the faint-hearted. Yet Chatthip's studies of the village—extended by Chatthip himself and his students to regional economies—was never merely academic. Like Nidhi and many others of his generation, Chatthip was engaged in a political project—one inspired by concern for the deleterious consequences of capitalist development on social life and by the new thinking that had emerged in the 1970s about economics and social structure (Reynolds 2013: 17–18).

Following the May 2014 coup, Somsak Jeamteerasakul (b. 1958), the most iconoclastic historian who lived through the mid-1970s, took refuge in France after he was threatened physically. Somsak's focus has always been on the monarchy, its history and, by means of its proxies and loyalists, the influence it has exerted over the historical record. Along with many others, he has also been an unrelenting critic of the massacre at Thammasat University on 6 October 1976. In a collection of expurgated articles in newspapers and news weeklies published as *History Invented Just Yesterday*, a polemical work without footnotes or bibliography, Somsak 'demolished the façade that the modern Thai monarchy was democratic, above politics, and the king a paragon of Buddhist virtue'. His goal was to insert his arguments into the mainstream of modern Thai historical writing (Jory 2011: 554–5; Somsak 2001). Thongchai, in his 2011 manifesto, does not mention Somsak's contribution to understanding how the ninth Bangkok king made himself a democratic monarch—an odd omission considering the two men have been the most outspoken Thai historians in exposing the royal nationalist narrative. They were imprisoned together as members of the 'Bangkok 18' after the military overthrew a popularly elected government in October 1976. Somsak's 'history invented yesterday' and Thongchai's royal nationalist narrative have become massive, immovable objects that stand in the way of histories that might achieve more than the privileging of royal initiative and deeds.

Alternative approaches to the royal nationalist narrative emerged from the upheavals of the 1970s, when the Thai education curriculum was reformed and decentralised. The education plan of 1978 integrated local studies into the national curriculum, and the Thai Government began to relax its oversight of local cultural identity. Regional and local histories proliferated in the 1980s with the dispatch of Bangkok-trained historians to staff new universities that sprang up in the provinces, where academics were encouraged to study and celebrate their own histories. They were assisted in that effort with funding from the tourism and nostalgia industries (Thongchai 1995: 110–13). In the boom years of the 1980s through to the first half of the 1990s, the Thai economy globalised and became more exposed to international markets. Trade—measured as exports plus imports between 1982 and 1994—increased from 54 per cent of gross domestic product (GDP) to 89 per cent (Baker and Pasuk 1996: 75). As the economy became more diversified and employment in manufacturing increased, financial institutions branched into the provinces. Between 1988 and 1995, the number of bank branches outside Bangkok rose by 40 per cent, from 1,500 to more than 2,100. Business and industry associations such as chambers of commerce, while fostered by the state, developed a degree of autonomy upcountry and began to exert political influence from the provinces (Hewison and Maniemai 2000: 209; Ockey 2000: 80). Provincial capitalism gave local businesspeople the wherewithal to become involved in electoral politics, and ethno-regionalist consciousness backed by real resources began to draw Thai tourists to the provinces. Community memory of ancient principalities was revived with the central government's blessing.

Some of the provincial wealth during the late 1980s and early 1990s was directed to local heritage. In the case of Nakhon Si Thammarat, which archaeologists have called Nakhon Si Thammarat-Tambralinga in recognition of the predecessor state that arose in the first millennium, researchers in educational institutions have benefited from this decentralisation. Most recently, the central government has been pushing to have Wat Mahathat put on the United Nations Educational, Scientific and Cultural Organization World Heritage list—a campaign that has been received locally with ambivalence and even resistance, given the disruption that would occur to the everyday rhythms of a provincial town (Brawn 2018: 156–8). During Thailand's economic boom in 1987, the Jatukham-Ramathep deity was conjured out of Nakhon's ancient past and caused a stir in the amulet markets around the country. Local history is by its nature not big-paradigm history, as its specificity constrains comparison with other locales and other regions. As an innovative alternative to national history, it would seem doomed, because it always ends up subordinated to the narrative of the nation's biography. In the 1970s, many conferences on local history were held in upcountry colleges of education, but 'nothing much came of them', observed the international historian and public intellectual Charnvit Kasetsiri: '[T]he participants were limited and seemed unable to get away from the usual dependency of the "local" on the "central"' (Charnvit 2015: 34).

This statement has long been out-of-date. So-called local history has evolved from being dependent on the centre and the change has been driven both by the central bureaucracy and by the enterprise of upcountry regional centres and communities. The Thailand Research Fund, a national grants body established during the boom-time in the 1990s after the end of the Cold War, and whose funding is weighed towards natural and medical sciences, has supported local and regional projects. In the case of the mid south, it funded the first academic study of Butr Phantharak's life and it has funded a study of southern character through the culture of bull-fighting—a sport popular with gambling farmers that has lessons about masculine prowess (Akhom 2000; Wira 2001). Academic standards in regional universities have risen and universities willingly dispense funds for conferences from their modest budgets. In August 2017, Walailak University in Nakhon sponsored a conference on murder, crime and lawlessness in the south that attracted social scientists and research students from around the country (Walailak University 2017). Regional and local researchers pondered whether or not there was a disposition to crime and violence specific to the southern part of the country and, if so, what would explain it.

Many authors writing on the south and its outlaw culture are not, strictly speaking, scholars; they are not formally trained as academics. They make their living as journalists, traders or schoolteachers. Their popular histories may be produced in a particular historical moment, such as the numerous accounts of Butr Phantharak's life and the origins of the Jatukham-Ramathep amulet that appeared around the time of his cremation in February 2007. Those histories gave the Jatukham-Ramathep deity a pedigree by surrounding it with fact and myth about its creation in the late 1980s. Academics in Bangkok universities do not rate these popular histories very highly and are disposed to dismiss them as unprofessional, even parochial, because they fail to pass tests for rigour and accountability. Yet in my explorations of Butr Phantharak's life, I have found the work of popular historians invaluable in providing angles of vision unavailable elsewhere. Local and regional authors, whether they are popular or academic, write about their native land with insight and passion. Their books contain social truths that illuminate community life and thought obscured by the royal nationalist narrative that is only about the dynasty at the royal centre. After all, 'the centre' is relative. Every place—any place—can be a centre and, in this book, the mid south, especially Nakhon Si Thammarat, with its eclectic and heterodox religious culture, is the centre. For Police Major General Khun Phan, Phatthalung as well as Nakhon Si Thammarat, the province of his birth, defined the centre of his cosmos.

A centre is not isolated, it is not apart. Nakhon Si Thammarat and its 12 satellite ministates had long enjoyed commercial links via global trading routes that stretched from coastal China to the Indian Subcontinent and beyond. As an entrepreneurial hub, Nakhon Si Thammarat from time to time successfully challenged the suzerainty of the kingdoms of Ayutthaya and Bangkok on the central plains. Over the centuries, the mid south's exposure to Brahmanism and Buddhism placed Nakhon Si Thammarat in the same cultural field as kingdoms to the north, and the history that surfaces in the policeman's life in the following pages is no less a history of the country.

Policing and the sovereign body

The third line of inquiry that emerged from my early reading and conversations posed questions about policing, sovereignty and the task of government to maintain law and order and protect citizens. Butr Phantharak acted on the authority of the state, yet at times he carried out his duties as though his pursuit of his adversaries was a personal matter. In the first half of the twentieth century, the mid south and many other parts of the country were frontier societies. The writ of government throughout the kingdom was weak, giving the police discretion in carrying out their orders. Details from Butr's career indicate that he saw himself as a protector of the rule of law. The bladed weapons he carried with him—the Malay dagger (or *kris*) and a sword wrapped in red cloth— were emblems of an earlier, premodern sovereignty in the Thai and Malay worlds. Until just before Butr's police career began in the 1920s, the army had performed the principal role of internal peacekeeping, but as the police force grew in the early twentieth century, it too developed a sense of entitlement in protecting the sovereign body.

The police force is charged with keeping public order and, as part of political society, the police are integral to the state's responsibility for carrying out what is one of the primary functions of government: protection of the population. Making laws, punishing criminals, declaring war and peace and a host of other functions are required to maintain the safety of people and their 'contentments of life', as Thomas Hobbes put it (Skinner 1999: 2). Gramsci understood political society to be those parts of the state—the police and the military—that lawfully exercise a monopoly over weaponry and the use of lethal force. He called political society 'the armour of coercion' that affords protection for the people (Gramsci 1983: 263). Defence of the land—be it the realm, the nation-state, the district or the village—requires not only diplomacy, but also coercion and the occasional use of lethal force. In practice, political society enjoys no such monopoly on the use of lethal force; witness the extrajudicial killing, armed militias in failing states and gangland violence found everywhere, even in so-called advanced democracies. Military and police together as 'the armour of coercion' is germane in the Thai case, as senior officers in the military and police have often changed places, moving from one service to the other as circumstance required.

The armour of coercion comes alive in the Thai term for government, *kanpokkhrong*, where *pokkhrong* means to cover or to shield. *Pok* means to shield and *khrong* to cloak or cover, or sometimes to possess. *Khrong* can also mean to wrap around or enclose, as when a monk dons a monastic robe to cover his body. A similar idea about the function of government and its officials to protect is the softer metaphor *pok raksa*, to look after or care for. The country's rulers are referred to in Thai academic language, if rendered literally, as 'those who shield' (*phu pokkhrong*). External threats to the sovereign body—be they enemy states or foreign ideologies such as republicanism, democracy or communism—were internalised in the elite consciousness from about 1900 as harmful to the body politic. The first line of defence in protecting the people and the Thai body is to throw up a shield and deploy lethal force if necessary.

The other element relevant to protecting the Thai body politic is kingship. Rulership in Southeast Asia has a deep history of connection with divinity. In premodern times, the king was a divine medium, an intermediary between the earth-god and the human community who possessed powers that assured the fertility of the land and all that it produced. Soil and stone from time immemorial had absorbed the generative properties of the earth, and cults developed that divinised the stone and clumps of earth. The belief systems that grew around these cults, particularly in relation to the custodial protection of land and property, were shared by peoples in China, India and parts of Southeast Asia (Mus 2011: 24–5). One of the popular epithets for the Thai king, 'lord over land', contains the word for soil (*din*). Water used in the ceremony of drinking the oath of allegiance from premodern times to the present day was scooped from the kingdom's waterways and brought to the royal centre for consecration. Officials then drank this water and pledged their loyalty to the sovereign before taking up their provincial posts. In the reverse direction, the king's body acquired a material presence throughout the country. During the long ninth Bangkok reign, parts of the king's body—his nail clippings and his hair—were dispersed physically and ritually to all provinces in images of the Buddha that served as spiritual shields against the communist insurgency. In defending his kingdom with sacred stuff, the godly king protected his own body that was at once here, there and everywhere.

Thailand's bounded territory, portrayed as a living organism, as a human body, took on graphic form when I was teaching secondary school during the mid-1960s in Krabi, which was then a very remote province with rudimentary infrastructure and intermittent electrical power. One weekend, teachers at the school were bused out to the beautiful beach at Ao Nang—as yet undiscovered and untouched by international tourism—for a retreat to discuss the year's activities. The time came for the geography teacher, a lanky guy with an earthy sense of humour, to demonstrate his trick for planting an image of the country's map in the kids' minds. He turned sideways to the audience, placed his right foot on a crate, propped his right hand under his chin and proceeded to show how Thailand's shape on the map resembled a human body. His head was north-west Thailand, with its centre in Chiang Mai. His rump was the north-east, with its largely Lao population, and he threw in a few barbs about the country bumpkins who lived there. The Malay Peninsula was the ambulatory appendage. Alas, this body had only one leg; the other had been lost in a war with the Burmese. Traversing vertically from the north through the centre of the body was the alimentary canal, the Chaophraya River. At the top of the digestive tract the watershed deposited nutrients to the floodplains below and, at the bottom, in the watery lowlands where Bangkok had grown into the giant conurbation it was even in those days, the wastes drained into the Gulf of Thailand. This was the excretory system of the organism. Delivered deadpan to the upcountry audience, this description of Thailand's body was met with much hilarity by the teachers who shouted out earthy details of their own. Years before the arrival of television let alone the internet, and decades before economic booms and globalisation, what secondary student sitting through this geography lesson could ever forget this cartoon figure of Thailand's map? Although the embodiment of the country was both graphic and funny in this geo-body, it could never be the subject of earthy humour in the solemn ceremonies conducted by Brahmans for the real-life king far away in his Bangkok palace.

The idea of the sovereign state, whether it be a kingdom or a nation-state, as a body, an organism, is instantiated in Malay culture that reached as far as the mid south. The policeman Butr Phantharak had Malay ancestry, although it is impossible to be precise about what this heritage might account for in his beliefs and practices. In the trophy photo taken by his son, the handle of a *kris* protrudes from his waistband, and he could boast of a personal collection of the daggers—an emblem of Malay sovereignty. In the Malay world of the deep south where he sometimes worked, spirit mediums known as *bomoh* treated the body as a realm in distress, and in their healing rituals they practised a form of statecraft. A sick body and its 'provinces' were a disaggregated kingdom, 'a realm in chaos' that lacked harmony. The healing rituals aimed to restore the body's wholeness and thereby its sovereign integrity (Kessler 1977: 318–19). It would then be able to 'govern itself'. A kingdom whose subjects were preyed upon by bandits and criminals was unwell. Suppressing crime returned the sovereign body to a healthy state. From this perspective, Khun Phan's policing was restorative.

The realm as a corporal entity has a long lineage in European political thought, made memorable by Kantorowicz's study of the king's two bodies in medieval and early modern English texts. In Christendom, the spiritual and secular powers were united in one person, bishop or king. This union of the religious and the secular is portrayed in the frontispiece, by Abraham Bosse, of *Leviathan* by Thomas Hobbes, published in 1651. The crowned head of state is holding the bishop's crosier in his left hand and the sword of justice in his right. In this memorable and celebrated image, the upper torso and the thick arms contain the bodies of citizens, but this collective of bodies is an artificial unity. The body politic does not create the state; rather, 'the people' exist only through having a sovereign (Skinner 2007, 2016). 'A certain spiritual capacity' was attributed to the sovereign king as an emanation of the consecrating rites that transformed the ordinary human being into a monarch (Kantorowicz 1970: 44).

The king was human by nature but divine by grace. Early in the history of this double identity, he was material-mortal as well as immaterial and immortal, foreshadowing the later transformation of the king's two bodies: the human body and the body politic. Church and State were distinct, but they created hybrids by borrowing from each other and exchanging insignia, symbols, prerogatives and rights of honour (Kantorowicz 1970: 193). As time passed and the State became more corporate and legal, its theorists continued to exploit the aura of religion as well as its thought and language. The State was eventually set as a 'body' over the Church 'body' even as the State helped itself to the supernatural and transcendental values claimed by the Church (Kantorowicz 1970: 207–8).

The bishop in Christendom stood in a very different relationship to the English sovereign than the Buddhist Sangharaja did to the Thai king. For one thing, the tensions between the two were fewer for the most part. Some scholars have argued that the ninth Thai king at the end of his life approached incarnation as a *bodhisattva*, a virtual god-king (Jackson 2010; Jory 2016: 180–5). Thai royal language describes the king's body, actions and speech by asserting that the king is a special being, a *bodhisattva*, a merit-filled creature in the same class (*ong*) as monks and Buddha images. When Christian missionaries in Thailand translated the Judaeo-Christian Yahweh, they chose Thai *phrajao*, a term that appears in many of the king's honorifics and epithets—for example, 'lord of the land' (*phrajao phaendin*) or, as the Marxist historian Jit Poumisak expressed it, 'lord over land'. If *phrajao* is translated back into English, it can be not a deity but merely 'revered lord'. Over the seven decades of the ninth Bangkok reign (1946–2016), military and civilian governments contrived an alliance with the sacral monarch—the 'revered lord'—to become his defender and agent, a move that protected both parties. The monarch needed protection from democrats and socialists and the army needed the monarch to acquiesce in its naked ambition. Did the monarch have a choice? The army was the one institution, and not a democratic one, capable of setting the institution to one side and pushing the king off his throne.

This book is a biographical study of a particular policeman, whose name meant, literally, 'pledged to protect royal power', and of his origins in the mid south of Thailand and his social world through most of the twentieth century. Police can be treated in ways other than the functional as agents of the state. We can ask, what *is* police? Must police be understood only as acting on behalf of some authority, such as government or the state, or can police be understood in some other way? These questions are ontological. They are about police as a state of being, an analytical category that can be interrogated. The criminologist Beatrice Jauregui (2016) puts the matter differently by asking about 'police life' and how it acquires (or loses) 'moral virtue or instrumental value'. She pursues this line of questioning after her conversations in Uttar Pradesh, India, reveal how police officers rationalise 'the fraught relations between means and ends in their work'. The officers are authorised to use state-mandated violence 'as needed', exposing them to the risk of harm and possibly death (Jauregui 2016: 65, 88–9).

Here I can address such questions briefly by recalling an idea of Giorgio Agamben's that ties sovereignty to policing by proposing that the police—contrary to what public opinion might think—do not merely fulfil an administrative function by enforcing the law. The police are 'the place', Agamben says, where violence and right are contiguous with the sovereign. Violence and right touch the sovereign.[5] Thus, Agamben continues, the figure of the sovereign and that of the executioner have in common an 'intangible sacredness'. The enemy or adversary is branded a criminal and excluded from 'civil humanity' (Agamben 2000: 104–5). As Butr Phantharak delved deeper and deeper into the mysteries of magical knowledge and other methods for arming himself mentally and spiritually, this policeman with 'executioner' tattooed on his knuckles, this very mortal man who had been wounded more than once in the line of duty, grasped the regalia of rule, the symbols of intangible sacredness. In so doing, he assumed the privileged rights and capabilities analogous to those of a sovereign. It is in keeping with his character that Butr should mimic some of the actions and symbols of royal sovereignty from a time when monarchical power was absolute.

In light of Agamben's words, Gramsci's term for the police and the military, 'the armour of coercion', is too superficial to describe the relationship between the police and sovereign power. The sovereign power does not execute its enemies and adversaries through the police as its agent. The sovereign power executes because it *is* the police, and vice versa. Seen from this perspective, Butr Phantharak's conceit of showing off the weapons of sovereignty—the sword of the Buddhists and the *kris* of the Malays—was

---

5   My thanks to Luigi Tomba for pointing out that Agamben's focus in this piece is to argue that the Gulf War and the Holocaust must be understood as police operations (Personal communication, 3 October 2016).

no mere affectation, but a sign of violence fused with right. In Thailand after the coup of 22 May 2014, the military and police collaborated in arresting political dissidents, including those accused of lese-majesty. Agamben's link between the sovereign and police is instructive here. By charging people with criminal activity and detaining them in army camps, the military's primary function of defending the kingdom became blurred with policing.

＊＊＊＊

Butr Phantharak was an executioner. He prided himself on his right and his ability to take a human life, and on more than one occasion when he exceeded his orders or disrupted cosy relationships between lawbreakers and local officials he was transferred to another part of the country. To carry out his duties, he shared community beliefs in powers exceeding the human. That much is apparent from the stories he told. In his pursuit of outlaws and criminals, he acquired enemies and, for his own protection, he armed himself physically, mentally and magically. His reputation—performed as much as earned—made him a person to be emulated (*ton baep*), in the words of one southern scholar.[6] The communities in the mid south, which called for his return when criminality reached crisis point, saw him as a resource who could reinstate order and justice, however roughly delivered. If police violence was necessary to achieve these ends, the community saw it as a 'positive provision' that solved a problem (Jauregui 2016: 92). His life story has contributed to the ruthless reputation of the Thai police and, in this respect, he was no different from police in other lands and other jurisdictions whose violent, sometimes morally questionable, interventions are authorised by the state.

In the chapters that follow, I want to draw the reader into the policeman's world by sketching a portrait of this complex man against the background of his homeland in Thailand's mid south. Episodes in his life and elements of his persona are manifest in political authority in Thailand today, especially when that authority wears the uniform of a soldier or a police officer. Butr surrounded himself with an aura of apprehension by cultivating a persona, a representation of himself that exceeded his actual person. His effectiveness as a police officer sprang not only from his skills, but also from uncertainty about what he was capable of doing, including the taking of human life if circumstances warranted it. In imagining

---

6   Kasem Jandam, Interview with the author, Ai Khiew, Nakhon Si Thammarat, 17 November 2017.

the policeman's world, I am reminded of what Quentin Skinner said in explaining Thomas Hobbes's view of human nature. In the war of all against all, 'you are constantly liable to sudden death' (Skinner 2007). Khun Phan knew the precarity of police life from his early days as a constable. He was regularly exposed to sudden death, as were his adversaries on the other side of the law—a fact of life that both sides took for granted. Aware of what could befall him in his policing operations, aware of police expendability and the provisionality of his authority, he protected his body with weapons and practices that emboldened him to carry out his duties efficiently and effectively in a way that would ensure his own survival as well as the subjugation of the lawbreaker he was confronting.

2

Lion Lawman

Video content for this chapter is available online:
press.anu.edu.au/publications/series/asian-studies/
power-protection-and-magic-thailand#media

Telling the life story of a larger-than-life figure, especially a person such as Khun Phan, who loved telling others about himself at length, cannot be straightforward. The written and oral records have left us innumerable versions of the life, many of these by the subject himself as the speaking 'I'. When he was 80 years old, Khun Phan began granting interviews to tell about his exploits hunting down outlaws and criminals and bringing them to justice. Southern Thai authors, academics and police comrades were particularly keen to talk to the 'Lion Lawman' and delve into his career and, after his retirement, into his role as a local notable presiding at community events and rituals.

Even with all the attention given him, no account touches all aspects of his life, nor is the most conscientious biography free of error or puzzling discrepancies in facts of time and place. To enrich their narratives and entertain their readers, popular authors sometimes shuffle the chronology in their accounts. Episodes, often undated, may appear in two or three different places in the same book. The documentation—much of it traceable to the policeman's own words of when, where and why he did this or that—is voluminous. Writers—sometimes identifying themselves as compilers—help themselves to the words of previous authors or scrupulously reproduce them verbatim with attribution and then supplement the record with new details of their own. Yet repetition of earlier accounts does not render facts any more accurate than they were in their first utterance by the speaking subject. A fact turns out to be a factoid, a mirage. To make matters worse, one of Khun Phan's sons told me that the biographers missed things, because the interviewer did not think to ask the right question, and it would not be truthful for Khun Phan to volunteer information that was not requested.[1] In any case, and despite what the textbooks say, raw data for a historian are as problematic as the explanations of a secondary narrator. A primary source, once it is given context or is directly contradicted by another primary source, becomes an interpretation mediated by opinion and angle of vision.[2]

I cannot resolve the many problems of veracity, beginning with the problematic dates of Khun Phan's birth. In his interviews with biographers, the policeman's memory for the exact day of the week and time of day when he conducted an operation covers his accounts with a sheen of credibility, but details that come readily to hand—as vivid and startling as they may be—beg many questions. Did he really kill his first prisoner by squeezing the life out of the man with his bare hands, when the official account states that the man in custody was fatally shot? Was he personally responsible for the deaths of 62 lawbreakers? Perhaps even more deaths could be attributed to him or to orders given by him. A former headmaster in Nakhon's Thasala District, who was distantly related to him on his mother's side, insisted that Khun Phan mostly employed psychological tricks on his prey and rarely used his gun; his offsiders were likely to have been responsible for the killings.[3] With his cunning and guile, was he a shaman or did he just pretend to be one? Had he really lived 108 years when he passed away, or was his age only 103?

I am tempted to yield to what, for a historian, is heresy: some details are unverifiable but socially true. The unverifiable details augmented by photography, by the internet and, since his death, by sculpture have solidified into a recognisable human actor, and the stories he told to his biographers have created a picturesque life that has invited cinematic treatment. He could be portrayed as an incorruptible action hero charging through the world with guns blazing in the name of the law to suppress crime and bring miscreants to justice. The film director Kongkiat Komesiri accepted this challenge and made two films for the mass market with

---

1   Nasan Phantarakrajchadech, Interview with the author, Nakhon Si Thammarat, 27 September 2009.
2   See the Appendix for an annotated list of biographies of Khun Phan.
3   Anan Ratanawong (b. 1932), Interview with the author, 6 December 2014.

the Australian-Lao actor Ananda Everingham in the role of Khun Phan.[4] The internet's desire for novelty and adventure has turned the southern policeman into a cultural hero, with narrators solemnly intoning his most dramatic exploits.

Taken together, the details point to truths about the person, the places and the times, but dates and placenames offer only an illusion of authenticity. Direct quotations from conversations nearly a century ago create a reality effect, but much about the policeman's life remains indistinct—not exactly unknowable, but confusing and, in places, misleading. No human being could have done all these things in just the way they are attested, we want to say, yet legends grow and flourish at the edges, where events, people and places fade into the shadows. In the southern policeman's case, and despite the high-resolution images online or the striking colour photographs in the books, it is as though we are viewing him through smudged spectacles or smoky glass. This blurred, indistinct image suited him in his line of work. He might depart quickly from the scene of an operation in an official car lest he be identified by people who sided with the man the police had just killed. Stories abound of his slipping into local communities in disguise to pursue his quarry and, to this end, the magical practices he cultivated were said to render him invisible so he could detect and punish, rather like the guerilla saboteurs who disappear into the local population to carry out their mission. This indistinctness and the undecidability of what he had or had not done also threw up around him an aura of apprehension and fear of what he might do and what he might be capable of doing. A weapon of peacekeeping is not only the firearm or the club, but also the uncertainty of knowing what action the law enforcer will take. When Khun Phan once boarded a train in the south, his stroll through the carriage was enough to shush the chattering passengers into silence.

Early years and education

Khun Phan, whose given name was Butr, was born the second eldest of seven siblings in the village of Ai Khiew in rural Nakhon Si Thammarat. Maybe his birth date was 18 February 1898. He died on 6 July 2006, which would have made him 108—the number of marks on the soles

---

4   *Khun Pan* (2016) and *Khun Pan 2* (2018). The first is described as 'caught between bio-pic and fictional action', whereas the second is 'fictional and entertaining' (*The Nation*, 7 August 2018).

of the Buddha's feet. The auspicious number 108 'comes down from heaven' in Buddhism, Brahmanism and astrology, and carries the promise of prosperity and good fortune (Okha 2007: 38). According to some biographies that give 1903 as the year of Khun Phan's birth, the date may have been a registrar's error. The cremation biography, which can be the final arbiter of such discrepancies, displays a photograph taken in 2000 of a celebration for his 100th birthday, in which case he would have been born in 1900, but the cremation biography also gives 1898 and 1903 as birth years, and other years turn up in books and interviews.[5] Thai authors expend many words canvassing the pros and cons of the different birth dates. Maybe Khun Phan gave his interlocutors different dates because he was vain, or perhaps he wanted to conceal the numbers associated with his birth—the year, day of the week, hour and minute of the event— lest his enemies cast a harmful spell conjured from the correct numbers. As we first peer into the past at the beginning of his life, the spectacles are already smudged.

Khun Phan's lifelong interest in Thai traditional medicine may have run in the family. On his father's side, one great-grandfather was a healer for the ruling family in Nakhon Si Thammarat, according to one biographer, and his paternal grandmother was the child of a Brahman. Another great-grandfather was a strict Muslim.[6]

Khun Phan's father was also his first teacher, and he began his studying at home. Khun Phan's early education at temple schools in the local district and in the town of Nakhon Si Thammarat was interrupted for several years beginning in 1914 when he fell ill with yaws—a disfiguring and potentially fatal disease before the advent of penicillin. After he recovered, his family sent him, in 1916, to complete his secondary education in the capital, where he lived at several monasteries as a temple boy (*dek wat*) in the charge of a Bangkok-based monk who was related to his mother. Bangkok monasteries had ties to the provinces through families and monastic lineages, and temple boys such as Khun Phan naturally congregated in monasteries in which the residents spoke the same regional dialect. He arrived in Bangkok too late in the academic year to enrol.

---

5   The *Bangkok Post* (22 August 2018) settled on 1903.

6   Anat (2006: 48); and *Prawat phi phroi phantharak* [*The Story of Phi Phroi Phantarak*], cremation eulogy for an elder relative attributed to Khun Phan (Photocopy of typescript, n.d.).

During the months he spent biding his time, he began to take an interest in the empowering and protective magical knowledge known as *saiyasat*, which he would cultivate for the rest of his life. The term—possibly derived from a Khmer word for excellence or expertise—refers to an order of knowledge that is both a weapon and a prophylactic. Khun Phan's cremation volume contains a detailed description of this corpus of knowledge as well as the names of his teachers and the places where he studied, but the elements that made up *saiyasat* were not discrete as though they were courses in a curriculum. The teacher transmitted the knowledge orally, although elements may be found scattered in hundreds of manuals archived in the National Library of Thailand and in published editions of the *phrommachat*. In daily life, the rituals and practices of *saiyasat* might be modified to suit the disposition of the practitioner (Thep 1978; Chalong 2007: 24–5; Chintapati 2007: 109–11; Saksit n.d.).

He began his early studies of *saiyasat* and astrology when he was in his mid-teens, living in a monastery where his teacher was Phra Thamwarodom, a southerner from Khuan Khanun district in Phatthalung who had received instruction at Wat Khao Or, the 'Vedic' academy where one could learn how to curse enemies and overpower opponents (Akhom 2001: 210–11). When the monk was appointed abbot of Wat Rachathirat, a monastery along the Chaophraya River, Khun Phan followed the older man, who would later become a high-ranking ecclesiastical official in the south. It was at Wat Rachathirat in the late 1830s that the future King Mongkut had resided when he conducted ordinations on a raft in the river that laid the foundations for the Dhammayut reform order. At Phra Thamwarodom's ordination into the reform order, his preceptor, whom he later served as secretary, was Prince-Patriarch Wachirayan Warorot, one of Mongkut's sons and brother of King Chulalongkorn (Ratchakawi 2000: 148–56). In this period of the reform order's history, Phra Thamwarodom was not the only monk to possess ritual knowledge of the arts of struggle.

Tracking Khun Phan's sojourn from monastery to monastery and mentor to mentor in these early years, we can observe that empowering and protective magical knowledge was to be found in many monasteries, including those that adhered to the strict Vinaya disciplines of the reform order. One of the most eminent Dhammayut monks of the nineteenth century, Sa, who had reached the top level of the Pali curriculum and belonged to Prince Mongkut's inner circle when he founded the reform order, knew a lot about spells, chants and horoscopes. He disrobed for several years and, while not a skirt-chaser, as the Thai language puts it, he spent his time as a layman hanging around gambling halls in the manner of a *nak leng*. This episode in his biography was private because of his later eminence as a senior ecclesiastic. He returned to the yellow robe when Mongkut became king and was later made Supreme Patriarch in the fifth reign (Thatchai 2013: 25–6). Well into the twentieth century, the so-called Vedic knowledge that made up *saiyasat* was far from alternative or marginal to Buddhism. It was mainstream, especially for men working in the institutions of political society charged with defending territory, conducting war and maintaining law and order.

Khun Phan completed his secondary schooling at Wat Benchamaphophit, built by King Chulalongkorn and known as the Monastery of the Fifth King. During his school years, he learned the art of tattooing and began to master the Thai martial art of swordplay (*krabi krabong*). He also excelled at gymnastics, judo and both Thai and Western boxing. During the 1920s, boxing became popular in Bangkok as a result of elite patronage, especially of King Vajiravudh (r. 1910–25), who championed physical fitness in the conviction that one was only truly alive when fighting. The king had spent nine years in England, where he received military training. It was this king who dispatched a contingent of Thai soldiers to join the Allies against Germany in World War I. On his return to Thailand, Vajiravudh established the Wild Tiger Corps and the Boy Scouts. Like Robert Baden-Powell, the English founder of the Boy Scouts, who saw the physical rigours of scouting as a way of controlling the libido, the king believed the nation's young men should develop their physiques and learn to be self-reliant (Reynolds 2014: 269–71). Vajiravudh proclaimed Thai boxing as the national sport and, in the reign that followed, the ring was modernised, boxing gloves were introduced and tournaments were held throughout the country (Sombat 2011: 33–4, 39–40).

Khun Phan's training in martial arts during his school years was in keeping with elite campaigns at the time to inculcate physical and mental toughness in the nation's male youth. This trend continued when the military became dominant after 1932 and championed a strong male body through the public events it held and the art it sponsored. Sculptures by students of Corrado Feroci (Silpa Bhirasri), who left Italy in 1923 just after the Fascist Party came to power, featured male virility and physical strength. Maurizio Peleggi has drawn attention to robust, homoerotic male physiques in the Euro-Asian statuary produced under Feroci's trained eye: *Archer* (1938), *Warrior* (ca. 1940) and *Farmer Sowing Rice* (ca. 1940) (Peleggi 2017: 128–9).

When Khun Phan left school, he was undecided about his next step. After briefly considering a career in government service, he spoke to a teacher at Wat Benchama about a placement in the military academy. None was available, so, according to one author, he approached a senior monk at Wat Bowonniwet, who suggested policing instead, and introduced him to Prince Khamrop, a military officer who became the first chief of the metropolitan and provincial police in 1916. The prince accepted him as a page while he bided his time until he could enrol for police training (Chalong 2007: 31–3). By the time he entered the police academy at Nakhon Pathom in 1925, he was sufficiently skilled in martial arts, including judo, boxing and Thai sword fighting, to be appointed a boxing instructor. Self-defence was important to his character. He was self-conscious about his size and wanted to be able to hold his own in a fight. He needed to strengthen himself physically and mentally or his diminutive height and spare frame would limit his prospects for rugged police duties. In his youthful journey of discovery and self-realisation during his years at the police academy, he furthered his study and acquisition of magical knowledge. He internalised it and made it one with his body in the belief that it could save him from sudden death (Chanthip 2007: 134).

At Nakhon Pathom—an ancient site in the orbit of the old royal base at Ayutthaya, where practices and beliefs about objects with supernatural powers had flourished for centuries—he spent time with Luang Pho Chaem, an eccentric monk disinclined to bathe regularly whose residence straddled the monastery boundary at the edge of a rice field. Cadets from the police academy who sought supernatural protection for what lay ahead and other laypeople seeking Buddhist incantations and spells (*phutthakhom*) were required to join the monk in the fields cultivating rice that would be stored for monastery use and shared with villagers if they needed it (Samphan 2007: 91–2). The eccentric monk would not be the last person to teach Khun Phan about spells that can cause loss of prosperity or reputation, illness or unexplained death. In his compendium of *saiyasat* knowledge, he included a brief discussion of spells under the southern Thai word *mop* (Phantharakratchadet 2007: 482; Anan 2008: 208, 348).

Khun Phan graduated from the police academy in 1929 ranked 10th in his class of 17, and with his friend, another southerner in the cohort, reported to the southern police command in Songkhla. They both wanted to work in Phatthalung, but the regional police commander selected his friend and assigned Khun Phan to Surat Thani, a less demanding post.

Banditry in Phatthalung required a strong man for its suppression, and the smaller Khun Phan supposedly did not have the physique required for the job. Khun Phan was aggrieved and, while he did not dwell on his feelings of inferiority in interviews, self-consciousness about his size came to the surface on this occasion. While the commander of the station was away on other business, the paperwork to carry out the boss's decision was unaccountably mishandled, the assignments were somehow reversed and the young constable was posted to Songkhla as he wished. He wanted to prove to his superiors that, although he was a small man, he did not lack the strength to do serious police work. His size was to dog him throughout his career. In the mid-1940s, the national police chief he was serving under, Rear Admiral Luang Sangwonyutthakit, exclaimed in his presence: 'So how come they call you, a tiny slip of a man, Tiger [*suea*]?' Khun Phan was taken aback, perhaps offended at the insinuation that a small guy was not up to the job, and he wondered what the chief might be thinking. The boss was later reassured that he was indeed very capable and appointed him chief in a central Thai province (Praphon 1983: 16; Chalong 2007: 49; Samphan 2007: 87, 93–4).

Five months after his posting to Songkhla, Khun Phan was reassigned to Phatthalung, where he sought out the master teachers at Wat Khao Or to be initiated in their teachings before he captured his first lawbreakers.[7] The cave monastery in Khuan Khanun district, Phatthalung, is built into a limestone outcrop that rises from the plain. An unassuming entrance greets the visitor, and beyond the gate one finds the usual assortment of shrines, preaching hall, dwellings for monks, a pavilion in which laypeople can congregate and rest, and water tanks. A complex of passageways and caverns extends deep into the hill. I did not explore the entire subterranean world, but I did descend into the largest cave, where the ritual bath was once taken and which was now empty except for a few small sacred images. The academy of learning that evolved at Khao Or, which Khun Phan would have heard about in his youth from family members related to some of the monastery's residents, was known for holistic knowledge consisting of *śastra* (Thai, *sat*)—sciences that protected the body and disciplined the mind. Laymen as well as monks gave instruction in the regimens that were physical as well as spiritual and included diet and herbal therapies. Men travelled from afar to imbibe what was taught there—for example,

---

7   I follow the chronology in Samphan (2007: 97–8). Wira (2001: 92) and Chalong (2007: 89) state that Khun Phan captured his first bandits *before* his initiation at Wat Khao Or.

Heng Phraiwan from Ayutthaya, who became a noted practitioner on the central plains providing soldiers with tattoos and amulets. When he grew indifferent to his studies in Penang, where his affluent parents had sent him, Heng abandoned his formal education and spent three months during the 1930s at Khao Or to learn about the arts of struggle and methods to protect the self (Suwit 2011: 102–3).

Archaeological evidence from the region's prehistory has shown that Shaivism was practised in the mid south, and plentiful images of Vishnu indicate that Hinduism strengthened local political authority from the fifth to the eleventh centuries CE (Wannasarn 2013b: 149, 156). Indian merchants came and went over this period, and Tamil inscriptions have been found on both coasts, the earliest being a goldsmith's touchstone at Krabi on the west coast (third and fourth centuries CE), and in the ninth century to the north at Takuapa another Tamil inscription testifies to the dedication of a new tank essential to the ritual life of a Hindu temple. A rock-cut inscription in Sanskrit from Nakhon Si Thammarat identified a community of Saivite Brahmans, and evidence of the ongoing role of Indian merchants comes from a Tamil inscription in Nakhon from the late twelfth or thirteenth century (Guy 2011: 248–55).

In Phatthalung, Brahmans had lived in the Wat Khao Or cave complex for centuries, observing practices and beliefs based on a corpus of Vedic spiritual and medical texts, although Vedic here does not refer to the Sanskrit Vedas as such. Brahmans sometimes undertake purification baths, and immersion in the herbal bath required of Khao Or initiates may have been inherited from earlier times. These practices and beliefs were distinct from the Buddhism taught in monasteries in nearby Nakhon Si Thammarat. According to the Phatthalung chronicle compiled in the early twentieth century, families of Brahmans (*chi phram*) had lived in the area from time immemorial, particularly in the subdistrict of Lampam, and local people had long worshipped a mix (*ponkan*) of Brahmanism and Buddhism at the shrine there. From earliest times, religious society was not monotheistic in the region, and Mahayana Buddhism and Brahmanism were interactive and complementary rather than exclusive (Skilling 1997: 98; Krom 2002: 235; Ran 2007: 79). Nakhon Si Thammarat hosts a festival in September–October, the 10th lunar month, which is said to be based on a Brahmanic ceremony from India. The Buddha 'credited' the value of the ceremony and so allowed it—another example of this mixing. Descendants recall their ancestors from the underworld by offering them food; a subsequent merit-making ceremony is needed to facilitate the ancestors' return below

(Kasem 2008: 79–84). The amalgamation of Brahmanism and Buddhism is ubiquitous in Thai religious life today—for instance, in the homage paid to Hindu deities by Thai Buddhists, who see the gods as integral to the practice of Buddhism. Localised Brahmanism occurs not only in the mid south, but also in many parts of the country, including Bangkok (McDaniel 2013: 194, 206).

Such was the prestige of the mid south's Brahman families that courts in the central plains invited Brahman priests from Nakhon Si Thammarat to conduct rites for the royal family, including the coronation of the first Bangkok king in the late eighteenth century. When it seemed that the priestly line at Khao Or would die out, the resident Brahmans—concerned that the cave complex would be abandoned and the knowledge and sanctity of the place might fade into obscurity—recruited a Buddhist monk from a nearby monastery and presented him with the manuscripts to carry on the tradition in a more Buddhist vein.[8] Some of the Khao Or graduates who had received instruction from the master teachers fanned out to other monasteries where they adapted what they had learned and imparted their own version of the knowledge to their disciples, while other graduates of Wat Khao Or disrobed and became lay vectors of the teachings (Ran 2007: 88–9). Khun Phan took some of his instruction at Wat Donsala, an offshoot of the Khao Or monastery, where willing disciples also endured the herbal bath and the other rites of initiation into *saiyasat* knowledge.

A man wishing to become an adept in the Khao Or knowledge needed a sponsor, a person who could vouch for his character and worthiness for initiation. In Khun Phan's case, a close friend who was a disciple of the Khao Or teachings served this purpose and introduced the policeman to Ajan Iat, a monk of rectitude who had his own special powers and could treat mental instability. It was said that Iat could not only cure madness, but also cause it (Ran 2007: 43, 125). Khun Phan approached Iat for instruction that would benefit him in his police duties, but the monk declined to impart any knowledge that would lead to the death of bandits and criminals. Instead, he referred Khun Phan to his own teacher, Nam Kaewjan, then a layman who specialised in *saiyasat* for defence, or offence as the case might be. Later in Khun Phan's career, when he was preparing himself to pursue outlaws with whom he shared the same teachers, Ajan Nam would perform a cursing ritual for him to strike fear in his

---

8   Wet (n.d.: 32–3, 48–9) does not provide dates.

adversaries (Wira 2001: 95). Ajan Nam's father had received instruction from an earlier generation of the monastery's master teachers, and Nam, having been ordained as a monk briefly for one rains (*phansa*) only, had disrobed, married and fathered two daughters. In his lay life, he assisted the senior monks at Wat Khao Or and acquired a reputation for *saiyasat* knowledge among people from all walks of life, including members of the Thai royal family. When King Bhumibol toured the south, he often visited Ajan Nam, who late in life was reordained at Wat Dawn Sala, in 1963, and received a royal cremation when he died (Ran 2007: 145–51).

To assess the suitability of a candidate to receive the holistic knowledge taught at Khao Or, a meeting of disciples and existing adepts would sit in judgement and inquire into whether the candidate was pure of heart and could confirm that he had never wronged another man's wife or family. The candidate needed to affirm his sincerity and intentions to use the knowledge wisely and truthfully. Misuse would besmirch the reputation of the monastery and its teachers and could cause injury and even death to the initiate. Ajan Iat instructed the policeman to be fearless, bold and brave. He was told to be incorruptible and refuse bribes; he must not wrong another man's wife or family; he must not curse his mother or father; and he must conduct himself in an orderly and disciplined way. He must be truthful and true to his word. If he violated any of these strictures, harm would befall him, and the consecrated sesame oil he was soon to ingest would flow out of his pores and he would die (Wira 2001: 92–3). These instructions on how to behave were similar to those set out in a code of conduct for warriors and 'true men' (*chai chatri*). A printed manual, which includes incantations and supplications for protection from harm that were imparted in an oral tradition, purports to derive from Brahman rituals and practices inherited from a distant past (W. Jinpradit 1996).

The initiation consisted of four separate rites (Ran 2007: 90–5). After astrological calculations stipulated an auspicious time, date and day— usually a Saturday or Tuesday, the days reckoned by *saiyasat* belief as the most propitious—the initiate ingested therapeutic herbs, black sticky rice and raw sesame oil that had been consecrated by the officiating monk. Initiates then immersed themselves for several days in a tank containing a heady brew of 108 medicinal herbs that treated or prevented just about every disease in the Thai medical register; the bath also toughened the skin against bullets and bladed weapons. When Khun Phan underwent the ritual, the bath was taken in a boat at the top of the limestone hillock.

A cement bath was later constructed in the cave underground, and in recent times a new cement tank was built on the slope of the hill. A grainy black-and-white photograph of poor resolution shows a couple of men in the cave tank, their heads just above water. It was said that Khun Phan was instrumental in reviving the tradition of immersion in the herbal bath (Wet n.d.: 45).

A bundle of palm-leaf manuscripts that supposedly lists the therapeutic herbs used in the bath graces the cover of *Khao Or: Siam's academy of Vedic knowledge*, and Chalong Jeyakhom remembers seeing the bundle of palm-leaf manuscripts at the monastery (Wet n.d.).[9] A sceptic might wonder whether one or two vital ingredients on the list might have been withheld by the master teachers to protect the patent on their recipe. The 108 herbs were credited with health-giving, miraculous properties, including protection against bullets and blades, rapid recovery from fever and protection against disease (Ran 2007: Appendix 3). Protection against sharp objects might have been more than miraculous. Some of the plants in the bath had thorns that pricked the skin, drew blood and allowed the herbal solution to enter the body, rather like a vaccination. Scar tissue formed over the wounds, hence 'the man with a tough hide' (*khon tai nang niaw*). The herbal brew was said to be so toxic that if care were not taken and it entered the body through orifices, it could cause blindness and deafness.[10] Khun Phan was also instructed in the use of herbs that suppressed the appetite for his long patrols and overnight stakeouts. At an early stage in my research, I tried to identify the therapeutic herbs with their botanical names, but I succeeded only in linking *jorakhe* to aloe vera, a styptic with antibacterial properties of modest—perhaps questionable— effectiveness when applied to burns and small cuts (Mulholland 1987: 137–9). Other herbs in the traditional Thai pharmacopeia were useful as balms, astringents, laxatives, pain relievers, diuretics and soporifics.

In the mid-1970s, immersion in the herbal bath started to become commercialised, and the cost of up to THB30,000 or about US$474 at the time (an estimate of the mid-1990s for locating and harvesting the therapeutic herbs) was borne by the initiate (Chaiyawut 1996: 52, 100). Police, soldiers and affluent civil servants outlaid this amount to soak in

---

9   Chalong Jeyakhom, Interview with the author, Bangkok, 2012.

10   Suepphong Saengwan (b. 1962), a distant relative of Khun Phan's, Interview with the author, Songkhla, 4 September 2012; Chanthip Phantarakrajchadech, Interview with the author, Nakhon Si Thammarat, 9 September 2012.

the bath and benefit from its therapeutic properties that promised good health, prosperity and avoidance of harm. When I visited the monastery in 2008, immersion in the herbal bath was still a lucrative business.

In pursuit

From the instruction he received at the Khao Or monastery, which he visited more than once, and his association with its master teachers and lay disciples, Khun Phan became familiar with local community networks. He spent a half-dozen years at the Phatthalung police station and returned to the province twice more in his career. His biographers give detailed accounts of many outlaws he and his police associates captured and killed, but several operations in the south as well as others in the mid north and central plains stand out for what they reveal about his methods, his relationships with the police hierarchy and its procedures and the social conditions in which he worked. In light of the stories he told, some incidents remained in his memory more clearly than others. They were violent incidents and, from my reading of Khun Phan's versions of these events, as revealed by his biographers, they carried emotional weight for him as well.

Khun Phan planned his operations carefully and employed subterfuge, surveillance, deception and disguise. In preparation for pursuit and capture, he would calculate the horoscopes of the policemen with whom he intended to work and selected to join the team only those officers whose horoscopes were propitious for the tasks that lay ahead. The operation might require specific abilities and end in physical combat or a gun battle. An officer who lacked the nerve for violent confrontations was a liability, and the horoscope provided a reason to exclude such a person. Police work entailed long hours for extended periods, and officers needed to be strong, healthy, mentally tough and fit. In one of Khun Phan's cases in Phatthalung, the team camped out in the jungle for 15 nights. As with any police or military operation, conditions at the appointed hour sometimes required last-minute adjustments to plans, so officers needed to be able to act quickly and decisively under pressure (Wira 2001: 67). Khun Phan's temperament was suited to the job. To be sure, he had a talent for mobilising resources and manpower and acting decisively, but the deaths that resulted from his actions sometimes breached community and police standards, or they disrupted cosy arrangements between lawbreakers and corrupt police or government officials. More than once in his career he was charged with exceeding his brief or using excessive force, and such was the case in 1930 at the outset of his career.

The first lawbreaker to fall victim to young Constable Butr Phantharak was Suea Sang, a strapping man notorious in the community for his cruelty and willingness to kill. *Suea* (literally 'tiger') was an epithet for an outlaw, bandit and *nak leng*. Suea Sang had escaped from the Trang jail and taken refuge under the protection of a headman in Mount Khanun District and the headman's circle of *nak leng*. Sang threatened villagers with violent retribution if they informed the authorities of his whereabouts, but there was no shortage of local people willing to share what they knew, including a relative of the blacksmith, who tipped off police. In the ensuing gun fight at dawn, Khun Phan narrowly missed being shot, saved only by a magic sign on his hat and a talisman (*takrut*) covering his breast: 'I was proud that the magic powers were with me that day', he later boasted. Firearms in the day were unreliable, and perhaps the outlaw's gun misfired. Khun Phan, exhausted from days and nights of pursuit and fearing for his life, soon found himself in a desperate struggle with a man twice his size, each of them biting and eye-gouging. Sang was wearing a sarong tied loosely in the local style so his manhood was readily accessible to the policeman's tactics, and Khun Phan finally prevailed by pinning Sang's genitals to the floor with his toes. He 'broke the outlaw's balls' and squeezed the life out of Sang, who turned green and expired on the spot (Chalong 2007: 77–86; Samphan 2007: 105–6). Khun Phan had proven himself by showing that a flyweight could overpower a light heavyweight. He had made his mark in a theatrical way at the beginning of his career and demonstrated that his small frame would not handicap him in carrying out his duties. Sang's teeth had drawn only a little blood and the knife wounds had not penetrated very deep—proof that immersion in the herbal bath had toughened Khun Phan's skin. He subsequently had his upper left arm tattooed to cover Sang's bite marks, asserting that he wanted to be reminded of how close he had come to being jailed for killing a prisoner (Okha 2007: 52). Sang's corpse was taken to the home of the village headman, who had protected the outlaw—a sign of Khun Phan's brutal victory. The brush with death had refreshed a sense of his own mortality.[11]

---

11   Khun Phan published 'The gun did not fire', his version of Sang's capture and death, in *Phutthawet* (3[5], August 1979), reprinted in Samphan (1996: 66–73). According to the list of 62 *suea* (bandit) fatalities by gunshot attributed to Khun Phan and police accomplices, Sang was shot to death, not asphyxiated, by Khun Phan (Wira 2001: 185). The source of this list is Konhoi ('Whorl'), a pseudonym of Khun Phan's son Chanthip.

A leaflet—the social media of the day—soon appeared, accusing the young constable of using unnecessary force that resulted in the death of a captured man. The anonymous leaflet (*bat sonthe*) asked why, if Sang was already in police custody, it had been necessary to kill him. Khun Phan was aggrieved that the outlaw, although now quite dead, had triumphed with this accusation of homicide. Even though he had filed an accurate account of how the man died in a hand-to-hand struggle, the top brass did not give credence to his report. As it happened, a noble police official from Bangkok on an inspection tour in the district, accompanied by his daughter, was on hand to congratulate Khun Phan. He was nonplussed at the daughter's appreciation of his brave actions, and it was not the last time a young woman would be smitten by him after one of his operations (Samphan 2007: 112–13).

In November of the same year, Khun Phan, with police accomplices, brought to heel another bandit gang (*kok*), of 16 men, headed by Suea Mueang, who was killed along with three of his men. The men had received an amnesty and were freed from prison in 1925 when the seventh Bangkok monarch, King Prajdhipok, ascended the throne, but they had rampaged through districts in the south killing and terrorising witnesses who had testified against them (Wira 2001: 187; Chalong 2007: 93–111).

Khun Phan achieved a great deal in his first months of duty, and when the national police chief came through the district on an inspection tour, he halted his motorcade to congratulate Khun Phan and the rest of the team. The civil administrator of the region followed later, riding an elephant, and so travelled more slowly. He, too, congratulated the young policeman. In 1931, the year before the absolute monarchy ended, Butr Phantharak was awarded the noble rank of *khun*—an unusual honour for a policeman of such modest rank. Other members of the police team, the governor and a headman were also ennobled and promoted (Samphan 2007: 126–7).

No action had been taken to discipline Khun Phan when he was accused of murdering Suea Sang, and he remained in his post at Phatthalung until 1936, when he was appointed divisional head in Songkhla. In 1938, he was promoted to captain, and in the same year he married a Phatthalung woman, Chalao Bunyanuwat, who was pregnant with his first son, Amorn, who passed away some time ago. His marriage to Chalao created conflicting loyalties for him: to his new family on the one hand and his police duties on the other. He gave priority to the latter over the former and insisted that duty came first, so his mother travelled to Phatthalung to help Chalao with the birth and look after the infant child (Chalong 2007: 127–8). Khun Phan had received an order to apprehend Ahweh Sador Talae, a Muslim from Narathiwat who possessed strange and powerful talismans. Khun Phan had shot him several times to no effect. He could elude police by making himself invisible and he was said to own a heritage *kris* belonging to a former Kelantan lord.[12] Ahweh Sador had already been captured once and sent to prison in Satthahip, Cholburi, on Thailand's east coast; then, using *saiyasat* magic, he slipped his shackles and those of fellow inmates and escaped, returning to the south, where he mobilised his gang to plunder and murder, killing his victims in a particularly cruel manner. According to Khun Phan's account, southern Muslims lauded Ahweh Sador's aspirations for building community identity; the Thai Government, for its part, regarded him as a violent separatist (Chalong 2007: 123; Samphan 2007; 141–9) [13]

Khun Phan's version of the case is limited to his role in the operation, and neither the wider context of Ahweh Sador's depredations nor his affiliation with any organised groups is clear from the biographies. When Field Marshal Pibul became prime minister at the end of 1938, Thai Government policies towards the deep south hardened and became more forcefully assimilationist, but before the army's ascendency, the state's cultural policies vis-à-vis the Muslim population in the deep south were integrative. After 1932, economic development and political participation in the region improved, and in the 1937–38 elections, three-quarters of MPs in the four Malay provinces were Muslim. The son of the former Raja of Pattani had returned to Thailand from exile in northern Malaya—a sign that the Thai Government recognised his status in the region (Kadir Che Man 1990: 64–5; Ockey 2008: 126–31). Should Ahweh Sador be understood as a political bandit linked to separatist movements of the time or just a criminal? A colleague from the deep south assured me he was an insurgent, not a common murderer, but apart from the accounts in biographies of Khun Phan, details of the Ahweh Sador episode have proved elusive. In any case, Khun Phan finally succeeded in capturing him and taking possession of his *kris*. Wary of being identified and of retribution at the hands of people who sided with the dead man, Khun Phan was driven away from Narathiwat and back to Songkhla in the governor's car before he could be photographed. According to Khun

---

12   *Ahweh* is probably an inexact transcription of *awang*, a Malay honorific for a man.
13   Khun Phan's version of Ahweh Sador's capture and death, published in *Suwitcha* by the Songkhla Nakkharin University-Pattani, is reproduced in Samphan (2007: 144–7).

Phan's son, out of respect for Ahweh Sador's special powers and struggle to defend his community's territory, the policeman had no intention of killing the man, who later died in jail of a self-administered poison.[14]

The capture and death of Ahweh Sador were popular with Thai Muslims, and Muslims in Malaya bestowed the title 'Little Raja' (*rayo kaji*) on Khun Phan for his role in apprehending the man—an epithet that stayed with the policeman for years. The Governor of Kelantan rewarded the southern policeman with a *kris*—an emblem of Malay sovereignty and a weapon with magical powers (Samphan 2007: 149). A *kris* could fly through the air, leap out of its sheath to kill an adversary, make itself invisible so its victim was unaware of impending danger and kill victims by stabbing their footprints. It could also extinguish fires and prescribe auspicious times for its owner's travel. The *kris* came alive in the annealing process that alchemically purified and transformed the iron ore into a weapon that was spiritually charged. The type of *kris* found most often in the south came from Pattani; another type was distinctive to Songkhla (Woolley 1947: 71–5; O'Connor 1985: 55–6; Suthiwong 1999: 138–9). Through the years, Khun Phan assembled a collection of these blades and placed one under the cradle of each of his sons when they were born; daughters were given knives.[15]

After the Ahweh Sador case, in 1938, Khun Phan's superiors appointed him chief of police in Phatthalung, where unrest in the countryside had continued after his previous departure, and where he was well away from the coast when the Japanese invaded in early 1942 on their march to Singapore. Community gossip held that he had fought the Japanese, but he demurred on the point, and when pressed for a reason the Japanese kept their distance and had not marched inland to Phatthalung, he replied with mock hubris that 'maybe they knew I was working in Phatthalung' (Chalong 2007: 151). On 1 April 1942, Khun Phan was appointed provincial police chief in Surat Thani, where he spent 13 months. There the bandit Suea Sai had taken up residence along with 30 householders who had migrated from the central plains. Suea Sai's gang was into burglary and moonshine, and the local police authorities had been unable to bring him to justice because of his derring-do and the difficulties of the terrain. After wounding and capturing Suea Sai, Khun Phan's team took him by

---

14   Chanthip Phantarakrajchadech, Interview with the author, 9 September 2012.
15   Nasan Phantarakrajchadech, Interview with the author, Nakhon Si Thammarat, 27 September 2009.

boat to Surat Thani town. As the procession of vessels made its way along the canals and the Tapi River to the provincial centre, communities along the route outdid each other with partying and *nora* dancing to celebrate the operation's success. Suea Sai confessed to his crimes and, with pistol in hand, had his photograph taken with Khun Phan, but succumbed to his wounds and died soon after.

Suea Sai's capture and death at the hands of the Lion Lawman came to the attention of the national police chief during World War II, General Luang Aduldetcharat (Bat Phuengphrakhun), an army officer who had been a member of the coup group that overthrew the absolute monarchy in 1932. In Surat Thani market, the Ivory Bamboo Casino—a popular brothel, opium den and gambling hall—had become entrenched over the years, and General Luang Adul wanted it closed. Opium distribution and consumption in the town were rife and causing problems; dishonest local officials and police were part of the problem.[16] The mafia figure who controlled the casino was 'a person of influence'—the wry Thai idiom for a powerful person, a gangster-like figure close to or part of the local power structure. The casino was on the second floor of a two-storey building in the market; on the ground floor was a restaurant from which gamblers could order noodles, rice and drinks for free. Using coded communications that bypassed the local police command as well as officers in the Bangkok police hierarchy, General Luang Adul recruited Khun Phan to close the casino, which the policeman agreed to do on the condition that he could use police officers of his own choosing to circumvent the corrupt local police. Khun Phan preferred to work with people he had known for some time or previously worked with, people he could trust and rely on if the operation were to turn violent. On this occasion, the reconnaissance required meeting with the provincial police chief and confiding in him about the secret communications with the Bangkok command, and he needed to enlist the chief's assistance in transferring local police officers to other posts. To keep the plan secure, Khun Phan decided not to share his planning with the provincial governor. Surveillance of the premises was necessary, so he called on a police chum (*kloe*) from the south to come to Surat Thani and make the intimate acquaintance of a young widow who lived in a shophouse adjoining the casino. Holes were drilled in the thin bamboo walls of the casino to spy on activities inside. Khun Phan's

---

16 *Kongchin*, the term for dishonest or corrupt, is a loanword from Chinese (*jianchen*) and is the binary opposite of *tongchin* (Ch., *zhongchen*): honest, loyal.

planning raised the casino owner's suspicions and soon he was being followed. To prepare for the final assault and to divert attention from his objective, Khun Phan pretended to leave for an inspection tour out of town. In fact, he had taken his team to cut ivory bamboo that grew profusely in the area to make a ladder with which to scale the casino building from the outside.

In the end, the operation was violent and the casino was utterly destroyed. There were 21 arrests, although the casino owner, who still had influence through his corrupt networks, managed to escape. The police coroner was slow in arriving to examine the corpses, which were left out in the sun for seven to eight days to be scavenged by dogs and crows. The regional police commander was furious at the way Khun Phan had handled the operation. Instead of receiving praise for shutting down 'the casino from hell', Khun Phan was charged with using excessive force and transferred to the northern provincial centre of Phichit (Chalong 2007: 151–71; Samphan 2007: 164–79). A university student from Surat Thani told me that community memory of the Ivory Bamboo Casino lives on in the town, even though the building that once housed that den of iniquity and hub of nefarious transactions between officialdom and the local mafia is nowadays a noodle shop.

Khun Phan—coming from another part of the country—knew almost no one when he arrived in Phichit in September 1943. From the first night, when he heard gunfire, he realised that what appeared to be a quiet town with few social issues had its share of troublemakers and hooligans. A particular problem for the police were deserters from army units in neighbouring Phitsanulok who had migrated into the district and caused trouble for villagers. A policeman relies on local knowledge, so after spending a couple of months assessing the situation, Khun Phan cultivated the acquaintance of two Chinese brothers from Hainan. Ko Yang (Sae Ui), the younger, who owned the opium concession and raised horses; and Ko Yueang, the older brother, who cultivated rice and raised cattle and water buffalo. The three men were about the same age and shared mutual interests. The Chinese brothers needed a modicum of public order to ensure their business activities ran smoothly, and Khun Phan, whom they addressed respectfully as 'Chief', relied on them as a local resource to take advantage of their networks and knowledge of the province's social dynamics. Khun Phan would often stay overnight with the younger brother when he was in town, and Ko Yang would lend the southern policeman a horse when he went on patrol to remote parts of the province. After Khun Phan left the province, it reverted to its wild ways. Bandits fleeing from police operations in neighbouring provinces came into the districts to steal cattle. In one year alone, Phichit went through three police chiefs because of unrest that followed Khun Phan's departure and accompanied instability in the Bangkok police command during the last years of the war (Okha 2007: 27–35).

Phichit could boast many *saiyasat* practitioners, laymen as well as monks, and the town of Chalawan had a concentration of such specialists—a hint that warriors on both sides of the law were active there. The father of Okha Buri, author of *Unlocking the Secrets of Khun Phantharakratchadet*, was a student of one such specialist. Suea Thai was a special forces 'tiger soldier' in the entourage of Prince Chumphon (Abhakara Kiartivongse), one of King Chulalongkorn's sons, who modernised the Thai navy and was himself a master of the magical arts. The prince valued the 'tiger soldier's' knowledge of *saiyasat* and its chants and spells, but when Suea Thai was accused of a violent crime, he decided to flee and spent many years running from the law in rural Thailand, sometimes crossing into Laos, Cambodia, Malaya or Singapore. Once the statute of limitations had expired, he settled in Phichit and changed his name to Pho Lim. Khun Phan knew about his background, but far from regarding the man as a hardened criminal, he saw Pho Lim as yet another master of *saiyasat* who might supplement his own stock of knowledge, including the power to stop bullets and disable firearms. One day a gang of 500 outlaws attacked Pho Lim's village and opened fire, yet not a single bullet touched him, so the story went—a miraculous outcome that immediately made him a person of great interest to the community. Owing to their common interests and skills, the two men became very close. Like Khun Phan, Pho Lim (aka Suea Thai) was a master of boxing and traditional Thai sword fighting (*krabi krabong*), and the pair—both of small stature, but one with a dark complexion (Khun Phan) and the other light (Pho Lim)— would perform the sword dance in public to the delight of Phichit crowds (Okha 2007: 124–30).

Suea Nom, known to his followers as Ajan Suea Nom—*ajan* being a respected epithet for teacher—was another case that came to Khun Phan's notice during his time in Phichit. The man did not break the law and enjoyed a reputation in the villages as a healer and tattooist who could cast spells, which also made him popular with ne'er-do-wells who availed themselves of his powers to impart invulnerability. His stubborn refusal to take responsibility for their thieving had made him an irritant to the police. Khun Phan was called to help apprehend Suea Nom and, after a skirmish in which two of Nom's followers died, the policeman finally captured the man and his accomplices and bound them with rope. As the men were being ferried across the Yom River under police guard, the boat snagged on tree roots, overturned and Nom drowned. When the body was recovered many days later, it appeared that the rope had been tied so tightly around his neck that it must have asphyxiated him. His head was lost in the water and his decomposed remains were cremated before family could pay their last respects (Okha 2007: 153–7).[17] The gruesome end to Suea Nom at the hands of the Lion Lawman and his men caused dread in bandit circles, but the police command was satisfied. Luang Adul rewarded Khun Phan with a six-pointed star and promoted him to major.

It was in Phichit, where Khun Phan was chief of police during the Japanese occupation of Thailand, that he acquired his famous Red Sword, so-called because he carried it wrapped in a red cloth. When he first laid eyes on the weapon, it was an heirloom in the possession of Luang Klaklangnarong, a soldier who had moved to Phichit to take up his official duties and a scion of the Phraya Phichai lineage in Uttaradit. Phraya Phichai fought alongside General Taksin, the eighteenth-century ruler who reunited the Siamese empire after the fall of Ayutthaya and later took the throne. Nowadays in the town of Laplae, Uttaradit, a spirit medium will channel Phraya Phichai for a small donation. The sword, which had its origins in an iron mine in Nam Phi, where ore was reserved for the king's weapons, was said to be stained with the blood of the kingdom's ancient enemies. Or was that vivid language just a rhetorical flourish of Khun Phan's biographer?

The mine is now a minor tourist destination, with a museum and shop selling small plastic bags of ore that is smelted locally into ingots and then shipped elsewhere to be transformed into swords, knives and other implements. When I visited the mine in November 2017, a couple of kids were lowering magnets into a large depression hoping to extract flecks of iron ore from the deposit, exhausted of what the earth had once gifted. In the course of his duties, the policeman sought out Luang Klaklangnarong's company, and the nobleman grew to so admire Khun Phan's skill at swordplay and the traditional Siamese sword dancing he performed at local festivities that he regarded him as an 'adopted' son

---

17   This account is drawn from Okha (2007: 153–7) and Samphan (2007: 180–6); the former provides the most graphic details.

(*luk buntham*). The surviving descendants in Phraya Phichai's lineage were not sufficiently skilled in swordplay and thus did not qualify to inherit the sword, so with Luang Klaklangnarong's blessing and confidence that the sword would be in the hands of someone willing to lay down his life for the country, it passed into Khun Phan's possession (Okha 2007: 165–76; Samphan 2007: 191–4). Along with the *kris* that he was given after he captured Ahweh Sador in 1938, the Red Sword was no mere souvenir but personal regalia that Khun Phan would treasure for the spiritual powers imbued in its forging.

In June 1945, as the war was ending, Khun Phan was transferred from Phichit to Chainat in the central plains, where bandits in large groups (*kok*) of up to 100 had the run of the countryside. Economic conditions had worsened during the Japanese occupation and food was in short supply. Cultivators abandoned their land, migrated and began stealing cattle to feed themselves; such people were easily recruited into the bandit way of life. Crime and violence had reached the point of national crisis, and the worst affected region was the central plains (Chalong 2013: 194). The most powerful bandit leader, whose influence extended beyond the borders of a single province, was Suea Fai, a village headman from a Suphanburi district bordering Chainat who had been charged with murder. Collusion by government officials exacerbated the problems of maintaining law and order, and Suea Fai's network within officialdom had given him a degree of social cachet, enhancing his prestige in the eyes of local people.

Suea Fai was not just a thief with murderous tendencies, but also a local boss who exercised his authority over land and agricultural production, and who enforced a strict code of conduct among his followers. Those recommending a recruit for gang membership would be punished publicly and cruelly if their candidate broke the rules, and a 'killing field' (*lan prahan*) was designated for this purpose. Prospective gang members were not allowed to have been ordained as Buddhist monks and were required to declare that they had no compunction about violating the precepts of the religion, especially the one that forbade the taking of life. His followers also needed to ask his permission if they wanted to marry. He lived in a fortified house with a commanding view of the Suphan River and charged freight barges up to THB500 (US$25) for using the waterway. He warned Khun Phan in writing to stay away from Suphanburi and passed along an envelope containing a payment of THB20,000 (about US$1,000 at the time), which the policeman returned via a courier, who pocketed the bribe. Other bandits were left their own turfs in the central provinces to control, but Fai controlled the largest tracts. He had the most manpower as well as a massive armoury available to his followers for their raids. His sway over his domain was *imperium in imperiō* (Samphan 2007: 196–202).

Suea Dam, another Suphanburi outlaw, controlled sugarcane fields and an opium parlour and was known to have special powers and talismans similar to Khun Phan's. For 16 years, he eluded the police, until Khun Phan finally asked for a meeting, at which they shook hands and embraced. They had shared the same teacher, which created a basis for mutual respect. Out of regard for Suea Dam's gentlemanly manner and the code he lived by, Khun Phan proposed to settle their differences by trading a life for a life. After a shootout in which hundreds of rounds were fired, Dam surrendered a member of his gang and his camp was torched. Khun Phan killed the hostage, burnt the corpse, photographed the cremains and filed a police report attesting to the end of Suea Dam. In return for Khun Phan faking his death and allowing him to escape, Suea Dam renounced his outlaw ways and was ordained as a monk in June 1953. Known in his later years by the monastic epithet Luang Pho, Dam was still wearing the yellow robe in 2014 and giving interviews about the peace deal he had struck with the southern policeman. Another outlaw in Chainat arrested by Khun Phan at the time was Suea Mahesuan, Thailand's Robin Hood, who died of natural causes in November 2014 at the age of 101. Suea Bai, yet another Robin Hood of the Chaophraya Basin, passed away in May 2015 at the age of 94.[18] A lengthy feature published by *Art and Culture* on the history of outlaw culture during and after the war does not fail to mention Khun Phan's contribution to curtailing the activities of the *suea* (Kong 1997). The public memory of the worst deeds of these men has faded, but the longevity of the outlaws in life and in literature has led to their apotheosis as minor cultural heroes.

A new chief of police, Phra Raminthara, replaced Luang Adul in 1945 when the government changed at the end of the Pacific War. To combat the lawlessness and unrest on the central plains, the Bangkok command created an elite task force under the direction of Police Colonel Sawat Kankhet and Khun Phan (Chalong 2013: 195). Suea Fai was induced to surrender, and Khun Phan was instrumental in organising a tense meeting

---

18   Matichon (2014b), in which the chronology of the peace meeting and shootout is not straightforward; and Manat (1997: 100). See also Matichon (2014a, 2015).

between the outlaw and the police chief, which took place in a Suphanburi hotel room. During the negotiations, Khun Phan had the barrel of his gun trained on Suea Fai through a hole in the ceiling. Phra Raminthara offered Suea Fai an amnesty if he agreed to work with the task force to suppress the other outlaw gangs. Fai's surrender was suddenly stalled when Phra Raminthara was appointed Deputy Minister of Interior, and a new police chief replaced him. Another officer, Luang Narintharasorasak, was appointed head of crime suppression in Suphanburi, and Khun Phan was relieved of his post in the elite task force and ordered to hand over the operations in Suphanburi to Luang Narintharasorasak. In an effort to overturn this decision and recover his position, he lobbied his former chief, to no avail. Months of rivalry with Luang Narintharasorasak, including allegations about Khun Phan's scandalous behaviour, culminated in the latter's transfer to Ayutthaya. He was ordered to pack up his belongings, return weapons, budget documents and other files to the central command and leave Chainat (Samphan 2007: 247–56).

The unrest and violence from 1945 to 1950 that the police were determined to quell in Chainat, Suphanburi, Ayutthaya and Kamphaeng Phet resulted in part from the large supply of military weapons left over from the war years that had fallen into the hands of lawbreakers as well as the police (Chalong 2005). Guns in the early years of Khun Phan's career were unreliable and often misfired, but, after the war, more modern pistols as well as rifles and grenades became the weapons of choice. Shootouts were common in confrontations between the police and lawbreakers, and the men with toughened skin were more in danger of bullets than blades. The political system was also unsettled. The capacity of the police to maintain order in the provinces was affected by frequent changes in government as Field Marshal Phibun, prime minister during the Japanese occupation, was replaced with a civilian government led by Pridi Phanomyong, leader of the Free Thai movement, who soon found himself in political trouble after the regicide of King Anan in June 1946. An army coup in November 1947 returned Field Marshal Phibun to the prime ministership (Baker and Pasuk 2005: 142, 176). Each regime change had an impact on the police hierarchy, and Khun Phan, who had enjoyed good working relationships with national police chiefs Luang Adul and Phra Raminthara, did not always find himself on workable terms with his bosses. One has to be nimble to maintain useful connections (*sen*) with powerful bureaucrats and officials when the country is careening frequently from one regime to the next.

At his final posting in the central provinces, Khun Phan was asked, in 1947, by the acting police chief, Rear Admiral Luang Sangwonyutthakit, to tackle crime in Kamphaeng Phet. Luang Sangwon was a strong supporter of Pridi Phanomyong, who had asked him to set up a Thai military police unit towards the end of the Japanese occupation (Reynolds 2004: 293). He promised the southern policeman that if he managed to solve the problems in Kamphaeng Phet in four months, he could choose his next assignment. Khun Phan met the challenge and, unsurprisingly, picked Phatthalung, where he moved for the third time on 4 March 1948, expecting to serve out his tour of duty until retirement. His return to the mid south was clouded by the death of his first wife, Chalao, who had followed him on many of his provincial postings (Chalong 2007: 194–9; Samphan 2007: 324).

During his earlier posting in Phatthalung, along with other officers senior to him, Khun Phan had unsuccessfully pursued a Trang bandit, Suea Klap Khamthong, who had been schooled in *saiyasat* knowledge at Wat Khao Or by master teachers such as Ajan Thong and Ajan Nam Keojan, who had moved to Wat Don Sala. Suea Klap had dodged the police for years, yet Khun Phan did not regard him in the same way as his other adversaries who had committed violent crimes and persisted in defying police authority. Suea Klap, by contrast, had no violent assaults or murders against his name. His crimes were small-scale thefts, and he never burgled in Phatthalung out of respect for his teachers. By the late 1940s, Suea Klap was elderly and had 'retired' from his life as an outlaw. Khun Phan conceded that Suea Klap, by eluding capture for so many years, was the one bandit who had bettered him. Through an intermediary, he sought a meeting, but Suea Klap was suspicious of the policeman's motives and refused (Chalong 2007: 141–9). Khun Phan vowed to wear his moustache for as long as it took to apprehend Suea Klap, which meant for the rest of his career, as it turned out, because he never apprehended the man.[19]

Suea Klap as well as Pho Lim, the *saiyasat* specialist and master of Siamese swordplay with whom the southern policeman had danced before the Phichit audiences, had imbibed *saiyasat* knowledge from their teachers. They believed in the efficacy of the magic arts that endowed them with charisma in the eyes of local communities. Like Khun Phan, these men

---

19   Suepphong Saengwan (b. 1962), a distant relative of Khun Phan, Interview with the author, Songkhla, 4 September 2012.

were *nak leng*. They had mental toughness and a dignified bearing (*saksi*), and they abided by a code of conduct not prescribed by bureaucratic statute but guided by community expectations that a man should be true to his word and live with honour. Seen in this light, Suea Klap and Pho Lim were the southern policeman's doubles. They were not *doppelgänger*, strictly speaking. They were not exact lookalikes or mirror images, nor were they apparitions. Khun Phan performed his duties brandishing the shield of state authority, whereas his outlaw doubles could boast only of the support of their outlaw cohorts and of the communities that protected them. Some rural outlaws Khun Phan pursued were shadows of himself that he could never quite put his hands on; there were others he respected enough to show lenience. In his persona and methods, he was little different from the outlaws, and his police-outlaw identity was manifest to many in his lifetime, even if it puzzled some of his bosses.

In 1948, Phatthalung communities called for Khun Phan's return because of a crime wave, and it was in that province that he fatally shot one of his last victims. The man's kinfolk declined to claim the man's remains and the policeman ordered the body decapitated, and required Suea Tho, the leader of the gang, to carry the head through the villages he had terrorised to demonstrate what would happen to lawbreakers. Decapitation was common in the early centuries of Thai warfare, when soldiers took heads as trophies of victory: according to a fifteenth-century military epic, 'Anyone who rides a horse to battle and takes a head is rewarded with a golden bowl, cloth, and promotion' (Baker and Pasuk 2018: 144). In this instance, decapitation served another purpose. Khun Phan performed a ritual that directed the dead man's spirit to do his bidding, and the severed head was displayed on the lakeside route into the district of Khao Chaison to spook outlaws from neighbouring Songkhla and deter them from entering Phatthalung to rob villagers in territory protected by Khun Phan (Wira 2001: 187; Samphan 2007: 128–9).

In 1950, Khun Phan was promoted to Police Lieutenant Colonel, and a year later he was made Deputy Commander of Division 8 in Nakhon Si Thammarat—a position he had to be persuaded to accept. After two decades of policing, his taste for desecrating outlaw corpses had not diminished. Suea Phat had been on a thieving spree in Phatthalung and Songkhla, and in a gunfight had shot an officer, who lost his right arm. After another shootout that left Suea Phat dead, the man's severed head was impaled in front of the Phatthalung police station. Yet a modicum of community policing was not beyond Khun Phan. To confront a spate of 'snatch and run' thefts, he invited the local *nak leng* leaders to his house for a meal, at which he admonished them to bring their more rambunctious followers under control. At the time, he also helped raise funds for a study centre and recreation precinct in Phatthalung town (Samphan 2007: 358).

As social unrest in the mid south receded and Khun Phan had time on his hands, he opened a restaurant in Phatthalung on the western shore of the central lake. His family life had taken another turn as he married again after Chalao died and fathered three more children. His second 'official' wife, Somasamai (b. 1927), was a Chinese woman from Penang who had changed her surname to Utsarattaniwat. She was one of eight siblings who had fled Malaya at the outbreak of the Pacific War and moved to nearby Hatyai. At the age of 14 or 15, Somsamai had come to live in Khun Phan's home, and they eventually married. According to his son Chanthip, Khun Phan discouraged Somsamai from learning Thai fluently, because he feared unscrupulous people would try to bribe her to compromise his work.[20] Somsamai bore him three children: Nasan (b. 1951) and Chanthip (b. 1952), both sons, and a daughter, Thitiphan. Most of Khun Phan's 13 children by various women were daughters, and he also had three adopted children (*luk buntham*) (Chintapati 2007: 34–5). He became Commander of Division 8 in 1960 and Police Major General in the following year and retired in 1964 (Chalong 2007: 199–200; Samphan 2007: 364–5).

Local notable

To commemorate retirement from active service, Khun Phan and a police friend, Police Lieutenant General Pracha Buranathanit, collaborated in sponsoring the production of Buddhist amulets and images modelled after the standing Buddha image at Wat Phra Pathom stupa south of Bangkok. The amulets were stamped from a powdered compound of over 400 therapeutic herbs, granules of soil from city pillars in all the provinces and lichen collected from the major Buddhist stupas in the country. Lieutenant General Pracha, a native of the central plains, was another 'man with toughened skin', who was known, like Khun Phan, for the lethal methods he had demonstrated more than once. On 21 May 1963, Pracha presented a collection of the specially consecrated amulets and images to King Bhumibol (Ek 2010: 32–40).

---

20   Chanthip Phantarakrajchadech, Interview with the author, Nakhon Si Thammarat, 9 September 2012.

Khun Phan's reputation as a police officer with an enviable arrest record and a regional reputation for crime suppression led to a brief political career, when the Democrat Party recruited him to run for election in the national parliament in February 1969.[21] He won the seat, but his term as an MP ended all too soon when General Thanom Kittikachorn, the military dictator of the day, conducted a coup against himself in 1971 and dissolved the parliament. The policeman campaigned for office again in 1974, as a candidate for the Social Action Party led by the royalist M.R. Kukrit Pramoj. He lost that election and decided he had had enough of politics. He was not a natural campaigner and had neither the talent nor the enthusiasm for taking on the jokey persona that entertains voters.

As a local notable, Khun Phan was invited to preside at festivals and ceremonies. He would bless newlyweds or read a horoscope to determine the auspicious date and time to build a house or consecrate an amulet. The most memorable of these occasions, and the most consequential for his reputation, was his role in identifying the Jatukham-Ramathep deity that would later bring his name to national attention. A new chief, Police Colonel Sanphet Thammathikun (later Lieutenant General), arrived in Nakhon Si Thammarat and decided the town should refresh its horoscope. Under a national policy that promoted decentralisation in the 1980s, the government was encouraging each provincial centre to install or renovate its city pillar, the spiritual heart of the town, and Sanphet decreed that a new horoscope was necessary. A community group urged him to consult a spirit medium, who drew a strange image and recommended that Sanphet visit Khun Phan, who immediately identified it as a composite image of guardian deities protecting the reliquary at Wat Mahathat. Khun Phan presided at the formal consecration of the 'new' deity, with the prime minister of the day, General Prem Tinsulanonda, a southerner from Songkhla, in attendance. Amulets were struck and disseminated to the public to raise funds to build a proper pillar for the city. Khun Phan had given advice on the design of the pillar made from timber cut from the peak of Mount Luang in the Nakhon range to the west of the town (Phuttharat 2007: 110, 113).

In 1999, Khun Phan was honoured by the Ministry of Health for his knowledge of traditional Thai medicine and received an honorary degree from the Rajabhat University in Nakhon Si Thammarat (Wira 2001: 62). In his later years, Khun Phan—the short, wiry policeman who had

---

21 *Bangkok Post*, 13 February 1969; Chalong (2007: 201); Chanthip Phantarakrajchadech, Interview with the author, 9 September 2012.

cheated death more than once in violent skirmishes in the countryside—wore a straw hat and walked with a cane. On special occasions, he could be seen in pristine white traditional dress (*pha jong kraben*). He spent his days visiting with friends, reading the newspaper and tending therapeutic herbs he grew at home. He had always been a man of simple, basic tastes, sufficient in what was necessary for life (Okha 2007: 243). Following the dictates of the *saiyasat* knowledge he had observed throughout his career, Khun Phan kept a strict diet and shunned foods he believed would diminish his powers. These included papaya, the *belimbing* or cucumber tree, a type of watercress (*krachet*) and eels (*pla lai*) that survived in pond mud and flooded rice fields (Wira 2001: 65). The nurse who washed and dressed him expressed amazement at the condition of his body and the strength in his limbs for a man who had lived more than a century.[22]

The bathed, tattooed and scarred body of the southern policeman finally came to rest in July 2006. Flags were flown at half-mast at police stations around the country and, when Khun Phan was cremated in February the following year, the Crown Prince of Thailand arrived for the preliminary devotions but departed before the cremation itself. Contrary to reports, the Crown Prince did not leave with the Red Sword—an object much desired by many, including local MPs.[23] Tens of thousands of people from near and far crowded into the Wat Mahathat compound hoping to receive a medallion with Khun Phan's image that had been struck for the occasion. Supply fell short of demand, and thousands were turned away, with more than 100 people injured in the crush. A special edition of the Jatukham-Ramathep amulet was struck with Khun Phan's image brandishing his Red Sword on the observe side (Nawamin 2007: 82–91; Ek 2010: 133–9). Lottery sellers did a thriving business as those in attendance sought to match ticket numbers with Khun Phan's vital statistics: his birth and death dates, the date of his cremation and the day of the week on which it took place. Drivers of lorries, vans, pickup trucks and station wagons full of amulets queued up to have their valuable loads blessed and ritually charged en masse by monks. Proceeds from the amulets' sale were donated to a local hospital.

Within a year of Khun Phan's cremation, the municipality honoured its famous son by erecting a statue on the main street that passes in front of the Nakhon Si Thammarat police station.

---

22   Wannasarn Noonsuk, Interview with the author, Bangkok, 20 November 2017.
23   Chanthip Phantarakrajchadech, Interview with the author, Nakhon Si Thammarat, 9 September 2012.

Plate 2 Statue of Khun Phan outside Nakhon Si Thammarat police station
Source: Craig Reynolds.

Khun Phan looks down the narrow lane that bears his family's name. Statues of commoners may be found in the provinces but are virtually unknown in Bangkok, where the country's kings and members of the royal family grace plazas and intersections. A decade after the 2007 cremation, a grassroots movement in Ai Khiew, the village of Khun Phan's birth, raised funds to erect another statue of Khun Phan; next to him is a pavilion sheltering the figure of the policeman's early childhood teacher, the monk Ajan Iat (Dam). It is planned that the statues will be at the centre of a park along the stream that runs through a clearing in the forest. Kasem Jandam, a poet and scholar of birds' nests in Southeast Asia, explained to me that the villagers regard Khun Phan as a model of integrity, in contrast to some people in Thailand today who are unethical and who lack moral scruples. Yes, he is a hero to them, a man who left the tiny community to make a success of himself as a policeman on the national stage.[24]

The right and duty to take human life

Parinya Sanyadet, who owns a traditional weapons museum in Thonburi, met Khun Phan when the southern policeman had only a short time left to live. Even in old age he had about him an aura of toughness and unwillingness to compromise. When I spoke with Parinya, he wondered aloud whether Khun Phan's near-death experience during his childhood illness had given him a sense of mission that lasted throughout his career. Perhaps, having cheated death when he was very young, he thought himself indestructible. He was single-minded and fearless in his pursuit of lawbreakers and believed he was entitled to use any means necessary to defeat them.[25] A lawman who was prepared to display in public the severed head of an outlaw to warn others off the territory he protected was not a man to be trifled with.

---

24   Kasem Jandam, Interview with the author, 17 November 2017.
25   Parinya Sanphet, Interview with the author, 1 February 2012. To celebrate its 40th anniversary, the Thai Studies Institute at Thammasat University held an exhibition of traditional Thai weapons from the museum (Sathaban Thai Khadi Sueksa 2011).

Khun Phan's biographers assure readers that while he could take life with little compunction, he did not take it gratuitously. He preferred to capture rather than to kill, although executing an order sometimes resulted in executing a lawbreaker. The tattoos on his knuckles told his adversaries he would not hesitate to take this action. Yet taking life is a sin among the first five Buddhist precepts. Was Khun Phan mindful of this precept against killing as he went about his work? When Khun Phan's sons asked their father whether he had sinned by killing human beings, the replies he gave sound like the same story filtered through different memories. Nasan, the elder son, said his father accepted that he might end up in hell and, if that happened, he would have a chat with Yama, the Lord of the Underworld, and try to work something out (*jeraja*: negotiate, discuss). To Chanthip, the younger son, his father replied similarly: when he arrived in hell, he would be offering Yama his assistance in sorting things out down there.[26] The sons' query was meant to probe their father's conscience about taking human life. His droll response was adroit deflection of the question's intent.

Khun Phan's biographers, who are careful to withhold judgement about the deaths of lawbreakers at Khun Phan's hands or at the hands of officers working under his command, report deaths in police custody or in prison without embellishment. The biographers do not stand in judgement of the policeman's actions. When Khun Phan carried out his orders only to find himself in trouble with the police hierarchy because kinfolk or local officials protecting the deceased outlaw filed a complaint that besmirched his reputation as a loyal cop, he resented it. Yet the Phichit author Okha Buri offers explicit and gruesome details of disrespectful treatment of human remains at the hands of the police. He observes that times have changed since Khun Phan's day, and public attitudes are now different:

> It is unthinkable that anyone would do these things nowadays. It is fortunate that Khun Phan and officials lived at the time they did and could escape the critical scrutiny of the human rights people who prefer to comment rather than do the job. (Okha 2007: 110)

---

26 Nasan Phantarakrajchadech, Interview with the author, Nakhon Si Thammarat, 6 August 2011; and Chanthip Phantarakrajchadech, Interview with the author, Nakhon Si Thammarat, 9 September 2012.

In describing one operation, Samphan Kongsamut states matter-of-factly that Khun Phan's reputation for taking no prisoners and for killing and discarding human remains preceded his arrival in a district. He then adds that rural Thailand was violent and lawless in the day, and Khun Phan's actions were necessary if he was to restore peace and order. The police—part of the state's armour of coercion—have legal sanction to use lethal force. The top brass might be unhappy with Khun Phan's methods even if they were effective, and communities were reassured by the decisive actions he took to clean up their districts. Bad means are sometimes necessary to achieve good ends (Samphan 2007: 182–6; Jauregui 2016: 65). Khun Phan's authority was provisional and subject to legalities, police procedures, community pressures and moralities, including his own moral code. All of these could conflict with each other. In keeping with his name—a literal translation of which was 'duty-bound to protect the power of the monarch' (*phantharak ratchadet*)—Khun Phan was doing his job.

Plate 3 Khun Phan at age 102

Source: Chanthip Phantarakrajdadech.

A trophy photograph of Khun Phan taken when he was 102 years old by Chanthip posed him with the weapons of Buddhist and Malay sovereigns, which he adopted as his regalia. The ceremonial Red Sword, acquired from the Phraya Phichai noble lineage in Uttaradit during the war years, lies on his lap; a *kris* is thrust into his waistband. His mock death stare into the camera is stagey, a performance of the authority he once exercised as though to inform the viewer that he is not innocent of the powers he had possessed. He drew his strength from the knowledge the *saiyasat* masters taught him, from his abilities as a warrior, from the shield that his uniform provided him and from the lands and waters of his birthplace.

3

The mid south's
fathomable past

Video content for this chapter is available online:
press.anu.edu.au/publications/series/asian-studies/
power-protection-and-magic-thailand#media

The southern region of Thailand on the Malay Peninsula is the smallest of the country's four regions, with 14 per cent of the country's total landmass. The core of the mid south, from where Lion Lawman Khun Phan came and where he felt most at home, comprises three provinces of roughly equal size that lie along the eastern side of the peninsula: Nakhon Si Thammarat, Phatthalung and Songkhla. The neighbouring provinces of Surat Thani and Trang share history as well as geographical, ethnic and social features with the core provinces of the mid south. Compared with Thailand's other regions, in the northeast and the north, which can boast Lanna history, the south of Thailand is not conceived of as a unit in Thai histories. Patani has a history as an autonomous kingdom and Tambralinga-Nakhon Si Thammarat has its history, but there is no regional history of the south.

The Malay Peninsula is an ethnically and religiously complex region where mainland and island Southeast Asia meet to form a distinctive cultural and economic zone. Over the centuries, the peoples on the peninsula in southern Thailand were exposed to Islam and Buddhism, both Mahayana and Sri Lankan, as well as to Hindu-Javanese and Malayan cultural influences (Suthiwong 2008: 334). As a label for the region, the Malay Peninsula is misleading in the sense that the term does not capture the presence of Chinese who passed through as envoys and traders from early times. Many made the peninsula their home, and Chinese merchant families became prominent in the administration of coastal ports such as Songkhla and Nakhon Si Thammarat as well as Patani, where intermarriage between Chinese and Thai/Siamese formed a local Peranakan Chinese population (Teo 2008: 217–18). Five large Hokkien families in Trang who had kin relations in Penang dominated fishing and tin trading and mining along the west coast as far as Sumatra (Wong 2008: 201–5).

Until the end of the nineteenth century, the Siamese kings were able to rule distant tributary states on the peninsula only indirectly, and interstate relations were conducted through suzerains or overlords. These rulers were proxies whose loyalty to Ayutthaya or Bangkok was contingent on the advantages to be gained by paying tribute to the Siamese ruler. In the late eighteenth century, at the beginning of the Bangkok period, when the new warrior-king Phya Chakri began to reconstitute the Siamese empire and reassert its authority over far-flung provinces and tributary states, the mid south marked the outer limit of Siamese suzerainty. Beyond this limit was a different world, with historical familial, cultural and intellectual ties to Muslim centres in what is now Pakistan, Egypt, Iran and other parts of the Middle East. These links to the Islamic world mattered to some of its Malay-Muslim population as much as ties to the Thai-Buddhist courts in the central plains.

Until the end of the seventeenth century, the centre of the Malay-Muslim world on the peninsula was the sultanate of Patani, a thriving entrepot in the trading networks of the Indonesian Archipelago. It boasted a golden age as one of the region's most prosperous entrepots and centres of Islamic education for Southeast Asian Muslims and rebelled against Siamese suzerainty. Five wars between 1785 and 1838 were needed before Bangkok's armies succeeded in destroying the sultanate (Bradley 2013: 150). Parts of Patani and Songkhla were ceded to Malaya in the 1909 treaty with the United Kingdom—a realignment that exposed the southernmost parts of Thailand to Malay nationalism during the 1930s and 1940s. These were the years when the policeman was most active and the threat of separatism began to haunt the central Thai Government (Porphant 2017: 229–30). From the 1960s to the late 1970s, the mountain range along the Thailand–Malaysia border provided sanctuary for communist insurgents, deepening concern for Thailand's military rulers that the country's territorial integrity might fracture in the southernmost provinces.

Patani people today are proud of their region, deeply religious and mistrustful of outsiders. They refuse to forget the loss of their huge cannon, the Phya Tani, which was removed from the province by the central government and relocated to the lawns of the Ministry of Defence in Bangkok to symbolise their subjugation. In response to the repression of Malay identity by the Thai state and the violent insurgency in the south, historical writing on Patani has burgeoned in recent years, making it one of many battlegrounds in the ethnonationalist struggle taking place in resistance to the government's policies. Contemporary Patani identity harks back to historical writing such as the *History of the Malay Kingdom of Patani* by Ibrahim Syukri, which documents and celebrates Patani as an independent entity before the Siamese empire extended its sway southward and Western imperialism arrived in the region (Jory 2013: xix; Mansurnoor 2013).

Environment and economy

Geology, geography and weather conspired to create an environmental niche for the provinces of the mid south. The Phatthalung monastery where the legendary policeman was initiated into the secret lore is built into the base of a limestone hillock that rises modestly from the surrounding plain. Water seeping through the limestone dissolved the rock and hollowed out caves that provided quiet places for meditation and hideaways for outlaws. Perhaps Khao Or was the 'cavern-like temple' just outside Phatthalung town mentioned by the local British bank manager who took up his posting in the early 1930s when the policeman was just beginning to make his reputation (Exell 1963: 137). Nearby, at 177 metres high, is Khao Ok Thalu, the 'mountain with a hole in its shoulder', with nature's hollowed-out space near the summit explained away by a local folktale.

These towering limestone formations extend into Laos, northern Vietnam and southern China, where they are magnets for international tourists (Gobbett and Hutchison 1973: 39; Kiernan 1988; Gupta 2005: 169). In northern Laos, the limestone caves were capacious enough to house the command centre of the Pathet Lao army during the Second Indochina War.

Plate 4 Khao Ok Thalu, Phatthalung
Source: Kasem Jandam.

Formed eons ago when this land was submerged more than once under the sea, these cave complexes in carbonate outcrops intruded by granite are anomalous in the landscape. Across the peninsula to the west, the limestone karsts onshore and offshore in the shallows of the Andaman Sea are even more dramatic. From Satul northward all the way to Surat Thani, the limestone type is the same. Some 15–20 per cent of Thailand rests on a bedrock of limestone of variable purity and age. The theatrical beauty of the karsts became known to the world when Hollywood discovered the unearthly forms. Scenes from the 1974 James Bond film *The Man with the Golden Gun* were shot on islands off Phangnga and Phuket. Tourism development quickly followed, and the west coast—once the homelands of fisher folk and sea gypsies known as *chao le*—lost its innocence. With the exception of resorts on Samui Island and the party islands off Surat Thani, the east coast of the peninsula has been spared most of the gaudy and polluting effects of the international tourism on which Thailand depends for foreign exchange.

Mount Khanun District in the province of Phatthalung lies between Songkhla to the south and Nakhon Si Thammarat to the north. The western border of Nakhon Si Thammarat follows the ridge of a steep north–south-running mountain range that boasts the highest mountain in Thailand's south, Mount Luang, at 1,780 metres. The mountain range forms a barrier to the weather systems moving across the peninsula from the west, but rainfall on the eastern side, while less than on the western side, is sufficient to irrigate the plains that extend from the mountains to the Gulf of Thailand. The eastern border of Phatthalung cuts through a string of inland lakes that stretches north from Songkhla town for about 100 kilometres. The water world of the Songkhla lakes that links Nakhon Si Thammarat, Phatthalung and Songkhla once defined the landscape, facilitating economic activity and shaping social life until the national highway system was constructed in the late twentieth century. Southern Thai social scientists and environmental historians who study the mid south provinces as a subregion refer to the waters as 'our lakes' (*thalesap rao*) and have produced a series of illustrated publications and CDs that showcase their work. Canals and river systems gradually silted up with the runoff from the mountains and it was only in the mid-1960s that the infrastructure improved to the point where roads replaced waterways for the transport of agricultural produce and commerce (Chatthip and Phunsak 1997: 45–7, 107).

The Satingpra Peninsula, a finger of land administered by the Songkhla provincial government that separates Phatthalung from the Gulf of Thailand, lies to the east. With access to the Gulf of Thailand confined to rivers and canals through Songkhla territory, the provincial centre of Phatthalung is today truly landlocked—an accident of geography that conceals its history. The southern Thai environmental historian Mana Khunweechuay (2003: 21) has drawn attention to the fact that two centuries ago this terrain was entirely under water, and it was possible to travel by boat from the lake entrance at Songkhla up to Pakphanang on the coast just south of Nakhon Si Thammarat town. Phatthalung at that time was a small port on a bay sheltered from the Gulf of Thailand by Tantalem Island, a landform that appears clearly on John Walker's map drawn from John Crawfurd's mission to Siam and Cochin China in 1828 (Crawfurd 1967). Until the late nineteenth century, vessels could pass unimpeded through the bay, which gradually filled as the runoff from the mountains deposited sediment in the lowlands. Forest land on the plains and slopes was cleared for agriculture and, with the construction of roads and rail lines, silting in the bay accelerated. The channel between Tantalem Island and the mainland became shallower and shallower to the point where oceangoing vessels could no longer navigate through the passage and the three 'lakes' gradually took shape. The smallest, Thale Noi, formed at the northern end of the chain, and a canal now connects

Thale Noi to the larger inland lake. The lakes are still very shallow, ranging in depth from 1.5 to 2.5 metres.[1] Salinity in the chain of lakes increases gradually from north to south as freshwater meets seawater entering through Songkhla Harbour. Flora and fauna have adapted to the changing salinity and continue to adapt through the seasons, resulting in immense biodiversity. The Satingpra Peninsula—that 'strange coastal feature'—is known today in the mid south as Big Island (*ko yai*), bearing witness to its ancient history as a separate landmass (Donner 1978: 417).[2]

By the end of the nineteenth century, much of the basin at the northern end of the lakes was a mosquito-infested swamp forest (*pa phru*) as the channel silted up. During World War II, a tropical storm destroyed 75 per cent of this forest, which was followed by a drought that left the wetlands vulnerable to fire, which further decimated wildlife habitats. Villagers who had come into possession of firearms after the war hunted in the habitats of the swamp forest and around the lake and lagoon for their livelihood, further reducing wildlife numbers in this ecological niche. What remains of the original habitat is today preserved as wildlife refuges in Phru Khuan Khreng and Phru Khuan Khi Sian (Wiwat 2007: 101–11). In drought conditions, which are common nowadays because of climate change, the refuges are even more vulnerable to fire. In early times fish and water fowl were abundant, as were many species of land animals, including the pygmy elephant. The hunter-gatherers of the forest collected bamboo, resins, rubber sap, honey and rattan, which they bartered with agriculturalists on the plains for rice and salt. The bamboo, therapeutic herbs (*samun phrai*), animal hides and tusk ivory were harvested for trade (Mana 2003: 27–35). In the late seventeenth century, Phatthalung produced low-grade cotton that found its way by sea to Nagasaki along with birds' nests, tin and sea cucumber.

In the early 1930s, the plentiful wildlife enabled the merchant brothers Albert and Edward Jucker to keep a motley collection of creatures in their family compound. One day a house guest was startled out of his afternoon nap by a young tiger that had broken out of its cage. The Juckers' family zoo housed the tiger, a black panther, monkeys, porcupines, guinea fowl, an argus pheasant, a cobra and a python—all of local provenance.

---

1   On the silting up of the bay and the formation of the peninsula, see Reynolds (2009).
2   Donner's Map 2 of 1897 still shows Satingpra as a landmass distinct from the mainland. Tantalem is a slag byproduct of tin extraction. Munro-Hay (2001: 250–8) observes that Tantalem Island does not appear on sixteenth-century Portuguese maps and leaves its existence in dispute.

The physician in Trang who looked after the American Presbyterian Mission was a keen if rather inept hunter of tigers in his spare time (Exell 1963: 128, 147).

Tin attracted the Dutch East India Company (Vereenigde Oostindische Compagnie, or VOC) to the east coast, where it opened a trading post in Nakhon Si Thammarat in 1642, supervised initially by company offices at Malacca, and after 1664 at Ayutthaya. Over the following century, the Dutch company exported tin intermittently from the east coast through Ligor—an old Malay name for Nakhon found on early European maps in garbled form: Lugo, Logor, Loguor, Lomgon, Lomgu and Lomgua (Munro-Hay 2001: 126–8). The Siamese ruler in Ayutthaya, with a wary eye on his commercial interests, sought to monopolise supply and disadvantage the Dutch company, which understandably wanted direct control over what it produced. Many Southeast Asian Buddhist rulers, beneath the pomp and circumstance of their status as universal monarchs, were astute traders. They were merchants who also ruled. The tastes of the Ayutthayan kings for luxury goods such as foreign textiles and rare and unusual objects were financed not by land rents but by trade in forest products, rice, minerals such as tin and hides exported through Ayutthaya from the hinterland. Discrepancies between the Dutch and Siamese-language versions of the treaty between the two parties signed in 1688 expose the conditions faced by Europeans traders in a market in which the Siamese merchant-rulers held the upper hand. The Dutch text stated that the VOC had a monopoly on tin, while the Siamese text stipulated that 'all the tin belongs to the king and may only be traded by His Majesty's servants'. Losses in the tin trade, the lack of success in pressing the company's case at court and political uncertainty in Ayutthaya compelled the VOC to close the Ligor post in 1756 (Brummelhuis 1987: 34–49).

On the west coast the tin seam extended to Malaya, and provinces in the west—Ranong, Phangnga, Phuket and Trang—are better known and studied (Cushman 1991). Phuket Island has a geographical cousin in Penang Island, where tin from the west coast was smelted. The tin industry in Siam, an annex of tin operations in British Malaya, was capital intensive and dominated by foreign corporations. By the 1930s, all ore was processed in the British Malay states (Dixon and Parnwell 1991: 218). Before the Thai Government nationalised the tin industry at the outset of World War II, there were 58 properties belonging to about 45 British and Australian companies. History tends to forget that the region east of the mountain range in the mid south supplied tin to international markets. After nationalisation, Nakhon Si Thammarat and Songkhla could still boast 10 tin mines; seven of the leases were owned by Australians (Whyte 2010: 113–16). The only other part of the country that was so dominated by foreign capital was the north, where the Borneo Company was able to control teak extraction after it was granted concessions by the Bangkok court.

In the heyday of the international tin trade during the 1920s and 1930s, the financial needs of the foreign miners exporting from the mid south called for the appointment of a bank manager at Tung Song, a railway junction of no great distinction. When the British schoolteacher F.E. Exell arrived in Tung Song in the late 1920s to take up the position, he spent a nervous first night in the shabby railway rest house with the windows and doors firmly bolted. He had been told that Tung Song 'was full of bad hats'—his quaint term for local miscreants—so he heeded the advice and took precautions (Exell 1963: 113–14).

In those days, the abundance of food and natural resources supported a very small population—a topic that is still discussed by local people. At the time the policeman was active in the mid-1930s, the south was estimated to have only 12.7 per cent of Thailand's population; the Nakhon provincial circle had almost half the population in the region (Porphant 2017: 231–2).[3] Even with the opening of the southern railway line in 1907, the area was wild and underpopulated well into the twentieth century. After World War II, parts of Phatthalung were still known as refuges for bandits, as places where stolen boats and cattle could be stashed and as ideal locations for the production of moonshine (Mana 2003: 25–8, 36). The fragmentary infrastructure and the rugged mountain spine of the peninsula were impediments to local travel and commerce. In the early 1960s, when I lived in Krabi on the west coast, a bus journey to Songkhla through Trang and Phatthalung entailed a hair-raising ride on a poorly maintained road that wound its way over the range and down the rainforest-clad ravines. As the bus reached the highest point of the pass the driver would lift his hands from the wheel and clasp them together in homage to the mountain sprite who dwelt in the shrine we

---

3   The data and table in Porphant (2017: 231) are slightly confusing. The 1904 statistics in the text for 'the southern region' include Kelantan and Terengganu, which became part of British Malaya later in the decade. The census of 1909 in the table shows that the Nakhon Si Thammarat *monthon* still had almost half the population in the south.

were passing. For an instant, the passengers were in mortal danger. If the driver failed to pay homage and continued to grip the wheel, the guardian spirit might avenge the lack of respect at the next hairpin turn. Yet if the driver obeyed the dictates of his faith, he could lose control of the vehicle and the bus with its passengers would end up at the bottom of the ravine. In the many times I tried to witness this act of devotion, it was so quick I usually missed it. The pleated landscape along the route is known locally as 'the mountains of folded cloth [*phap pha*]'. The first arterial road across the mountains of folded cloth was instrumental in furthering the Trang rubber industry and was built without foreign engineering expertise at the instigation of the *monthon* commissioner of the south, Khaw Simbee (Ajin 2009: 257).

Legacies of an ancient heritage

In the early centuries, the mid south on both the east and the west coasts of the Malay Peninsula was a vital link in the international commerce between China, the Indian Subcontinent and the Western Orient—a watery highway sometimes referred to as the Silk Road of the Sea. Transhipment routes ferried goods across the peninsula, making possible a chain of short-range trading connections that stretched from China to Europe. Recent archaeological excavations by French, Italian and Thai teams have unearthed cosmopolitan and proto-urban complexes on the east coast where products of stone, glass, ceramics and metals were manufactured to serve markets in the South China Sea. The findings at Khao Sam Kaeo north of Surat Thani and other sites on both coasts have pushed back the dates of the portage routes across the peninsula to the fourth and third centuries BCE (Baker and Pasuk 2017: 8–9). Local products also found their way into the trade. The rich resources of the hinterland supplied camphor, rhinoceros horn, aromatic woods and beeswax to the Chinese market.

The Isthmus of Kra is the narrowest land bridge across the Malay Peninsula, so narrow that from time to time plans are floated to dig a canal from one coast to the other to accommodate oceangoing vessels. In the mid-1970s, Edward Teller, 'father of the H-bomb', proposed excavating a canal using nuclear explosives that were being heralded as sufficiently 'clean' and suitable for peaceful purposes in the not-too-distant future (Kaufman 2013: 224). One might expect that the most natural crossing for transhipments in the premodern era would be at the isthmus, but the strong winds of southwest monsoons obeyed their own logic and carried ships across the Bay of Bengal and the Andaman Sea to landfall south of the Kra. There the land bridge was wider, the mountains steeper and portage more laborious. These goods as well as Indic artefacts were relayed from one side of the peninsula to the other along the waterways and across the mountains, thus spurring the emergence of entrepots on both coasts. Hindu worship and the Brahmanical practices of seafarers and traders from the Indian Subcontinent may date from as early as the sixth or seventh century (O'Connor 1972: 13–15, 23–7).

Itinerant merchants from Persian and Arab lands and the Indian Subcontinent stayed longer than required by the change in monsoons that would carry them to their next port and left inscriptions, sculptures and shrines. The religious needs of Tamil merchant guilds and early Buddhist ascetics bequeathed traces of their cultures and religions: stone and terracotta objects in the form of Buddhist votive tablets, images of Vishnu and phallic lingas for the worship of Shiva. The environs of Takuapa on the west coast are particularly rich with evidence of these sojourners in the form of Tamil inscriptions, Hindu statuary and Chinese porcelains (Pisit 2013: 150–1). Although the temples and shrines that housed images no longer survive, six long-robed mitred Vishnus dating from the sixth to the eighth centuries CE have been traced to provinces in the mid south and are now housed in local museums and in the National Museum in Bangkok (O'Connor 1986a).

In these early centuries, Chinese envoys visited the entrepots on the peninsula, which they regarded as stepping-stones on the trade routes to India and the Middle East. When they returned to the Middle Kingdom to write up their journeys, they identified the entrepots with toponyms. Chinese historical geographies indicate towns or city-states, but these centres can have been little more than small settlements with a market and a religious shrine. As with all early toponyms on the peninsula, the Chinese texts identify placenames on crude maps, while archaeological finds on the peninsula do not connect objects to placenames. These toponyms have a surprisingly long half-life in local memory that reaches back to an ancient past to confect a mythic present. Takkola, a placename of the seventh century located somewhere along the northwest coast, perhaps in the neighbourhood of Trang, is now the name of a restaurant in Krabi that boasts an oversized image of the Jatukham-Ramathep deity.

Peninsular entrepots that entered the historical record have left backstories of centres that later grew around them. Langkasuka, a toponym known to Chinese envoys from the sixth century CE, flourished long before Islam came to the region and, according to Malay-Muslim historians, laid the groundwork for the international emporium and paramount state that Patani would eventually become. In arguing that Langkasuka held imperial sway over Songkhla, Phatthalung, Kelantan and Trengganu, Malay historians have perforce overlooked its early Hindu-Buddhist character (Walker 2013: 201). Legend and history comingle in these foundation stories based on archaeological and textual evidence, with some legends attributing the foundation of Patani to people from Kedah (Maier 1988: 96). The name Langkasuka occurs in many stories told in the interior of Kedah and Patani about a princess born from a stem of bamboo—a foundation myth that occurs elsewhere on the peninsula, including Phatthalung, where the story of Lady White Blood originated (Gesick 1995: 41, 62, 84). In the eighth and ninth centuries, Langkasuka was strong enough as a trading centre to catch the attention of Srivijaya, the maritime empire that by the seventh century had drawn the international trade away from transpeninsular routes and through the Straits of Malacca. Langkasuka paid tribute to Srivijaya as its dependency (Wade 2013: 61).

Local rulers extended their hegemony by acquiring loyal entourages and building up a fleet to exact tribute and bring to submission rivals who lacked comparable resources and cultural capital. Nakhon Si Thammarat, which evolved in this way, had a history that predated the influx of Tai peoples to the mainland from the eleventh century. Its coastal location gave it advantages in international commerce and, evolving from its predecessor, Tambralinga—a placename known from an inscription in the Tamil region of South India—it became a major trading centre (Brawn 2018: 17–18). Wannasarn Noonsuk, an archaeologist who worked at Walailak University, studied ancient topographies, temple ruins and artefacts with his research students to bring Tambralinga to life and enrich Nakhon's backstory. His excavations include Khao Kha hill, north of Nakhon town, the most important Saivite site in Tambralinga, where a temple complex of nearly 50 shrines stretches along the high ridge. A large linga was chiselled roughly out of the granite and reservoir tanks for rituals were dug into the slopes. Wannasarn thinks that fires were lit on the ridge as a beacon for coastal shipping; other high points along the coast have similar archaeological profiles (Wannasarn 2013a, 2014).

During the first millennium CE, the mid south belonged to trading networks in the archipelago dominated by Srivijaya, the regional maritime power. In their chauvinism, southern historians have gone so far as to say that the region was the birthplace of Srivijaya. Mahayana Buddhist images, for example, can be dated to the Amaravati school of South India in the first millennium CE and include the bejewelled bronze Bodhisattva discovered at Chaiya, now located in the National Museum of Thailand. It is described as Srivijayan because of stylistic similarities with images from Central Java, leading some art historians to propose an Indo-Javanese period for Thai art in the eighth to ninth centuries. A Sanskrit epigraph of 775 CE, once known in Western scholarship as the Ligor inscription, was discovered in Surat Thani Province and refers to a ruler of Srivijaya. A couple of centuries later, Tambralinga was still capable of defending itself in battle. Its vitality as a trading state made it a target of Cola aggression in the eleventh century, according to a Tamil inscription from Tanjore. In 1230 CE, Chandrabhanu, then the ruler of Tambralinga, left an inscription at Chaiya after apparently annexing it (Wolters 1958: 587–8, 597; Piriya 1980: 64). In 1247 and 1270, Chandrabhanu invaded Sri Lanka. Tambralinga was regrouping and consolidating its power just as the emerging Thai kingdom at Sukhothai was beginning to exert itself southward. As it did so, Sukhothai ruler in the thirteenth century, King Ramkhamhaeng, appointed one of Nakhon Si Thammarat's senior monks to be his supreme patriarch. It would not be the last time that a Siamese ruler availed himself of Ligor's religious prestige.

Nakhon Si Thammarat's name is derived from Sridhammasokaraja, Chandrabhanu's honorific title. Embedded in the foundation king's title is a reference to King Ashoka, the Mauryan Indian emperor of the third century BCE, who converted to Buddhism and built 84,000 stupas to house relics of the Buddha. Within walking distance from the pillar shrine in a park on the grounds of an old prison is a modern statue of the ruler erected in 2001.

King Chandrabhanu looks southward over his domain of 12 satellite states, including Kedah, Patani, Kelantan and, at the very tip of the peninsula, Pahang (Sujit 2000: 59). In earlier times, these Malay states paid tribute to Nakhon, Ayutthaya and Bangkok in the form of miniature gold and silver trees. Nakhon's medallion is of geocosmic design, with the Great Relic stupa at Wat Mahathat in the centre surrounded by the 12 signs of the zodiac, each corresponding to one of Nakhon's tributary states.[4]

---

4   Nakhon's ancient geocosmic political order is explained in *Phot Thude* [*The Post Today*], 19 June 2016: B8.

Plate 5 Chandrabhanu, Nakhon Si Thammarat's founding king
Source: Craig Reynolds.

Chandrabhanu's exploits, the Ligor inscription's reference to a ruler of Srivijaya and artistic styles with Javanese elements have led international and local historians to identify the mid south, and especially Nakhon Si Thammarat, as a centre of Srivijaya. Georges Coedès, Prince Damrong Rajanubhab and his son, the art historian and archaeologist Prince Subhadradis Diskul, who followed him in this endeavour, argued for a strong Srivijaya presence on the Malay Peninsula. In the 1930s, Srivijaya became one of the eight stylistic classifications of Siamese antiquities in a project that told a convincing story of the emerging nation's classical past. In this way, Srivijaya became a centrepiece in the glorification of Nakhon Si Thammarat.

Artistic styles such as 'Srivijayan' cannot be tightly correlated with territorial extent, although Prince Damrong and Coedès made such a correlation by choosing art styles to mesh with the rise and fall of polities and conflated art history with political history (Peleggi 2013: 1539–40). Srivijaya's political control, or even its reach, in its heyday is difficult to define. The religious, art-historical and linguistic evidence that would pinpoint the location and extent of Srivijayan authority across the centuries is sufficiently ambiguous to challenge the idea of centring Srivijaya's empire in the mid south.[5] The identification of Srivijaya's centre at Palembang in southeastern Sumatra during the seventh century rather than on the Malay Peninsula is supported by textual and archaeological evidence to the satisfaction of many scholars, including O.W. Wolters (2008: Ch. 5), who was persuaded that Srivijaya should be located in the Indonesian Archipelago. Archaeological evidence of economic and religious activity is overwhelming that the material remains near the modern city of Palembang 'can only be reconciled' with the political and economic capital of a pre-fourteenth-century Malay kingdom in the archipelago (Manguin 2014: 114). The main centre of Srivijaya was at Palembang on Sumatra, not in the mid south of the Malay Peninsula.

Provincial pride has, however, continued to push against scholarly rigour and insists on identifying Nakhon Si Thammarat as the centre of Srivijaya. The fact that the 775 CE epigraph that is the primary dated evidence for Srivijayan supremacy in Siam was for many years termed the Ligor inscription has confounded the problem, and the inscription's provenance may not be Nakhon Si Thammarat but Chaiya in Surat Thani to the north.[6] Police Lieutenant General Sanphet Thammathikun,

---

5   Examples of scepticism about Srivijayan hegemony abound—for example, in O'Connor (1986c: 148)—and Robert Brown (Personal communication, 10 August 2012) notes that the connection of the Srivijaya polity with its art can be associated only vaguely with the geography of the sea trade and specific historical periods.

6   Among the many scholars who attest to Chaiya as the provenance of the Ligor inscription is Hiram Woodward (2003: 82). Wannasarn Noonsuk (Personal communication, 20 February 2017) informs me that the Fine Arts Department continues to give Wat Sema Muang in Nakhon Si Thammarat as the inscription's provenance.

a key figure in the creation of the Jatukham-Ramathep amulet, is one of many who have linked the glories of a legendary Srivijaya—'the forgotten kingdom'—to Tambralinga and Nakhon Si Thammarat–Ligor (Sanphet 1995; Phirayu 2007: 43–6). During the early years, when the amulet was slow to sell, the spirit of capitalism was nurtured by touting the town's fabled past. Another southerner, Dhammadasa Phanit, born in Chaiya in 1908 and the brother of Buddhist philosopher Buddhadasa Bhikkhu, also argued for a Srivijayan period in Thai history, as did Preecha Noonsuk, who placed the centre of Srivijaya at Tambralinga–Nakhon Si Thammarat (Preecha 1982; Thammathat 2000).

Kasem Jandam, a poet, short story writer and a scholar of birds' nests in Southeast Asia, is more cautious. In his school textbook on the province, he acknowledges the claims made for Ligor and its role in Srivijayan history. He knows that the evidence is thin for a kingdom with a continuous unitary centre in the vicinity of Nakhon Si Thammarat. In deference to the chauvinism in the local scholarship, he says only that 'quite a few historians and archaeologists' believe that Ligor was a 'city-state' (*nakhon rat*) and part of the Srivijayan empire stretching from Surat Thani to Java (Kasem 2008: 12). To put the proud claims of local historians into perspective, the archaeologist and writer Sujit Wongthes believes it is more accurate to think of Srivijayan power as dependent on rulers in several locales who sustained their hegemony by controlling trade. Small principalities—or *mueang* in the Tai sociopolitical vocabulary—shared common cultural features such as devotion to Mahayana Buddhism expressed in an art style that could be termed Srivijayan (Sujit 2000: 45–7).

The protagonists who conjured up the Jatukham-Ramathep amulet in the late 1980s celebrated Nakhon's putative connections with Srivijaya to promote their new creation, and the amulet's story thrived in the fertile landscape. Local people living near archaeological sites were aware of what had been excavated in the surrounding rainforests and under their feet, and local children could read about the region's heritage in schoolbooks. Museums in the mid south, formally administered by the Fine Arts Department and housing Hindu and Buddhist artefacts from the ancient past, are open to the public. Over time, community imagination imbued with Hindu-Buddhist beliefs and practices has mythologised the landscape. A local teacher and historian, Chali Naparasmi, who has circulated dozens of his photocopied studies, is sure that, from a certain angle, the limestone outcrop in Phatthalung sheltering the Khao Or monastery, where the policeman underwent his initiation, bears the unmistakable profile of a Shiva linga. He assured me that the linga profile was perceptible to an onlooker possessed of the requisite mindfulness.[7]

The legacy of ancient rule within the network of Srivijayan dependencies is still remembered. Brahmanism in the region from early times and contacts with Sinhalese Theravada Buddhism established a pedigree for Nakhon Si Thammarat and empowered its ruling families with a degree of autonomy cherished by city-states in a complex political field of rivalries and shifting loyalties.

Geopolitics

The topography of the Malay Peninsula and its environment made it difficult for the Siamese courts in the central plains to rule their vassals in the northern Malay states. The rugged terrain restricted communications, which were largely seaborne before the early twentieth century, and military planning was hampered by distance. 'It's too far away to get a decision', complained a Bangkok general about a tactical matter that was being referred to Phatthalung (Corfield 1993: 247). At times, Siamese courts could govern the south in name only, leaving the loyalties of Patani and the Malay sultanates to be enforced indirectly, fitfully and unreliably by proxy states. Nakhon Si Thammarat was one such proxy. With its Malay name, Ligor, it enjoyed a measure of independence as an autonomous state with a mind of its own if its ruler was strong. For the Siamese courts in the central plains, managing these loyalties through a proxy state was a tricky business (Kobkua 1988: Ch. 2). The Thai term for autonomous state is *prathetsarat*, which is sometimes translated as dependency, dominion or colony. A literal translation is more telling: lands ruled by a raja. Indeed, the early nineteenth-century British envoy Henry Burney, who negotiated the Anglo-Siamese Treaty of 1826, referred to the Nakhon governor at the time as 'the Raja of Ligor' and found that he was an active player in court politics at the royal base in Bangkok. This reputation was not surprising, given the governor's lineage and the strategic practice of mid south rulers of placing loyalist relatives in the Bangkok court to gather information and forewarn the governor of developments that might have local consequences. A century later, the term 'raja' still had currency.

---

7   Chali Sinlaparasami, Interview with the author, 7 September 2012; and Chali (2007).

After a successful mission in the late 1930s that put a violent separatist in prison, the policeman Khun Phan from Nakhon Si Thammarat was given the Malay sobriquet 'Little Raja' (*rayo kaji*).

During the Ayutthaya period, Phatthalung, Songkhla and Ligor marked the extent of Siamese paramountcy in the south, yet the loyalty of governors sent to Nakhon Si Thammarat from the royal base in the central plains was difficult to maintain, and paramountcy was only intermittent. When there was instability or a weak ruler in the Ayutthayan court, the governor would rebel, as he did in 1629 at a change of reign. The Siamese court appointed the Japanese military commander Yamada to be the new raja of Ligor. He was supposed to use his 'unruly troops' to quell rebellion there, although the real motive was to remove General Yamada from court politics and send him elsewhere (Van Vliet 2005: 295–6, 302–5). In the late seventeenth century, King Narai dispatched a strong nobleman to govern Nakhon, who restored the city-state's suzerainty but then rebelled and refused to acknowledge Narai's successor, Prince Phetracha.

Khun Phan showed a keen interest in these conflicts that demonstrated how Nakhon's loyalty was conditional on its governor's approval of the Siamese king's legitimacy. According to the policeman's version of this history in a cremation biography for a relative, the nobleman sent to govern Nakhon was the son of the Sultan of Kedah. The scale of the fighting in this typewritten document was of epic proportions: the force sent by the Siamese king to quell the rebellion numbered 300 elephants, 100 ships and 5,000 men (Phantharakratchadet n.d.).[8] These episodic challenges to the Siamese king's authority were rooted in Nakhon's history of independence from the centre and its own network of dependencies. By the eighteenth century, Nakhon was the only proxy in the south capable of exerting any kind of authority over the Malay states (Wyatt 1984: 110, 125; Kasem 2008: 17–19).

When the Siamese kingdom based at Ayutthaya collapsed after the Burmese incursions of 1767, Nakhon subordinated its nearest dependencies and formed a federation, declaring itself untethered from the centre (Anusonsitthikam 1962: 64). King Taksin, the warrior who reassembled much of the Siamese empire and established a new royal base on the western bank of the Chao Phraya River, detained the ruler

---

8   I am grateful to Kasem Jandam for sharing this rare source with me. The dates in the document are unreliable, but the details, including those for the policeman's family tree, are priceless.

of Ligor in the capital, took one of the ruler's daughters hostage and impregnated her before presenting her to the deputy Nakhon ruler in the expectation that the male offspring would one day become a loyal vassal of the centre (Anusonsitthikam 1962: 66–7). The strategy of tethering vassals and dependencies to the centre did not always produce the desired effect. The tether could fray or snap. The offspring sired by Taksin became the powerful Jaophraya Nakhon (Noi), who governed Nakhon with such a firm grip from about 1824 until his death in 1839 that the early Bangkok kings were forced to devise counter-stratagems to check his influence. Towards the end of the first Chakkri reign in 1809, the king moved to circumvent Nakhon Si Thammarat's regional hegemony by placing Songkhla directly under Bangkok's control. Songkhla, not Nakhon, had successfully quelled an uprising in Patani, and the king rewarded its governor with new authority. The two provincial rulers were feuding not only over supervision of the Malay vassal states, but also, closer to home, over the control of people for corvée labour. At the expense of Nakhon and Phatthalung, the Songkhla governor was inducing people to settle in Songkhla—an assertion of his authority that created friction between the two governors. The capacity of Songkhla—located at the southern end of the ocean channel where it emptied into the gulf—to tax exports shipped from Nakhon and Phatthalung was another cause of friction.[9]

Yet the first Bangkok king, while needing to divide and rule, could not entirely ignore Nakhon's cultural capital as the sovereign centre. In the destruction of Ayutthaya, Brahmanic lineages in the central plains had been broken and the symbolic expertise for conducting a new coronation was momentarily lost. The ceremony had to be done correctly and authoritatively, because at the time the king, having executed his predecessor, Taksin, had no royal claim, only his reputation for military leadership. Of the two warriors, he was simply the more successful and ruthless leader. For his coronation in 1785, three years after he took the throne, he identified a suitable Brahmanic line in Nakhon and summoned Brahmans from there to officiate. Had he remembered that

---

9   Details of this adversarial relationship appear in editorial notes to a nineteenth-century document appended to the Nakhon chronicle in *Prachum phongsawadan* [*Collected Chronicles*], part 53 (Bangkok: Khurusapha Edition, 1969), 26–7. On the basis of the prose style and the expertise of the editor, I surmise that Prince Damrong Rajanubhab was the author of these notes and the footnotes to the Nakhon chronicle. The document and its prefatory notes were not published in Anusonsitthikam (1962).

Ramkhamheng's supreme patriarch came from Ligor? The Hindu shrine in Nakhon, refurbished but now emptied of its sacred images, is a featured stop on the town's tourist route.

The mid south was invaluable to the royal base for defence of the east and west coasts of its peninsular extremity as well as for enforcing the subordination of the Malay sultanates. Nakhon and its neighbours were no longer vital nodes in trading networks, as had been the case in premodern times, but were now coveted for the rice and soldiers that could be commandeered in regional skirmishes. James Low, an officer of the British East India Company stationed in Penang, reported that Taksin treated Nakhon Si Thammarat, Phatthalung and Songkhla as a regional subset. The three centres (*meuang*)—for it would be many decades before they formally became provinces—could each supply from 3,200 to 3,750 householders for military service (Low 2007: 72).[10] Nakhon had served this purpose by providing manpower for Siamese wars with Burma in the late sixteenth century. Local families might be described as garrisons-in-waiting if the mid south needed to be defended or if troops needed to be levied and dispatched to subdue unrest or stand behind a favoured claimant in the Malay sultanates. Burmese navies were also a threat on the west coast in the late eighteenth century as the resurgent Konbaung dynasty began its aggressive campaigns. By the third Bangkok reign (1824–51), the political field had become even more complex after the British conquered lower Burma in 1826 and secured their colonial presence on the mainland. Suddenly the Siamese court found itself sharing the Malay Peninsula with a European power. By the 1830s, the peninsula had become a pressure point of growing Western imperialism that clashed with Siamese ambitions to reestablish order in the south.

In the third reign, Jaophraya Noi actively pursued his own expansion in the Malay states beyond Kedah (Kobkua 1988: 66–7; Corfield 1993: 16). When he died in 1839, a tremor went through the tiered network of suzerains and vassals that stretched from Bangkok to the mid south and the Malay sultanates. Kedah rebelled and Malays attacked as far north as Trang (Corfield 1993: 37–9). The third Bangkok king (r. 1824–51), now faced with British armies in lower Burma and with Malay unrest, dispatched a military expedition to 'pacify' the Malay states and retether them to Bangkok's suzerainty. His discussions as commander-in-chief have

---

10   By the time he visited the region, Low reported a total of 9,000 householders, including in nearby Trang—a number somewhat lower than in Taksin's time.

been preserved in a remarkable document that illustrates what the last so-called traditional Siamese monarch knew about the practical science of advantage and the arts of strategy. In the age before typewriters, to say nothing of digital records, court officials were blessed with remarkable memories. Luang Udomsombat, the diarist, took down every detail he overheard at court over five months of deliberations as the kingdom's commander-in-chief demanded answers from his subordinates about enemy strength, whether or not his army had adequate supplies and whether he could rely on the provincial rulers to do his bidding. Some men were expert in administration, but others were lazy, incompetent or corrupt; one of the southern governors smoked opium, while another smuggled it (Reynolds 1997: 267).

With the passing of Jaophraya Noi in 1839, the Bangkok court reasserted itself to govern the mid south directly and, by the end of the nineteenth century, the reform of provincial administration, known as the *thesaphiban* system, soon curtailed the independence of regional rulers such as the Governor of Nakhon Si Thammarat. Revenue and resources that had once flowed to local rulers were gradually redirected to Bangkok, which disbursed moneys according to a national budget. Between 1893 and 1899, when the new system was implemented, Songkhla was designated as the centre of the southern administrative circle of provinces (*monthon*). It was closer to the seven small Malay states in the deep south and could keep a watchful eye on them (Mana 2003: 46).[11] The central government not only appointed governors to replace the local rulers who had inherited their positions through their families, but also, as the result of an 1899 edict, appointed the headmen of villages and village clusters. Commune elders had already been given coercive powers by an Act of 1897 (Bunnag 1977: 122–5). The provincial ruling elites resented this imposition of central authority. In any case, the centre often found it difficult to identify reliable personnel, especially at the lower levels of the administrative hierarchy. Appointees from the centre did not always enjoy local support and newly created positions at the village level were sometimes filled by local toughs trusted by villagers even as they engaged in behaviour that came close to banditry in the eyes of neighbours who were its victims. The inhospitable, sparsely populated and remote terrain was itself a force that resisted Bangkok's control. Given the rigours of living in a lightly

---

11   Appendix III in Bunnag (1977) makes clear that, while the *monthon* was named Nakhon Si Thammarat, the administrative centre was at Songkhla.

governed frontier, with its natural hazards and lawlessness, the local population tended to be independent-minded and to look to each other for assistance rather than to the central government (Mana 2003: 49–50). These conditions could not have been unique to the mid south, but they have received eloquent expression by local scholars with intimate knowledge of the Songkhla lakes environment.

Local officials appointed by Bangkok ruled according to their own lights—a style of government found throughout the kingdom that the reforms of the 1890s took a long time to rectify. In 1894, provincial judges in Phatthalung operated no fewer than six jails, containing 240 men and 60 women. Operating a jail was a status symbol testifying to the social standing of the judges. It was also to their personal advantage. Incarcerated men and women were a source of labour that officials could use as domestic servants or to build public works. Some prisoners were hired out to cultivate paddy (Mana 2003: 132). In the fifth reign, the supply of labour increased with the emancipation of slaves and the release of freemen and women (*phrai*) from corvée duties. Given the paltry salary provided by the central government, local officials seized the opportunity to supplement their salaries by using the perquisites of office—a practice known as 'living off the fruits of office' (*kin meuang*).

The Siamese empire in the south lasted from the thirteenth century, when the Kingdom of Sukhothai claimed sovereignty over the entire Malay Peninsula, to the reform period at the end of the nineteenth century. Soon after the Anglo-Siamese Treaty of 1909 created a border between the northernmost sultanates in Malaya and the southernmost Malay vassals in Siam, one of the negotiators of the treaty, the American Jens Westengard, said wistfully that the 'heroic age' had ended (Loos 2006: 55–6, 58). In Ayutthaya times, the larger the empire's territorial reach, the greater was the number of satellite states that chafed under its sway and resisted its demands. Any attempt to expand territory, administer it or demand loyalty to be tendered with tribute increased the risk of rebellion. The Pax Britannica also brought an end to the need to defend the west coast of the peninsula from Burmese predations, and a *Pax Siamensis*—although it was not very peaceful—now settled over Malay principalities such as Patani that Siam had been able to retain under the terms of the treaty. The tiered network of suzerains and vassals—some of which, such as Songkhla and Nakhon Si Thammarat, were proxy suzerains of smaller vassals—was replaced with a centralised national government that arrogated to itself the appointment of provincial governors.

By the time the Lion Lawman came on the scene in the early 1930s, the provincial system known as the *thesaphiban* had been in place for nearly three decades, but the mid south was still a frontier society. As late as the 1950s, settlers were still moving into the region. Government infrastructure remained weak and banditry was endemic. The budgets of provincial administrations were centralised by the national government and proxy suzerains such as Songkhla and Nakhon Si Thammarat no longer controlled their own finances. The policeman's active career from 1930 to the late 1950s coincided with the arrival of a new sovereignty that rested on territorial control rather than on the contingent and intermittently unenforceable sovereignty through the tiered tribute system of proxies, and a new provincial police force was created to replace local village security with an institution whose agents were employees of the sovereign nation-state.

4

Policing and banditry

Video content for this chapter is available online:
press.anu.edu.au/publications/series/asian-studies/
power-protection-and-magic-thailand#media

The Thai police, always a force to be reckoned with, came to renewed prominence in the first half of the 2000s during the governments of Police Lieutenant Colonel Thaksin Shinawatra (b. 1949), who was prime minister from 2001 to 2006. Thaksin came from a northern Sino-Thai family and had garnered broad electoral strength, especially in the north and northeast, but to the extent that his political networks were based in non-elected institutions, they were in the police force rather than in the military. Thaksin had graduated from the police academy and held advanced degrees in criminal justice from American universities. His entrepreneurial activities during his years as a policeman did not distract him from being promoted to police lieutenant colonel. His wife, Pojaman, came from a police family, and her brother, Phrieophan Damaphong, was a classmate of Thaksin's at the police academy who joined him when they went abroad for advanced study at Eastern Kentucky University. When Thaksin's sister, Yingluck, became prime minister as a Thaksin proxy following the general election in July 2011, Police General Phrieophan was appointed the national police chief.

Policing can run in families, putting relatives in danger from those who might want to settle scores, but police relatives afford protection to those who remain loyal within the family fold. Even today Khun Phan's descendants are careful when moving through the districts of the mid south. Families of the men Khun Phan and his team dispatched with rough justice did not always forgive and forget. The brothers of one decorated policeman born with a patriarchal Chinese clan name took a Thai surname that literally meant 'very good at protecting the family'. The family may have been protected, but the policeman, known as 'Iron Leg Phian', could not protect himself. As the anti-government protests in early 2010 began to shut down Bangkok's central business district, Iron Leg Phian was killed by a roadside bomb while on duty in the deep south (Reynolds 2010). From March to May 2010, until the Red Shirt camp was broken up by the army with brute force and loss of life, police were often in the news. Many police had supported the Red Shirts; many Red Shirts were police officers.

Given the prominence of the police force in recent Thai political history, research on the institution in Western languages is surprisingly thin. Scholars inside and outside the country are understandably wary of delving too deeply into police matters. Thai police are well known not only for their role in state-building, but also—like police almost everywhere— for their corruption, their aptitude for violence and their sometimes comic ineptitude. A postwar memoir by a deputy chief of police states that members of the force knew that the citizenry regarded their line of work as inferior to other occupations but leaves the reader to deduce the reasons (Phinit 1976: 311–91). A Thai survey in 2000 reported that respondents saw the police as the most dishonest element of Thailand's public institutions (McCargo 2009: 115). In the course of my research for this book, I learned a new Thai word for dishonest as it applies to police. *Kong chin* is a loanword from Chinese (Ch., *zong chien*); its binary opposite for honest and trustworthy is *tong ching* (Ch., *zong chien*).

At the time when modernisation theory held sway over area studies in the United States, during the Second Indochina War, Albert Weed provided a sketchy history of the Thai police in his study of American aid for counterinsurgency. He reported that a disproportionate budget was allocated to law enforcement in the north and northeast—the regions of the country identified by American and Thai strategists as most vulnerable to the perceived communist threat. Weed's research drew on USAID reports and, while the data were sparse and derivative, one of his sources advanced an idea that strikes me as insightful. Weed said the Thai police 'create around them an aura of apprehension, of anxiety [and] of fear. They are imbued with an emotional significance that does not attach to other agents of government' (Weed 1970: 10).

I once discussed my interest in the Nakhon policeman with a senior Thai anthropologist. She shook her head and said she did not have much to say about the topic. Like many Thai people, she prefers to maintain a distance from the police. Yet emotional significance, which according to Weed's informants I take to mean visceral responses of anxiety and fear, does not capture another aspect of policing in Thailand. Police connections are useful at all levels of society. It pays to have a policeman onside. Indeed, to solve some kinds of problems it is advisable to pay to have a policeman onside.

The emotional significance that attaches to the police is a distinctive feature in the career of Khun Phan. His severe countenance and willingness to resort to lethal force earned him the nickname Lion Eyes. A former lawyer and retired employee of the state electricity authority recounted how conversation among passengers on a train ceased as Khun Phan entered the carriage and walked up the aisle. This was about 1945 and Bunsong, who was only 18 or 19 years old, said he was terrified by the southern policeman's presence.[1] Khun Phan liked to brandish his weapons and brag about his brute strength in the manner of a local tough and risktaker, or *nak leng*. Khun Phan's biographers refer to him as the *nak leng* lawman (*nak leng mue prap*), because of the ruthless manner in which he went about his job, often pursuing an adversary to death with singular purpose. More to the point, in his methods, his guile and daring and his dignified bearing, he was a bit of a *nak leng* himself (Wira 2001: 81–7). *Mue prap* ('lawman') is not to be confused with *mue puen*, a word commonly used for 'hired assassin'. The alliterative twinning of the terms in the Thai ear intimates that the one, the police gunman, might well become the other, an officer out-of-uniform and a gun-for-hire. *Prap*, a word found in the Three Seals Law Code of the early nineteenth century, is a loanword from Angkorean Khmer, in which it meant to level, to flatten and also to defeat, to suppress and to subdue (Jenner 2009: 378). During the absolute monarchy when the government needed to quell rebellions, they were suppressed (*prap*), as when Ho raiders in the northeast were defeated by armies from Bangkok in the 1870s. The literal meaning in modern Thai, like the Angkorean Khmer meaning, is to flatten or crush, and *prap* is still a keyword for the hard edge of policing. In police argot, it means to subdue, to subjugate, to suppress criminality and to restore order. In the mid twentieth century, when the Thai Government pitted its strength against communism, *prap* referred to the suppression of communism (*prap khommiwnit*).

---

1   Bunsong Chamnandit, Interview with the author, Tungsong, Trang, 24 September 2009.

Nowadays there is a Department of Crime Suppression (Kong Prappram), but in the 1920s and 1930s, suppression and investigation were not bureaucratically distinct. Authorities did not just look around and find someone to arrest; they crushed and suppressed. In 1917, a lawyer and former provincial prosecutor published a manual on modern police investigation, yet in the accounts of Khun Phan's capture of lawbreakers I have found nothing about fingerprints or photographs of crime scenes (Lim 2016: 63). Perhaps the police archives have such records. In the early 1930s, when Khun Phan began his career, proper investigative procedures were in their infancy, and his methods of suppressing crime dispensed with the niceties of forensic examination, although there was plenty of reconnaissance and the use of informants. After Khun Phan had graduated from the police academy, a new curriculum was instigated, in 1934, by Field Marshal Pibun Songkhram, then deputy commander of the army, and Luang Adul Detchatarat, then chief of the police department, which took advantage of military knowledge to make the police more motivated in their work and improve their cooperation with the army (Wanlaya 1999: 58).

In his own work, Khun Phan specialised in suppression, sometimes with gruesome results. Incidents of atrocities and the abuse of corpses at the hands of police are scattered in the informal archive of Thailand's modern history. Undated photographs in *Kings and History of the Police*, an official publication, show men condemned to death by decapitation in the nineteenth and early twentieth centuries. Prisoners are shackled and tethered with heavy chains as they await the executioner's sword (Prayut 1976). The pictures were taken in the early history of photography, so poor resolution and multiple printings have left only a blurry image of this intimate moment of impending death.

In Khun Phan's time, Tiger Phat was a fearless murderer. He was fatally shot in 1950 by Police Lieutenant General Pracha Buranathanit and his severed head set out for the vultures at Phra Phathom stupa, an hour's drive from the capital, as a deterrent to other criminals. The scanty evidence of the atrocity—a grainy photograph without attribution in a popular biography—hints at the scale of police barbarity (Okha 2007: 108). Another photograph purports to depict the skull of Suea Sai, a bandit Khun Phan relentlessly pursued and finally captured. Wounded in his struggle with the police, the man developed a fever and died, whereupon Khun Phan brought the body back to the police station and turned the skull into an ashtray (Okha 2007: 88–9). Then there was the incident in the late 1940s when Khun Phan had returned to Phatthalung for the last time and fatally shot a man whose remains were left unclaimed by relatives fearing association with their unfortunate kinsman. The body was decapitated and the severed head publicly displayed at the provincial border to warn outlaws against crossing into territory that the southern policeman was protecting (Samphan 2007: 128–9). These were all barbaric acts, and the details are ghoulish, but one wonders whether Khun Phan really did flick his cigarette ash into a cavity of bone that once contained a human brain.

In rural Thailand, magnanimity and dignity (*saksi*) as well as a capacity for violence were attributes of the macho *nak leng*. Before the writ of government gradually worked its way out to the edge of the bounded Thai state and the centre had yet to dispatch its own officials to the provinces, *nak leng* often performed the service of 'neighbourhood watch' to keep public order in the countryside. Law and order were a local affair, not a national or even a provincial one, and entailed the enforcement of customary law rather than a legal code. A man could protect the people in his home village and rustle cattle or take a life in another.

Khun Phan, who displayed attributes of the *nak leng* with his tattoos, amulets and readiness to fight with dignity, mirrored the *nak leng* social type in the communities in which he lived, shadowing the outlaws rather like a double but on the right side of the law. To lawbreakers and law-enforcers alike, master teachers in the monasteries—or *keji ajan*, as they are known in the vernacular—imparted their specialised knowledge, which promised invulnerability and survival in the jungle. The parts of Khun Phan's sobriquet, *nakleng mueprap*, might then be separated to expose this double identity: Khun Phan, the *nak leng*, was also the enforcer policeman (*mue prap*). To be tough and to triumph in struggle, a man needed spiritual protection; to acquire powers to defeat adversaries, a man had to spend time in the monkhood. So, the permeability of *nak leng*, *mue prap* and monk was not unique to him. The head monastic official in Trang, Phra Borisut Silajan, explained that he was ordained as a novice in 1892 to learn spells and chants. He would then disrobe, take up the outlaw life and use his newfound powers to protect his kinfolk (Mana 2003: 126). The emerging provincial police force was a state institution that had to accommodate the social worlds it encountered in the countryside to impose order on them, so it is little wonder that such complex social types on both sides of the law should appear in rural Thailand at this historical moment. To apprehend these outlaws, Khun Phan had to enter the world of the tigers (*suea*) and adopt their methods. He had to be one of them.

Policing in colonialism's shadow

The emotional significance that attaches to the police must be seen as a recent phenomenon. The police force itself was not an old institution but a creation of the late nineteenth-century Siamese absolutist state in colonial Southeast Asia. The police force grew not organically out of indigenous society but from the needs of Siam's colonial condition, and it began in Bangkok in the middle of the nineteenth century in response to the demands of the Western imperialist powers, who needed to safeguard their interests. Only decades later did it extend to the provinces.

In a courtyard in the central police station in Bangkok, a statue of the fourth Bangkok king, Mongkut (r. 1851–68), honours his role in establishing a constabulary in the districts of the capital. Soon after the Bowring Treaty was signed in 1855, granting extraterritorial rights to the European imperial powers, King Mongkut appointed a former British sea captain, Samuel Joseph Bird Ames, to command the unit in Bangkok—a position he held until 1901 (Suwan 1996: 107–8). Special policing units were dispatched to the Sam Pheng district of Bangkok to curb the activities of Chinese secret societies, and to Phuket, where the societies were also causing unrest. One problem facing law enforcement officers was that lawbreakers, if they were Indian or Chinese, could be British or French subjects whose misdeeds would be adjudicated by European courts comfortably beyond Siamese reach under the extraterritorial treaties.

Siam from 1855 until about 1910 has been called a buffer state. Its survival as a sovereign kingdom relied on Great Britain and France being satisfied to rule the kingdom's neighbouring lands while leaving Siam a sovereign state. Given the international dynamics of those years, a more apt description of Siam's condition would be a buffeted state. The extraterritorial rights stipulated in the Bowring Treaty would eventually become irksome, although at the time the treaty was signed, the monarchy saw no reason to object to the same privileges it had granted to European merchants since the seventeenth century. Siam's national humiliation, as Shane Strate has put it, to express the elite's deep hurt at the treaty's inequalities, became acute only after the 1893 gunboat crisis that led France to extend its extraterritorial demands for French, Annamese and Lao subjects in Siam (Strate 2015: 24–36).

It was at this point that the reforming Siamese court began to strengthen the police force. Under pressure from the British and French, police duties were concentrated in the capital, especially for the protection of the monarch and foreign subjects. The initial model for the constabulary came from Singapore, and possibly Burma, both colonies of Great Britain that the Siamese judged to be the more dominant of the two paramount powers. French criticism of Siamese law enforcement led to the employment of British police officers from India and Burma in the Siamese expectation that, under the extraterritorial treaties, British officers would deal with Westerners and the Western consuls more effectively than the French. In 1897, A.J. Jardine was succeeded by Eric St J. Lawson, who introduced new procedures and crime detection measures and established a hospital dedicated to police health and forensic examination. The first appointees to the constabulary were recruited to Bangkok from elsewhere in the British Empire (India, Burma, the Middle East), leading the Saigon press to claim that Siam was becoming 'a second Egypt'. The official uniform of the Bangkok metropolitan police made them look like British officers, and the treatment of Siamese subjects by these officers was sufficiently tactless and severe for King Chulalongkorn to say that 'the police are not ours, they are the police of the British' (Hong 2003: 128–32). The king's son and heir, Vajiravudh (r. 1910–25), a pioneering author of detective fiction, portrayed police characters in his novels as callous and arrogant. Archives of the time show the police to be 'untrained, bumbling fools' who misused their powers (Lim 2012: 90).

One consequence of the compromised sovereignty forced on Siam after 1855 was that the army was relieved of its task of defending the borders. British and French armies now guarded their respective colonies adjoining Siam. Internal security was shared by the Thai army and the police, and the shares were not equal. The army was the elder brother and the police the younger sibling, and it has always been the army, not the police, that has claimed a sense of entitlement in governing the country. More than once during Khun Phan's career, officers left their army commissions to become police commanders.

To improve relations with Bangkok residents, an academy for the metropolitan police was established in 1907. The recruitment of Siamese police cadets lagged at first owing to the unattractiveness of the work and the poor reputation of police among local people. The job required tact in dealing with miscreants who were British and French subjects, including Chinese and Indians under the jurisdiction of the European courts

(Suwan 1996: 195–6). A separate section of the procedural manuals issued to the metropolitan police in the 1920s gave instructions on how to treat such subjects and included a form to be filled out by the arresting officer. Time and again it is stipulated in the manuals that the Thai police have no power over extraterritorial subjects, which included Japanese as well as French and British (Khunjomphonlan 1922–24: 13–16). The manuals, which were updated annually, were a jumble of proper procedures to be followed and topics requiring special vigilance on the part of police: notice of quarantine areas for smallpox victims, rewards for capturing criminals and alerts about specific problems at the time—for example, con artists who were circulating German currency easily mistaken for Thai *baht* by unknowing traders. Motorcycle police rostered to escort the royal motorcade were required to obtain proper training and to drive safely.

Many decades would pass before the police force developed a formidable presence outside the capital. In rural areas, where law enforcement was spotty at best, policing had been the responsibility of local lords and administrators. Provincial judges operated their own jails and exploited the labour of incarcerated people for domestic service and the cultivation of their lands. Such was the case in the mid south. In a few provinces, officials administered regional police forces. In many locales, law enforcement had been counted among the duties of village headmen, as had been the case in Burma before British rule (Griffiths 1971: 194).

A provincial police force was created in 1897 within the Ministry of Interior to shift policing duties away from untrained civil officials who had taken matters into their own hands. The Provincial Gendarmerie Department would supersede the army in the task of keeping peace in the countryside. Between 1899 and 1909, some 330 substations of gendarmerie were established in provincial and district towns. A police academy in Nakhon Pathom began preparing officers for provincial police duty in 1904, and it was there that Khun Phan received his training. Instruction was given by Westerners with a military background. From 1897 to 1926, 21 Danish officers worked under the command of Gustav Shau, a senior Danish officer who had been employed as a military instructor in the mid-1880s and now headed the fledgling gendarmerie. The recruits were accommodated in barracks and trained in marching, marksmanship and physical fitness, including boxing, football and swimming. The model evidently had its origins in the way the military police was established by the British in Burma (Ivarsson 2016: 216).

As with modern methods of jurisprudence, education, taxation and census, Siamese authorities adopted and adapted many ideas about security from British colonial administration.

In 1905, the king abolished corvée labour and instituted universal conscription. A military training syllabus dating from the same year laid out a regimen to inculcate military virtues of bravery, unity, obedience, honour and willingness to shed blood in defence of the homeland. The intent and scope of this reform, which laid the foundations of the modern Thai army, have been described with lyrical flair by the Australian historian Noel Battye. His words capture the ethos imagined for newly created Siamese institutions as the absolute monarchy wrenched the kingdom from the past to accommodate pressures from the Western powers:

> Technique, ideology, behaviour and values were combined into a new socialization process that was technical, national, urban, collective and martial—something previously beyond the realm of peasant experience. These things were imparted by qualified instructors who trained conscripts according to a syllabus within an organization with its own distinct regulations and code of law. Conscripts lived in barracks which took their place with the village, the temple and, increasingly, the primary school, amongst the principal institutions of provincial life. (Battye 1974: 484–5)

The order, regularity and predictability imagined for the peasant-soldiers subjected to a regimen such as this are familiar motifs in the history of modernity. The Danish military instructors were given the task of moulding young provincial police officers with a similar regimen inspired by a particular kind of modernity that came with Western colonialism in the region.

Unlike other countries in Southeast Asia where provincial police forces were being established, Siam was not a colony. The police did not face 'the conflicting responsibilities of law enforcement and social work' as in the Dutch East Indies, where the ethical policy decreed development and control to be the job of police, who were charged with being the civilised face of the colonial state (Bloembergen 2011: 169, 171, 176). In Siam, the task was control alone as centralised government was extended into remote regions with the aim of subordinating provincial elites and rulers. There were no stirrings of nationalism to challenge law enforcers, just local enforcers who had their own ideas of 'peace and order', as it was known in the Dutch East Indies.

Establishing a provincial police bureaucracy did not bring about *Pax Siamensis* throughout the country overnight. Recruits to the fledgling police force were often conscripts levied by the 1905 Act selected to serve as provincial police officers (Bunnag 1977: 97, 224). These officers were untrained and reluctant to execute their duties. They feared retribution from the people they arrested and, after serving out their tour of duty, tended to depart the district quickly. For whatever reason, the impact of the new gendarmerie in suppressing crime and banditry was limited. In Lawson's survey of 1917, the number of murders in Siam was double that in British Burma, and the murder rate was increasing at twice the rate of other crimes—statistics that alarmed officials but that may have surfaced in data never before collected. Provincial officers were slow to report cases and they lacked the legal authority to investigate and question witnesses. Only district-level administrators had this authority (Lim 2016: 35–6).

Police leadership

Khun Phan, the Nakhon policeman, rose in the provincial police to the rank of major general but showed no interest that I can discover in pursuing a career in the upper echelons of the police bureaucracy in Bangkok. He seemed content with his postings in the north, the central plains and the south, although from time to time his duties and operations brought him to the attention of the police command. In the early 1980s, when he began to talk about his exploits with journalists, writers and academics, it was not so much his connections with the police hierarchy that he enjoyed sharing anecdotally with his interviewers, but rather his skill in apprehending outlaws using his knowledge of spells, charms and magical thinking to lure, deceive or overpower those whom he was ordered to bring to justice. A retired schoolmaster from Tha Sala District in Nakhon, who had met Khun Phan several times, recalled that he was a man of action, full of energy, who loved to be out and about conducting operations rather than sitting at a desk. Khun Phan's motto was: 'Do your job so your deaf and blind boss can hear and see.'[2]

National police chiefs are political appointees, and incumbents tend to be replaced when a new government takes office. Over his long career, Khun Phan served under a dozen chiefs of police. Two are worthy of

---

2   Anan Ratanawong (b. 1932), Interview with the author, 6 December 2014; Chanthip Phantarakrajchadech, Interview with the author, 9 September 2012.

mention, as each in his own way represents contrasting styles of police leadership. During World War II, when Khun Phan was dispatched to close the infamous Ivory Bamboo Casino in Surat Thani, he did so at the behest of Police General Adul Aduladetcharat (1894–1969), born Bat Phungphrakhun, an army officer who had participated in the coup that overthrew the absolute monarchy in 1932. The last absolute monarch had conferred on Adul the noble title of *luang*, which Bat renounced at the beginning of the Japanese occupation. As Field Marshal Phibun moved to take control of the state from the People's Party in the mid-1930s, General Adul became chief of police and held the position until the end of the Pacific War. During his time, the police budget for training, investigating crime and expanding the provincial police force was increased (Prayut 1976: 403).

An incorruptible, hardworking patriot with no time for flattery, the ascetic and enigmatic General Adul patrolled the capital at night dressed in a blue cotton shirt and naval trousers. His 'burning, black eyes' and piercing gaze earned him the sobriquets 'Tiger Eyes' and 'the general with fierce eyes'. He vowed to arrest anyone who fell foul of the law, even if that person happened to be the prime minister. He knew he had made enemies and, on official business, preferred to ride behind his chauffeur, where he thought he might miss the assassin's bullet.[3] During the war, his officers would deliver downed American pilots they had captured into his presence. He received the men politely only to release them promptly through a side door to continue their work with the Free Thai. He helped the movement using the code name 'Betty', but he did not completely trust the Free Thai and did not join until nearly the end of the war. For his assistance to American pilots and the Free Thai movement during the occupation, he was awarded the Silver Palm Medal of Freedom by the US Government, according to his cremation biography. He became army chief in 1945 and participated in the 1947 coup that returned Field Marshal Plaek Pibulsongkhram, the wartime dictator, to power. His colleagues remembered him as thoughtful and generous and at ease with his friends, although he was a private man and became something of a recluse in his final years.[4]

---

3   Chaiyan Rajchagool heard this anecdote from his father (Personal communication, 4 August 2011).
4   The information in this paragraph comes from MacDonald (1949: 157–60); Okha (2007: 117); and General Adul's cremation volume (Buranasinlapa 1970: n.p.).

After the war, the Thai population faced economic hardship. The nation's infrastructure had been weakened by the occupation, the country was unsettled and the government found it difficult to maintain law and order. Small arms had found their way into the hands of the citizenry via British and American forces, Japanese troops who had surrendered to the Allies after the war and a worldwide surplus of ordnance (Chalong 2005: 41–2). With munitions widely available, outlaws were well-armed and policing became a dangerous business. In the central plains, large groups of bandits (*kok*), numbering up to 100, roamed at will and held sway over the population, especially in Chainat, where Khun Phan was chief, and in half a dozen neighbouring provinces including Suphanburi, where the outlaw Suea Fai had carved out a piece of the national real estate that he ruled with an iron fist (Samphan 2007: 196). The government itself was in possession of more than half a million firearms, including submachine guns, automatic pistols, hand grenades, grenade launchers and various kinds of explosives. The police responded to unrest with harsh measures—'by any means available', said an officer at the time, which was code for lethal force (Phut 1981: 6). In the capital, fatal shootings by police were indiscriminate, often with no evidence of criminality or of danger to the community. Many of the killings were political. Between 1944 and 1957, the police killed more than 20 well-known public figures (Chit 1960: 41–7; Lim 2016: 122–31). It was in this period—the five or so years after the end of the war—that Khun Phan's operations in the central plains and the south were the deadliest. Between the end of May 1945 and January 1950, he and his police teams shot to death 43 men—more than two-thirds of the total attributed to Khun Phan and accomplices that is publicly known (Wira 2001: 185–7; Samphan 2007: 393–8; Chalong 2013: 195).

In the late 1940s, Thailand quickly became integral to the United States' global strategy to contain the spread of communism, which often meant support for authoritarian governments. American funds through a Central Intelligence Agency (CIA) front company, Sea Supply, began to flow to the Thai police. Police General Phao Siyanond (1909–60) was the national police chief from 1951 to 1957, when he was forced from office after the 1957 coup led by his rival in the army, Field Marshal Sarit Thanarat. He went into exile in Switzerland. Phao, like General Adul, had graduated from the military academy and was a commissioned army officer. At the beginning of the Pacific War, he briefly headed the Crown Property Bureau—an ironic touch to his career given the ignominious exile that was later visited on him (Prayut 1976: 419).

So close was Phao to the CIA that, during the 1950s, two American operatives eager to bolster police capacity married two women in the Thai aristocracy. Phao considered one of the American men, James William (Bill) Lair, needed rank if he was to be effective in establishing an elite paramilitary unit and commissioned him captain in the Thai national police (Ball 2013: 63, 66–7). The Thai women were sisters of Siddhi Savetsila (1919–2015), foreign minister from 1980 to 1990 and a privy councillor at his death. *Savetsila* ('white stone') is a calque of alabaster and the family name of descendants of Henry Alabaster, the British Consul in Bangkok in the late nineteenth century. The close association of the Savetsila family and American intelligence operatives is not as surprising as it might seem. Siddhi was in the anti-Japanese Free Thai movement during the Japanese occupation and had worked with Americans in the Office of Strategic Services. He was a comrade-in-arms with US Allies fighting the Axis powers. Social fraternisation of American and Thai officials from the earlier period would continue many decades after the war had ended, when Siddhi Savetsila's friends from the old days—professional and personal, foreign and Thai, diplomatic and intelligence—would gather on 7 January every year to celebrate his birthday.[5]

To this day, Phao is acclaimed as the father of Thailand's modern police, the man responsible more than any other for building up the force. His statues in police precincts around the country are the focus of anniversaries to celebrate the founding days of police units. At the Pathumwan Police Centre in Bangkok, he was looking proud amidst the chaos of building renovations in 2012 when I came upon his bust festooned with two small garlands.

---

5   Tej Bunnag, Personal communication, 22 November 2017.

Plate 6 Statue of Phao Siyanon, Pathumwan Police Centre, Bangkok
Source: Craig Reynolds.

Khun Phan's exploits in suppressing crime of all kinds included the interdiction of illegal drugs, and it was drug trafficking that brought the southern policeman to the notice of Police General Phao. Official histories of the Thai police in Thai and memoirs by Phao's subordinates are reluctant to mention that Phao was involved in the opium trade and competed with Sarit for its control; at one point the two nearly fought their own opium war over the crop (Baker and Pasuk 2005: 146–7). Phao supported the CIA's clandestine activities in southern China and Laos in exchange for using those activities to achieve a virtual monopoly over opium and heroin trafficking into Thailand (Ball 2013: 59–60).

In 1950, while he was serving as the provincial chief in Phatthalung, Khun Phan apprehended a couple of soldiers trafficking opium on the southern train line. Police intelligence had tipped him off and he was persistent and meticulous in questioning passengers seated next to a large suitcase that no one would claim. Inside the bag were 50 kilograms of pure opium, and the two army officers, who were finally identified as owners of the bag, were arrested (Samphan 2007: 339–42). The opium turned out to belong to Police General Phao, and Khun Phan was summoned to Bangkok to account for himself. When he turned up for his audience with Phao to declare that in apprehending the men he was simply doing his duty, he was in civilian clothes. He did not wear his uniform that day, he told Phao, because he expected to be fired (Okha 2007: 117–18). Phao was satisfied enough with the explanation not to dismiss him, but this version of the tale cannot be the whole story. By 1950, Khun Phan had been policing for two decades. With so many successful operations behind him, his reputation within the force was secure. In age if not in rank, he was senior to Phao. Would Phao have gained anything by sacking an officer with what the national police chief—given his own predilections and methods for dealing with criminals and outlaws—could only regard as a commendable record? It would have been in Khun Phan's character as a calculated risk-taker to challenge his commander-in-chief, confident he would emerge from the encounter unwounded.

In due course, Khun Phan was rewarded for his many successes and received one of the prized rings worn by elite police who had earned sufficient favour to become one of Phao's knights or *aswin*, a Thai loanword from the Indic term for horse and the same word for the knight's piece in chess. Phao conceived the honour in 1949 when he was deputy chief, perhaps inspired by the British honours system he had learned about during his training in London, where many police officers were sent because of Scotland Yard's reputation. This flashy piece of gold or diamond jewellery was no mere bodily ornament but an emblem of loyalty to Phao and to the national mission of suppressing crime and combating communism. A police officer in the first group of 18 recipients vividly remembered the occasion when he received his *aswin* ring. Phao placed the ring on the officer's finger and, reeking of whisky, drew the man into a close embrace. The officer would never forget the stench of alcohol on Phao's breath (Chaiyong 1980: 157).

Phao's reputation as an unrefined, hard-drinking bully emerges from police memoirs, but it clashes with another side of Phao, whom Alfred McCoy, in his classic study of drug trafficking in the region, described as 'a cherub with the smile of a Cheshire cat' (McCoy et al. 1972: 136). Phao had been an outstanding student. He liked to write poems, regularly entered his verse in poetry competitions run by the newspapers and was fond of quoting a stanza about rings from the seventeenth-century Thai classic *Khamsuan Samut* by Si Prat. 'On East–West', an unfinished essay of 135 pages composed during his Geneva exile, displays a commendable if rambling prose style. He likened governing a country to presiding over a family and mulled over the political, economic and cultural differences between Europe and Asia. After his departure from Bangkok in late 1957, he lived but another three years. His remains were interred in Geneva and his tombstone identified him not as police general but as 'General Pao Sriyanonda', his army commission. His widow held merit-making ceremonies on the 10th anniversary of his death at Wat Intharawihan, a monastery the family had supported and for which Phao had once raised building funds. No cremation book to celebrate his life was ever formally published, but in a memorial volume sponsored by the family, his daughter recalled that companions visiting him from Thailand always found him in good spirits and reasonable health. Family members knew he was devastated by the way his country had turned against him and pined for his homeland.[6] Police General Phao believed himself to be a patriot, but in contrast to General Adul, the patriot honoured by the US Government for service to the Allied cause, Phao had been disgraced and never received the royally sponsored cremation granted to other national leaders. By contrast, the 2007 cremation of the southern policeman Khun Phan was a royally sponsored affair that included the Crown Prince of Thailand.

A portrait of Police General Phao cannot be rounded off to the point where it obscures the violence of the period and the gangland-type killings that cut down opposition politicians. The Iron Man of Asia, as Phao was once

---

6   This paragraph is based on *Anuson phon tor or phao siyanon wan thoeng kae anitchakam khrop 10 pi 21 phroetsajikayon 2513* [*In Memory of Police General Phao Siyanond on the Tenth Anniversary of His Death, 21 November 1970*]. Privately printed.

known, presided over the force when it was at its most powerful, although Thailand was far from becoming a police state (Chit 1960: 41). Phao did not have absolute power; he had to share control of state institutions with Phibun, and later with Sarit. Yet he left a legacy that is remembered. When the prime minister at the time, Police Lieutenant Colonel Thaksin, announced the war on drugs in 2003 and authorised the police to carry out his policy, he quoted Police General Phao: '[T]here is nothing under the sun that the Thai police cannot do' (Pasuk and Baker 2009: 158). Phao's boast, endorsed by Thaksin, who quoted it, has two valences. In Phao's time, the police had the capacity, including force of arms, to do anything they cared to do, and what they did was beyond the reach of any person or institution.

General Phao and General Adul before him were both trained in the military academy. Both officials headed the police force when international relations in the region were undergoing a seismic shift as the United States replaced the United Kingdom as the paramount power in the western Southeast Asian mainland. General Adul was incorruptible and earned the respect of fellow officers for his probity and dedication in steering the country through the war. Thailand was occupied by the Japanese army, but General Adul's position as national police chief allowed him to cooperate discreetly with the new paramount power to defeat Japan. Phao, by contrast, lived out his life in Geneva, unwilling to accept that he had been disgraced. He loved his country and longed to return. Like native Southeast Asian princes, kings and sultans who had been deposed and sent abroad once continuation of their rule became inconvenient to colonial regimes, Phao was sent into exile not as formal punishment but as the result of a political manoeuvre. The irony of his pining for home from exile in Europe was that, once ensconced in the swank Geneva apartment he could afford thanks to his self-aggrandising ways, Phao was untouchable by the Thai judicial system. Exile guaranteed him impunity from Thai law.

Banditry in the mid south

When Khun Phan began his career in the mid south in the late 1920s, parts of the region were governed only in a formal sense. Gangs of bandits (*chum jon*) had roamed the countryside since the fifth reign, and burglary, kidnapping and cattle rustling were a way of life for many people

(Suwan 1996: 258). To protect their villages, headmen sometimes relied on local toughs, or *nak leng*, who might become headmen themselves, attaining the position through inheritance or local political dynamics. Southerners were straight talkers who were quick to anger and seek revenge if they felt dishonoured. Poison was deployed for vengeful retribution in Krabi, Phatthalung and Trang during the 1940s and 1950s, and Khun Phan himself had some understanding of how lethal slow-acting poisons and their antidotes were administered (Phantharakratchadet 2007: 484; Suwit 2017). Banditry, so local lore has it, was inherent in the character of people from the mid south from time immemorial, and villagers could be sympathetic, seeing necessity and even virtue, rather than criminal behaviour, in banditry. The endemic *nak leng* culture with its rough justice meant that mutual support groups formed quickly to defend territory and to settle local disputes (Mana 2003: 109–10; Thammanit 2010: 15–16).

One explanation offered by Thai scholars for a regionally specific disposition towards banditry in the mid south is that village settlement there was markedly different from that in the north, where the founding of kingdoms and major principalities was enshrouded with the mystique of Buddhist prophecies, the arrival of the Buddha's relics and visits by famous rishis. Petit kingdoms (*mueang*) were governed by princes and local lords whose authority was linked to the custodianship of relics and the monasteries that enshrined them. By contrast, what characterised centres in the south were the resourcefulness and rugged independence of settlers (Nidhi 1995: Ch. 2; Chatthip and Phunsak 1997: 72–3). With very few exceptions—and Nakhon Si Thammarat was the preeminent one—settlements were not shrouded in Buddhist legends. Compared with the northern region, there were few monasteries housing relics of the Buddha that attracted pilgrims. The south was a frontier society, whereas the north had histories of kingdoms and royal courts that were traceable to the eleventh and twelfth centuries. Throughout the nineteenth century, the court's authority was weak on the frontier, and imposing its will through proxies, as it had done in the Ayutthaya and early Bangkok periods, was now being challenged as the British in Malaya moved to draw a national line between the two states.

In the first half of the twentieth century, lawlessness was not unique to Siam. It was also pervasive in the rural areas of Siam's neighbours. Cattle rustling across the borders with French Indochina and British Malaya was common. In Cambodia, which, like Laos, was ruled by the French as a protectorate, gangs of men (*chor plan*) roamed the countryside in the off-season stealing livestock and other valuable objects to sell back to the owners. Villagers regarded the bandit gangs with a mixture of fear and respect. After all, some bandits could be turned to useful purpose and engaged to protect villages or recover stolen property. The predations of bandit gangs need to be distinguished from political protest, such as the one that occurred in 1916, when tens of thousands of peasants rose up against the abuse of power and exploitative practices of Khmer officials. The French financed their colony, including the salaries of French officials and public works, by taxing salt, alcohol, opium, rice and other agricultural products. During World War I, the French increased the tax burden, thus triggering the insurgency—a relatively peaceful expression of resistance to the civilising mission of Franco-Khmer colonialism (Chandler 2008: 187–8; Broadhurst et al. 2015: 47–57).

Banditry—described by the French as *piraterie*—was different from insurgency or political protest and involved violent house invasions and robberies. Yet a recent study of peasant resistance to Franco-Khmer rule includes rebellion in the category of *piraterie*, suggesting that, as in Siam, the distinction between banditry and insurgency was not always clear to the authorities at the time (Broadhurst et al. 2015: 66). In British Malaya during the 1910s and 1920s, bandits could be social bandits, as in Kedah, where a population of Siamese-speaking Sam-Sams lived. Cheah Boon Kheng, inspired by the work of Eric Hobsbawm and Jim Scott on peasant resistance, made a case for rural social bandits who dedicated themselves to redressing injustice and redistributing wealth among villagers (Kheng 1988: 1–12). In Malaya, what colonial authorities saw as crime may be read as the negative articulation of rebel consciousness.

Another source of unrest in the south were separatists active in the remnants of the former sultanate of Patani. One case with which Khun Phan dealt was the capture in 1938 of Ahweh Sador, discussed in an earlier chapter, when the policeman was posted to Narathiwat Province. In 1922 and 1923, opposition turned into armed conflict over the compulsory *Primary Education Act* of 1921 that required Malay Muslim children to attend Thai primary schools—a measure that was also designed to promote use of the Thai language in the local population. In the late 1930s, cultural policies became more repressive when Field Marshal Phibul came to power and the central government promulgated cultural mandates that forbid Malay Muslims to dress as Malays. Malay language and certain Islamic practices were also outlawed (Che Man 1990: 64–5; Kobkua 2013: 233). Malay Muslims in the deep south resented the way

Bangkok had 'subcontracted' the tasks of ruling the region to provinces such as Songkhla, Phatthalung and Nakhon Si Thammarat. These largely Buddhist provinces in the first half of the twentieth century 'lorded it over' Malay Muslims in the lower south (McCargo 2009: 57). The fact that Khun Phan acquired the sobriquet Little Raja from the sultan of a northern Malay state for his capture of Ahweh Sador indicates that his reputation as a legendary lawman was known to Malay rulers of the former tributaries that had been incorporated in the Unfederated Malay States by the 1909 treaty with the British.

The remoteness of the deep south made the region a haven for banditry that lasted for many decades. In a story published in 1963 about five *nak leng* who ran afoul of the Bangkok police, one of the characters fled to Yala in the deep south and wrote back to his comrades to say he was so happy he felt he had gone to heaven (*mueang suwan*). Finally, he was in a place free from the discipline of the state where *nak leng* types such as himself could roam at will, and he invited his comrades to join him as soon as possible. The young researcher who rediscovered this tale underscores how attractive the south was to fugitives from the law from the early twentieth century until well after World War II (Worayut 2017).

When Khaw Sim Bee na Ranong arrived as the new Governor of Trang in 1910, he was told that a man wanting to marry a local woman would inevitably be asked two questions by her parents: did the suitor know how to perform *nora*, a southern Thai dance, and was he good at stealing cattle? A man who could answer in the affirmative to both questions confirmed to his future in-laws that he was capable of mobilising supporters to protect the lives and property of his future bride, their extended families and the community at large. This anecdote was repeated so often that it became burnished into a local truth, yet ethnographic facts also lie buried in the tale. *Nora*, abbreviated from *manohara*, is a southern Thai dance that continues to have meaning for people in the mid south provinces. Its rituals of physical and spiritual healing are embedded in customary laws, values and practices. In the anecdote, the suitor's prospective in-laws were inquiring about the man's social skills and his ability to function in the local community. If he could dance the *nora* and rustle livestock, he would be able to form alliances and networks with local people (Cholthira 2013: 23–4; Sitthiphon et al. 2017: 127).

Local historians of the mid south—among them Pramuan Manirote, who has built up a picture of the bandit culture in the three provinces on the shores of the Songkhla lakes—like to cite the anecdote (Pramuan 1994: 58–9). The hazards of frontier life called for rugged men who could protect their families and communities. The mid south provinces fiercely resisted the demands of local officials and this reputation for resistance fed into an insurgency that lasted through the rise and demise of the Communist Party of Thailand (CPT) (Khrongkan Chapho Kit Phu Banthat 2001: 74). At the time Khun Phan was retiring, in the early 1960s, the CPT was becoming active in Phatthalung, and violence against villagers—communist or not—increased. The historian Thanet Aphornsuwan proposed that criminal acts and political insurgency became mixed during this time. Villagers reported that if they joined the CPT it was out of frustration that the government did not provide proper welfare and justice, echoing the feelings of neglect on the part of the local population from earlier in the century (Haberkorn 2013: 192). The linearity of this narrative from social bandit to communist needs to be scrutinised for its teleology, but the writ of the central government was weak as late as the 1960s, when infrastructure and security began to be upgraded to counter the communist threat.

Various factors have been put forward to explain the bandit culture in Phatthalung and Songkhla. Overlapping jurisdictions between the two provinces created confusion about which officials had responsibility for detecting and arresting criminals (Sangop 1994: 32–4). Specie came into wider circulation during the fourth reign and increasing affluence in Songkhla attracted thieves from Phatthalung. During periods of drought, when the land was unproductive, people turned to banditry to supplement family incomes. The southern Thai environmental historian Mana Khunwichual has argued that conditions peculiar to the south favoured banditry. The region's numerous rivers and canals as well as the Songkhla lakes facilitated the movement of travellers: merchants, traders, officials, soldiers, police and bandits. Jaophraya Yommarat, the Governor of the Nakhon Si Thammarat Provincial Circle, whose posting lasted a decade from 1896, reported that banditry would greatly diminish if officials could control the casinos, opium dens and cock fighting—a recommendation that sounds more like the huffy comment of a Bangkok official than an astute observation about the region's political economy (Mana 2017: 44–51). Casinos, opium production and brothels had historically been tax farms that yielded revenue for the government, so measures to close the farms were slow in coming. Still another explanation for bandit culture in the mid south is that cattle rustling was a nonviolent act, so everyone—including the livestock owners, villagers, thieves and police—engaged in it. Buffalo and cows would go missing and everyone knew who the culprits were, so the livestock could be immediately retrieved. It sounds like a game, but it was also a way of making a living, a vocation (Kong 1997: 85–6; Sitthiphon et al. 2017: 127). One problem with these explanations, such as increasing affluence and economic hardship, is they are contradictory: they explain both banditry and its absence.

Some banditry in the south expressed resistance to the gradual tightening of Bangkok's rule over distant provinces, but, according to a detailed report of 1894 by a Bangkok official sent to inspect government in the mid south, local officials, not the central government, were responsible for the hardships and injustices endured by local people. The Bangkok nobleman who wrote the report found people reluctant to speak their minds for fear of retribution by local officials. One example of bandits whose reputations as local leaders were based on such resistance was Rung Dawnsai from Dawnsai Subdistrict in Phatthalung and his deputy, Dam Huaphrae, a 'graduate' of the academy at Wat Khao Or, where Khun Phan had acquired his knowledge of *saiyasat* (Wet n.d.: 111). The two bandits rebelled against paying the poll tax and other fees (Lom 1994: 40–53; Pramuan 1994: 62; Ran 2007: 152–69). As a form of governance for their social group, the bandits devised a code of conduct and, as a badge of equality within the gang, addressed each other as *khun*, a noble rank conferred by the king. The *nom de guerre* of Rung was Khun Phat; Dam was Khun Atasadong Phraiwan (Pramuan 1994: 66; Mana 2003: 142). The *khun* rank drew the men together with a shared status that mocked the hierarchical ranking system monopolised by the monarchy.

Before firearms became widely available, the weapon of choice in such bandit circles was the sickle (*phra*), a farm implement used to lethal effect. Rites were conducted to empower swords, guns and knives and to confer invulnerability on those who wielded them. Astrological calculations guided the outlaws on when and where they should strike, and tutelary deities that guarded homes and villages were appeased so the bandits could pass without hindrance. The rituals were conducted on specially consecrated land, much as the ordination of a monk takes place on land free of usufructuary rights (Mana 2003: 143).[7] The moral

---

7   Local conditions in the mid south that bred bandit culture are canvassed by the environmental historian Mana Khunwichuay (2003) and the author and historian Pramuan Manirote (1994) and were presented at Walailak University in Nakhon Si Thammarat (Mana 2017; Pramuan 2017).

principles embraced by the bandits had been taught by monks respected in their local communities. In some cases, these were the same monks who taught police and officials. In the words of the southern writer and teacher Pramuan Manirote, the word for bandit or outlaw (*jon*) is not as straightforward as the dictionaries would have it: 'like the incessant movement of water in the lake', its meanings are 'in constant motion' (Pramuan 2017: 106–7).

This political banditry, the complexities of which are difficult to tease out because the culture has largely faded, must be distinguished from the hired hit. Only a few years ago at a cremation in the mid south for an elderly relative at which guns had been banned, a man slipped into the gathering, went into a back room where a gambling game was under way and shot dead one of the players with a .38 pistol. Heeding the injunction against weapons, a policeman-guest was not carrying his sidearm inside the building and, enjoying the libations on the day, was in no condition to prevent the man's escape. A grandson of the deceased grabbed the microphone and urged everyone to remain calm and the ceremony proceeded without further incident. This was a mafia hit and, although no one would testify against the gunman for fear of retribution, he was eventually caught. I was assured that such an incident was not at all common at funerals in the mid south.[8]

Local writers and scholars tend to valorise the bandit culture that flourished during the Japanese occupation and, in so doing, they point to a regional identity specific to the Songkhla lakes ecosystem. They are quick to recall stories of their own relatives in previous generations who followed the bandit way of life. One of my colleagues overheard in the teasing banter of family conversation the story of a boatwoman who operated a long-tailed craft on the lakes from the Ranot market in Songkhla. She needed firearms to protect herself and was ambidextrous in the use of them. On her wedding day, her husband-to-be, an experienced horseman wanted by the authorities, saw mounted police officers stationed at the ceremony to block his escape. After the wedding, he managed to elude his captors and flee into the nearby forest.[9] Yet such anecdotes of bandits and *nak leng* in family histories as well as academic studies by Pramuan Manirote, Mana

---

8   Kasem Jandam, Personal communication, 7 September 2012.
9   Davisakd Puaksom, Personal communication, 10 November 2017.

Khunwichuai and others raise the question of the uniqueness of banditry to the mid south compared with other regions in the country that were also beyond the reach of the central government until after World War II.

The south was not the only part of the country with low population density where policemen feared to venture and sometimes only to investigate a serious incident. Villagers everywhere were self-reliant and, where government was weak and a police presence non-existent, they took matters into their own hands and resolved disputes sometimes by force with the aid of the *nak leng* types who were their friends and relatives. Not all villagers enjoyed resources sufficient to avenge a wrongdoing. I once spoke to an elderly woman in Phitsanuloke whose husband, a Lothario and bandit-type, was shot in the mid-1980s and left to die in a pool of blood. He was employed by a village headman to look after elephants that worked in the timber forests along the Nan River. The local police had been quite happy to share the man's moonshine, but when the time came to find his killer, they were suddenly unavailable, and his widow had no money to offer incentives for them to act.[10] Her village settlement was in Phromphiram District near the border with Uttaradit, one of the in-between spaces where jurisdictions faded away and officialdom became indifferent to local problems. While the environment of the Songkhla lakes created specific conditions for banditry and resistance to the demands and exactions of local and national governments, banditry was not unique to the mid south.

Rural masculinity

Khun Phan, the southern Thai lawman, was dispatched to catch outlaws or bandits (*jon*), not *nak leng*, and the accounts of his exploits never fail to mention that he apprehended lawbreakers. *Jon* was a loanword from the Pali-Sanskrit *cora*, usually translated as bandit or brigand, which had legal status in the old legal code (Davids and Stede 1966: 273). The same loanword is found in Khmer.

Nak leng referred to local toughs willing and able to solve disputes by fisticuffs if necessary. They were known as *suea* or 'tigers'. One of the best sociological explanations of *nak leng* in the central plains is by David Johnston (1980), who came across the social type during his research on

---

10   Conversation with 'Prayoon' (b. 1942), Phromphiram District, Phitsanulok, 10 November 2017.

agricultural development in the Rangsit district north of Bangkok from 1880 to 1930. Johnston discussed relationships among the bandits, *nak leng* and villagers, and the interplay between banditry and different levels of government authority. The region was atypical in the sense that it had been settled recently by cultivators taking advantage of the irrigation system newly constructed with government assistance. Johnston drew a fine line separating *nak leng* from bandits. A man could protect his village one day and thieve from another the next. It would seem that the line might as well not have been there, because a man could be both guard and thief. Another line supposedly separated government officials and bandits, yet in a social history of the central plains, Thai historian Peerasak Chaidaisuk (2008) discovered many examples of compromise and collusion between government officials and bandit gangs.

Using the skills of his former profession in a new line of work, a thief might find himself in gainful employment on the right side of the law. An example of such a crossover comes from Prince Damrong Rajanubhab's account of a bandit known as Jon Jan in Nakhon Pathom to the southeast of the capital, where the prince found respite from his official duties. During his conversations with Jon Jan to find out how the thief went about his business, Damrong learned that a successful robbery almost always involved an insider, either a servant or a disgruntled family member who tipped off the thieves about the best time to pounce. Damrong was so impressed with Jon Jan's familiarity with the modus operandi of thieves that he hired him to guard his bungalow when he was away on official duties in the capital. Jon Jan carried out his duties reliably and retired after 20 years of service guarding Damrong's house (Damrong 1963: 216–30).

Western social scientists have seen continuities between the *nak leng* and provincial bosses—sometimes of Chinese heritage and sometimes not—who exercise power at the local level through their connections with politicians and government officials. In this narrative, *nak leng* gave rise to local bosses known as *jao pho*—a Thai calque of English 'godfather'. The godfathers who flourished with the rapid growth of the provincial economy in the 1980s and 1990s were able to deliver votes to national politicians. Like the *nak leng*, the *jao pho* in their heyday were willing to use coercion and even violence to achieve their ends (Sombat 2000: 55). Sometimes these two social types overlap in the literature on modern rural leadership. Yet Yoshinori Nishizaki, who studied the compulsive, fussy and quick-to-punish managerial style of Banharn Silpa-archa, the provincial politician who was prime minister briefly in the mid-1990s, cautioned that not all provincial bosses should be lumped into the *nak leng* category, with its connotations of violence, brutality, belligerence, hedonism and lawbreaking (Nishizaki 2011: 117). James Ockey, following Thak Chaloemtiarana, who pinned the *nak leng* label on Field Marshal Sarit Thanarat, argued that Sarit exploited the most authoritarian aspects of the *nak leng* in the way he governed, thereby making possible a new and different type of *nak leng*: a politician who distributes his largesse to supporters and constituents through charitable foundations or access to government contracts and resources (Ockey 2004: Ch. 4). Some of Thailand's toughest and most ruthless politicians are today reminiscent of the *nak leng* types, with swagger and derring-do in the way they go about their business.

Debate about the evolution of *jao pho* from *nak leng* and the relevance of these terms to describe provincial or national politicians obscures older meanings of the term that pertain to the early period of Khun Phan's career. The few references to *nak leng* in the Three Seals Law Code, which the Bangkok court inherited from the previous kingdom at Ayutthaya, associate *nak leng* with gambling dens and their proprietors and, inevitably, with disputes over the payment of gambling debts. In Pallegoix's 1854 dictionary, *nak leng* is glossed as 'professional gambler' as well as 'rascal' and 'vagrant'. Bradley's dictionary of 1873 concurs and mentions wagers on cock-fighting (Bradley 1971: 328; Pallegoix 1972: 458). The term comes from Khmer, where today it means gangster, and the verb *lee:ng* in Angkorian Khmer meant to joke, flirt, show off, deceive or act rashly (Jenner 2009: 508; Haiman 2011: 158).[11] Historical linguists might not agree that these traits have persisted since Angkor times across language boundaries like some kind of DNA, but the gloss for the verb in Old Khmer points to a type familiar in the Thai social world of the early twentieth century. Khun Phan was a show-off who lived a long life by reducing risk to himself by force or deception, or both, while acting with derring-do.

The southern Thai scholar Suthiwong Phongphaibun suggests a four-part typology of the *nak leng* social type that draws out the hedonistic, hooligan qualities of the figure. His fourth type stresses the magnanimity, dignity and loyalty to supporters as well as the capacity for building alliances that made these men natural leaders as circle and village

---

11   I am grateful to Paul Sidwell for discussing the etymology of *nak leng* in Khmer (Personal communications, November 2016).

headmen (Suthiwong 1999: 3673–5). Dignity (*saksi*) is a personal quality often attributed to the *nak leng* of old in Khun Phan's mid south, where a man would start a brawl if he thought his dignity had been besmirched (Suwan 1996: 258). Proximate to dignity are self-importance, arrogance and snootiness (*thoranong, jonghong*)—personal traits often attributed to southern Thai people by outsiders or by knowing southerners themselves. *Nak leng* can apply as an attribute or style of behaviour that is performed as occasion requires. Indeed, Khun Phan, the legendary lawman, was credited with the *nak leng* value of magnanimity, with which he treated some, but not all, of the outlaws he confronted. To complicate matters further, the Thai language abounds in terms for tough guys, rascals, scoundrels, hooligans, hoodlums, criminals and ne'er-do-wells, and the overlapping meanings are tricky to delineate with sociological finesse. The word for hooligans is *anthaphan*, whose capacities for violence have been for sale to politicians. They usually started their careers in their own neighbourhoods as tough guys. In the 1963 novel discussed above, it is clear that when Phao and, later, Sarit set about dealing with crime, they criminalised behaviour that was merely antisocial, and *nak leng*, the local toughs who were protectors of their community, were transformed by statute into *anthaphan*: hooligans who then became targets for police action (Chalong 2013: 198; Worayut 2017: 84).

Ruth McVey made a fine distinction between *nak leng* and local toughs and argued that 'real leaders gained their prominence through shrewdness and manipulation rather than muscle' (McVey 2000: 8). By real, McVey may mean legitimate, but, if so, legitimate in the eyes of whom? Shrewdness and manipulation are the skills that Suthiwong embraces in his fourth type, skills that persist in local and national politics in Thailand today. By no means were all *nak leng* criminals. Some enjoyed the respect and trust of the ruling class as well as the reputation of local hero and native protector of the less fortunate. *Nak leng* could be tough if circumstances required, and the willingness to use force and the threat of force as well as their shrewdness and powers of manipulation enhanced their reputation.

The functions performed by *nak leng* in early twentieth-century Siam resemble in many respects the career of the *jago* under the Dutch in the second half of the nineteenth century on Java. The literal translation of *jago* is 'fighting cock', but the term carries a broader meaning of brawler and daredevil when applied to men. The conflicts among *jago* had to do with protecting territory and supporters as well as defending personal honour and prestige. Here I am reminded again of the numerous references in Thai writing to the importance of dignity (*saksi*) and the humiliation of losing it or seeing it tarnished (*min sak si*). *Jago* also shared with *nak leng* the cultivation of supernatural powers and rituals to make themselves invulnerable. The Indonesian term *kekebalan* describes these powers as well as the ability to get things done through connections with people higher up (Nordholt and van Till 1991: 75–6). Like *nak leng*, the *jago* maintained a modicum of law and order at the local level, where the infrastructure of government did not exist. In this sense, they were indispensable to the stability of the Dutch colonial government (Nordholt and van Till 1999: 68).

Manliness in the profile of the brawling and daredevil *jago* is also evident in the character of the *nak leng*. Khun Phan caused his first death in custody by squeezing the life out of his adversary with his bare hands. Men in this social world were constantly testing and measuring their prowess rather like bulls fighting in the ring. Bullfighting competitions still rotate through the mid south on weekends in connection with local festivals.

Plate 7 Bullfight, Phatthalung
Source: Kasem Jandam.

The sport, possibly introduced by the Portuguese, is considered by people in the mid south to be a keystone of southern Thai identity, and its export to agricultural communities elsewhere in the country is a source of southern pride (Akhom 2000; Charan and Pakapun 2000). Much of the information on pedigrees and desirable characteristics for the purpose-bred bulls comes from a manual published in 1934 that originated in Nakhon Si Thammarat, one of the hubs of the sport historically (Reynolds 2009).

Before the fights, the bulls receive magical *saiyasat* rites empowering them to triumph in their struggle. The bulls then charge each other and lock horns until one animal passes water and retreats ingloriously. The victorious combatant is draped with garlands and paraded around the ring to the applause of the packed crowd—women as well as men. A sign over the entrance to the Phatthalung arena on the day I spent in the stands stated that gambling was strictly forbidden, but the injunction was obviously not being enforced. The odds changed during the fight, so it was an emotional rollercoaster for anyone who had placed a bet. Attending police had been paid THB500 (US$15) for the day's work, and I was told that their main job was to not obstruct the action.[12] In the earthy language of the countryside, a man who declines to enter his bull in a fight for fear of losing is mocked by other owners for his lack of manliness by saying he has been gelded; he is 'a bull with no balls' (*wua lot*) (Wiwat 2000: 79). Men need to take risks to give evidence of their manliness, and societies tolerate this risk-taking. A population can afford the loss of men more easily than of women, and the acceptance of this expendability constitutes the measure of manhood (Gilmore 1990: 121).

In the wider social field, there is a Buddhist dimension to Thai homosociality. Although the Buddha is portrayed in sculpture and painting as asexual, the maleness of the Buddha is evident in the early history of the religion. All the texts that relate the story of the Buddha 'incorporate discourses of masculinity' (Powers 2009). Potency in Theravada Buddhism—in the archaic sense of might, strength and command—is an attribute of the Buddha because of his supranormal powers (Reynolds 2005: 216–17). Male prerogative still looms large in Thai ritual and public life. Challenged by women who want to be fully ordained as *bhikkhuni*, the Thai Sangha has, with few exceptions,

---

12   Field notes, Phatthalung bullfight arena, 2 July 2010.

answered this challenge by resisting reform and has remained a stronghold of male prerogative and privilege. Male homosociality in the lives of the *nak leng*—some of whom were bandits and some of whom, like Khun Phan, were police—has analogies at the national level among soldiers and policemen who work in national and public security.

As the provincial police force was extended into the more remote areas of the kingdom, it encountered ethnicities, social customs and belief systems that thwarted the order, regularity and predictability imagined by the modernising court and the foreign experts in its employ. Khun Phan began his career in the provincial police in the first decades of its existence, and I do not know whether he came into contact with even one of the Danish military instructors training police recruits. If his approach to policing may be taken as an example of what happened when the centre met the heterodox countryside, provincial policing over much of his career was still rooted in local expectations of manliness and public order.

5

Magical thinking to dispel
fear and uncertainty

Video content for this chapter is available online:
press.anu.edu.au/publications/series/asian-studies/
power-protection-and-magic-thailand#media

Before the military coup in May 2014, the darker side of magical knowledge such as black magic and curses had been employed by both the Yellow Shirts and the Red Shirts in their bitter political campaigns. When the Yellow Shirts were campaigning for the removal of the Thaksin party from government in late 2008, they broke into the grounds of Government House and vandalised the Brahma shrine there. A Khmer ritual specialist was then engaged to decommission the Brahma image using his supernatural powers—Khmer magic being regarded in Thailand as particularly powerful. A few years later, in March 2010, when the Yellow Shirts were in power, the Red Shirts set up camp in the centre of Bangkok and embarked on a spectacle of bloodletting and bloodspilling described by an American newspaper as one of the 10 most bizarre protests in the history of the world. The Red Shirts donated blood en masse as a sign of their willingness to shed their blood for democracy. A Brahman priest performed curses at the headquarters of the Democrat Party—a ritual aimed at spooking the Abhisit Vejjajiva–led Democrat regime and weakening its hold on government. This brazen act by a ritual specialist who came from nowhere infuriated the capital's established Brahman families, who sought to discredit the upstart priest. All that red blood in digital images on the internet made for great theatrics and became a proxy in the war of position in the political field (Nostitz 2010; Cohen 2012). In political warfare, as well as in war to defend the homeland, demonising the enemy can be motivational. In the preparation of soldiers for battle, dehumanising the enemy leads men to do the unthinkable and take human life (Nidhi 2012: 11–12).

Warriors need the protection of armour as well as technologies of invulnerability that are as important to survival as wielding a knife or carrying a gun. Thai soldiers in the expeditionary force sent to Vietnam during the Second Indochina War (1959–75) returned home convinced that the protective devices they wore around their necks were not only efficacious, but also superior to any other form of spiritual protection available to allied or enemy troops. The soldiers were young and the young think they will live forever, enabling them to overlook the reality of their own vulnerability. The soldiers appealed to the protective devices just in case and, in fact, would not fight without their amulets, as the American command discovered when it confiscated the objects for security reasons (Ruth 2012: 129, 145). Some talismans were distinctly Buddhist, others less so. In Thailand and other countries, Buddhism and magic overlap in offering protection, which is not only spiritual and emotional, but also social, in keeping an individual and the community safe from harm. Social protection takes the form of guardianship, custodianship, patronage and refuge and a place of safety. The taking of refuge is the act that defines a Buddhist (Skilling 1992: 12).

During his policing exploits in which he called upon his knowledge of the dark arts, Khun Phan earned a reputation as a man who knew about the technologies of protection. When he retired in 1964 as a police major general in command of the Nakhon Provincial Circle, his exploits in apprehending bandits, criminals and separatists came to an end. To celebrate his retirement, he collaborated with another retiring policeman in casting amulets for distribution to police comrades, soldiers and laypeople; amulets were also presented to King Bhumibol. Both Khun Phan and his fellow retiree had survived harrowing brushes with death and became renowned as men with tough hides (*khon tai nang niaw*), impervious to blades and bullets. The amulets that were minted in May 1963 were humble objects given a false patina of age to render them antique in appearance and mythic (Ek 2010: 32–9). But whatever favour these amulets found with consumers in the marketplace was overshadowed by the Jatukham-Ramathep deity when it was conjured in the late 1980s with Khun Phan's indispensable counsel. His wisdom about these matters was instrumental in identifying the deity that announced its presence through a spirit medium.

Early in his career, Khun Phan had been initiated by senior teachers who cultivated the dark arts—what the Thai call *saiyasat*, a term derived from a Khmer word for excellence or expertise (Baker and Pasuk 2010: 944). In a hierarchical ranking of *saiyasat* powers, Khmer magic trumps Thai magic; Lao magic lies at the bottom of the tree (Okha 2007: 57). The apparently non-Buddhist aspect of much *saiyasat* practice is often denigrated by orthodox monastic and lay Buddhists. At the same time, the practitioners of *saiyasat* are almost always monks or men who have disrobed and left the monkhood where they acquired their expertise from Buddhist master teachers. Knowledge of this complex of practices that can release the forces of nature is useful to warriors and fighters on both sides of the law. Many early Southeast Asian inscriptions contained curses and imprecations against anyone who would tamper with the religious image whose installation was commemorated in the epigraph. I refrain from using the term Tantric, because it does not occur in the Thai materials and evidence for Tantrism in Thailand seems thin. In Tantric Theravada practice in Cambodia, 'left-hand' worldly goals such as the protection and destruction of enemies are reminiscent of Hindu Tantra (Crosby 2000: 162–3). This arcane knowledge reaches back to the Vedas, the fourth volume of which deals with ways to influence natural forces, acquire protection against calamity and human perfidy and conjure supernatural powers.[1] For the policeman, magical beliefs and practices were a resource, a mother lode of potentialities on which he could draw to keep himself alive and safe in the threatening situations he encountered as he went about his duties. Khun Phan was a lifelong exponent of the knowledge handed down to him by the master teachers in the cave monastery. His bandit adversaries were also initiated into this knowledge in rituals conducted by these same master teachers and their disciples.

Magic—the term often associated with *saiyasat* knowledge—is an exotic word and we moderns do not think it is part of our lives except in the theatre or parlour trickery. In using it, we consign magic to the other

---

1   In Thai, the compilation is known as *athan* or *athanpawet*. Baker and Pasuk say that the link between Atharva Veda and the Thai concept of *athan* is tantalisingly unknown, although the Royal Institute dictionary affirms a direct connection (Baker and Pasuk 2013: 228–9). See also Baker and Pasuk (2010: 942–5).

and make it a binary opposite of reason: 'I think rationally, scientifically; belief in magic and the supernatural—that is the way others think.' The Other is unreason, or apparent reason, which is the conventional domain of anthropological study that seeks to 'de-exoticise what may otherwise be deemed exotic and strange' (Kapferer 2002: 2–5). De-exoticising does not discredit the exotic and strange, however, because magic is a matter of belief. 'Nobody seeks out a magician unless he believes in him', the French anthropologist Marcel Mauss stated emphatically (Mauss 2010: 113). Science is also a belief system, but one that rests on *a posteriori* beliefs, even if some people reject these beliefs out of hand. 'What are we to make of another culture's apparently false knowledge?' asks Richard Shweder, whose question is answered by Kapferer and Mauss. But Shweder is interested in contemporary society as well as other cultures. The magical thinking we attribute to people in other cultures is little different from how modern people often interpret reality: 'most of us have a "savage" mentality much of the time', says Shweder (1977: 637–8).

Khun Phan's repertoire of self-strengthening practices emboldened him and contributed to the ruthlessness in his character. He acknowledged his savage mentality, cultivated it and deployed it as a weapon. The executioner's tattoos on his hand meant he would cause instant death if he fired a bullet or madness if he threw a punch. The tattoos demonstrated that he would not hesitate to use lethal force. The performative aspect of Khun Phan's play with magic was not unique to this policeman from Thailand's mid south. Executioners in many societies use spells and charms to catch their adversaries (Mauss 2010: 37).

Writing about the Trobriand Islands, Malinowski suggested that magic supplies men and women 'with a number of ready-made ritual acts and beliefs' to confidently carry out important tasks, to maintain poise and mental integrity in fits of anger and in the throes of hate, unrequited love, despair and anxiety. The function of magic, he writes, is to ritualise human optimism, to enhance faith in the triumph of hope over fear (Malinowski 1974: 90). Magic and the sciences of protection and prognostication are as much about bolstering confidence and maintaining optimism as they are about thwarting evil. Magic belongs to the psychosocial dimension of human experience. It treats the emotions and humanity's expressive needs rather than the rational faculties, but this is not to say that it is irrational. It is a highly determinate system whose rules and procedures, which are empirical and precise yet always subject to modification and adjustment, have an integrity all their own. The system—a sacred canopy thrown over human behaviour—has an inner logic and is entirely self-confirming. It gives reasons to decide to do this rather than that, on this day rather than another one.

Amulets and protection

Many of the measures Khun Phan employed were aimed at building confidence and reducing the possibility of failure. Not least of these were his boasts of owning objects with special powers, including *krises*, the daggers emblematic of Malay sovereignty that possessed supernatural powers, and amulets, some of them seized from the bandits he had captured. In Khun Phan's time, police as well as bandits armed themselves with objects that were as necessary to their defence as a weapon. The warrior castes—policemen and soldiers—are keen consumers and connoisseurs of these objects. Buddha amulets confer or enhance personality traits and offer protection; other objects have magnetic properties that attract wealth, supporters or auspiciousness in all its forms. A distinction is made between Buddha amulets—which encase small images of the Buddha, saints or eminent monks—and other kinds of amulets, such as the Jatukham-Ramathep deity, or *takrut*, which are small cylinders tied around the neck, waist or upper arm. The cylinder contains a thin pliable sheet of rolled metal such as tin, inscribed with the kabbalistic diagrams and formulae that confer protective powers (*yantra*).

The Thai police force has never stopped modernising, and the latest forensic techniques are now more important than ever in combating terrorism and identifying human remains left in the wake of natural disasters. Yet a serving policeman of my acquaintance proudly showed me the scars where his policeman uncle had slit the skin in the flesh of each upper arm and inserted tiny *takrut*. Even today's policeman wants to hedge against the risk of injury or death by utilising all available methods.

In former times, metallic objects were inserted under the skin in the forearm as a physical as well as a spiritual shield, a barrier against blows from a sword or cudgel. An elusive silvery substance of mercury-like appearance known as *leklai* (lit. 'fluid iron') was, and perhaps still is, a favoured choice for this purpose. It is harvested in caves by monks familiar with Brahmanic expertise using a naked flame and special chants that render the substance pliable and malleable for working into small silver oblongs or images, including Buddha images (Daeng 2006;

Thotsaphon 2012). On one visit to Nakhon Si Thammarat, I was promised a viewing of this material with its ineffable qualities, but the opportunity never materialised. The sceptical modern might say that the specificity of the properties of *leklai*, its sources of supply and the methods of its extraction are in inverse proportion to the likeliness of its existence, yet it is discussion of substances such as *leklai* that keeps the reality of the supernatural in circulation. A description of one of the skilled warriors in the epic poem *Khun Chang Khun Phaen* pictures a rather grotesque, misshapen human figure once it is equipped with these dermal shields:

> He had a jet gem embedded in his head, golden needles in each shoulder, a large diamond in the middle of his forehead, a lump of fluid metal (*leklai*) in his chest, and herbal amber and cat's eye in his back.

> His whole body was a mass of lumps and bumps in ranks and rows. Since birth he had never been touched by a weapon, and did not carry even the scratch from a thorn. (Baker and Pasuk 2010: 631)

Amulets can not only shield their owners, but also make them rich. They belong to a class of auspicious objects capable of attracting wealth and good fortune. Some objects are explicitly Buddhist or display distinctively Buddhist elements, while others, such as lucky fish (*pla taphian*) or turtles, are secular. Consecrated stones, 'golden dolls' (*kuman thong*), linga cast from bronze or carved out of timber and therapeutic herbs also belong to this class. The Thai epic poem mentions bits of tusk left in trees or antheaps by raging elephants in musth. Bees' wax, if given the right treatment and applied to the lips, is a most effective love charm (Klam 2008: 109–10). Such intrinsically powerful objects (*sing saksit*) are found in many cultures, as a little Thai book with Nepalese, Peruvian, Hindu, Judaeo-Christian and Native American examples makes clear (Jaturawit 2008). Tucked away in restaurants and shop houses in Thailand and in Thai-owned establishments abroad may be found an image of Nang Kwak, a female figurine beckoning to passers-by to venture inside and make a purchase to boost the day's takings. The powers of such objects obey the laws of attraction, to borrow from the title of a pop psychology manual; the scientific pretence of the enterprise may be gauged from the publisher Physics Centre (Wisit 2008). Thai gurus with a smattering of overseas education build their reputations by marketing manuals that promise profit and success if the prescribed regimens are strictly followed.

The power in amulets is not abstract or amorphous. It is concrete, and the universe is lumpy with it, rather like the *mana* in Melanesian and Polynesian cultures that suffuses everywhere and can take material form in nature and in the human-made world. The spirit stones found in Chinese gardens and courtyards, much prized by collectors and connoisseurs, exhibit similar properties. The strange shapes of spirit stones with their sharp overhangs and pocked, craggy surfaces are never completely natural after an artisan's careful tooling. Chinese scholars were inspired by the stones and saw them as imbued with the generative properties of the earth and as a manifestation of the organic structure of the universe (Little 1999). In the compounds of Thai monasteries, one comes upon miniature grottoes studded with small stupas and other reliquaries that morphologically resemble Chinese spirit stones. The strange, otherworldly appearance of the grottoes holds the onlooker's gaze.

In Thai language, objects that concentrate *mana* are called auspicious matter (*watthu mongkhon*). If it is a mass-produced amulet, the object is stamped from a powdered compound (*phong*) containing ash, ground-up tiles from a famous monastery and therapeutic plants. Herbs such as *hang jorakhe*, a styptic used for small cuts and the treatment of burns, are said to protect against bullets and sharp objects. An amulet created by the king in the mid-1960s and affixed to a Buddha image he had commissioned contained the king's hair and nail clippings. By means of ritual, the amulet is charged (*pluk sek*) by the spoken words of the monks and transformed into a powerful object (*khreuang rang khong khlang*). The power it has acquired is *phalang*—the word also for nuclear, atomic and hydraulic energy as well as people power and the power to struggle and fight.

Those trading in these objects sometimes endow them with a scientific reality by saying they 'emit' as though radioactive (Chalong 2013: 204). Like the half-life of a radioactive isotope, the charge weakens over time, or can be lost entirely if the person wearing the amulet walks under a footbridge and exposes it to the polluting effects of pedestrians treading overhead. Khun Phan's son Chanthip said his father did not allow other people to touch his kit lest the objects be sapped of their special powers that protected him.[2] The local historian from Chawang District in Nakhon, Chali Sinlaparasmi, used to run into Khun Phan in town, where they would both enjoy sticky rice roasted in bamboo. When he asked the policeman why he was wearing so many amulets, Khun Phan

---

2   Chanthip Phantharakratchadet, Interview with the author, 9 September 2012.

replied that he feared the spirits of those he had killed and he needed to protect himself.[3] Once an amulet is consecrated it becomes a magnet that can attract customers, lovers, clients or constituencies. The properties of attraction (*mettamahaniyom*) attach to the person who owns such a consecrated object, and thus they become an asset useful to politicians, village headmen, gangsters or businesspeople.[4] Anyone needing to build and hold the loyalty of an entourage wants to own these lumps of special stuff. The magnetic force of *mettamahaniyom* makes a man attractive, endowing him with personal charm (*saneh*) that can even be erotic. Khun Phan himself had 'the right stuff', as an early American astronaut might have said.

In this case, the stuff is manliness. There is a distinctly masculine aspect to the interest and trade in amulets across all socioeconomic classes that connects to the struggle for power in Thailand that today is still mainly a male affair. The ethnographer Irene Stengs calls the male obsession with amulets a fetish of modern Thai men and describes a small amulet market in Chiang Mai as exuding a 'typical masculine atmosphere', with all the male vendors wearing dark sunglasses, with long hair, tattoos and sporting well-toned muscles (Stengs 1998: 56, 69). It is not only in an upcountry amulet market that one sees such types; motorcycle-taxi drivers waiting for their customers at the mouth of a Bangkok lane could be described in the same way. In more upmarket places, brokers may be dressed in smart casual or business attire. While women traders may sell the cheaper, mass-market items in the amulet markets, the brokers who trade the most valuable amulets and charms are usually male.

Though it is seldom acknowledged, the maleness of the Buddha is evident in many texts and observances. It is said that his sexual prowess was such that he could satisfy 60,000 courtesans; his penis could extend from its sheath, wind around Mount Sumeru seven times, and extend upward to the Brahma heaven (Powers 2009: 13–14). Potency is one of the glosses for the powers (*iddhi*) of the Buddha. The trade in amulets—particularly Buddhist amulets—and the exchange of information about valuations, qualities and brokers are elements in male bonding. Even the giving of amulets is a male thing: fathers, brothers and uncles present them to female as well as male relatives. Women have their own consumer preferences and are not keen collectors.

---

3   Chali Sinlaparasami, Interview with the author, 7 September 2012.
4   Baker and Pasuk (2013: 224–5) identify the spoken or chanted formulas for charging objects with the force of attraction or repulsion.

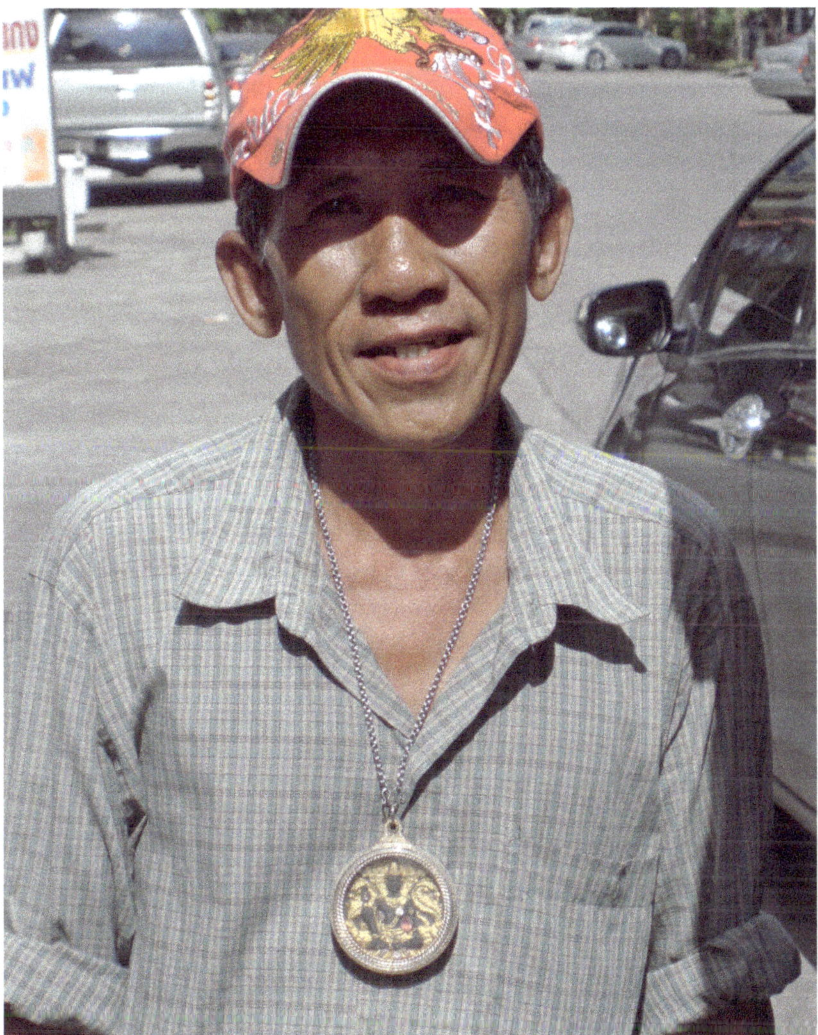

Plate 8 Fruit seller wearing the Jatukham-Ramathep amulet, Nakhon Si Thammarat

Source: Craig Reynolds.

Sales of early editions of the Jatukham-Ramathep amulet were slow among the female demographic, because the large cookie-sized objects were considered too macho for women, especially young women. Many Thai women, although I hesitate to essentialise the point, want something smaller, daintier and more feminine to wear around their necks. They prefer to buy and wear a locket (*lokhet*) rather than adorn themselves with a clunky amulet (Stengs 1998: 70).

Khun Phan was an astute observer of the world of auspicious objects (*watthu mongkhon*) and a student of the rites that brought them into existence. In 1976, he wrote an essay for a southern Thai magazine that was basically an inventory valorising auspicious objects and expounding on their characteristics and benefits. He offered his own definition of *saiyasat*:

> *Saiyasat* is a form of knowledge about spells and chants that has flourished in India from ancient times. It is a kind of knowledge that branched off from the eighteen Great Puranas which anyone seeking to excel above others [*phu thi cha pen yot khon*] needed to learn and be fully conversant in. Siddhartha himself [the Buddha] studied *saiyasat* as well as the eighteen sciences and became expert in all of them. *Saiyasat* is the life-force of the Thai people. (Phantharakratchadet 2007: 470)[5]

Thai people, he writes, have made use of *saiyasat* from the cradle to the grave, and he goes on to explain that those in possession of this knowledge have more connection and more rapport with the general public than monks who teach the way of the Dhamma—a claim that at first sight seems extraordinary but that explains why Khun Phan valued this knowledge as beneficial in his police work. He had firsthand knowledge of the mental universe of the people in the districts he patrolled. In his essay, he reiterates the importance of *saiyasat* for conducting the good life through one's behaviour, speech and thought. The master teacher extracts a pledge from the student adept to conduct himself properly. There are prohibitions against this or that: one should not curse one's mother, for example, or be cruel or betray others or commit adultery. Someone adept at *saiyasat* must be trustworthy, diligent and mentally tough (*mi samathi*), and neither fearful nor shy. The master teacher should assess the student's adeptness and decide which is the most appropriate path according to the student's personal qualities and abilities. Not even the 16 Buddhist saints or the Buddha's disciples were adept in all branches of magical knowledge because their powers (*iddhi*) were all different. This moral code and the personal qualities that maintain it recall the pledge the southern policeman made when he was initiated into the dark arts at Wat Khao Or

---

5   The information in the following paragraph is also taken from these pages of Phantharakratchadet (2007). I presume the 18 *sastra* are the Great Puranas. Khun Phan's inventory is reminiscent of the rural Thai rites and practices compiled by the late Robert Textor in the 1950s (Textor 1973).

at the beginning of his career. Mental toughness and fearlessness stand out as personal qualities befitting a policeman who lived every day he was on active duty in the face of sudden death.

Khun Phan's inventory of auspicious objects and practices runs parallel to the auspicious objects and sciences of prognostication that Baker and Pasuk found in their study of the Thai epic poem *Khun Chang Khun Phaen*. One of their insights is that mastery of the self gives the adept the ability to control spirits and activate natural forces by using a repertoire of formulas, chants and unusual substances derived by alchemic means (Baker and Pasuk 2013: 230). Khun Phan quotes verses from the poem, so he knew of its elemental knowledge about auspicious objects and their powers. I am tempted to say that the poem was speaking through Khun Phan. In identifying these objects and their characteristics and deploying them during his career, Khun Phan was channelling Khun Phaen, the character in the poem who avails himself of supernatural powers to gain advantage over his nemesis, Khun Chang, a rich, well-connected man in the local town who has held the upper hand in their rivalry. The southern policeman had downloaded a hefty section of the Thai cultural code shared by many people at all levels of Thai society.

Arbiters of Buddhist orthodoxy such as Phya Anuman Rajadhon state categorically that *saiyasat* has nothing to do with religion; it is a kind of knowledge that lies 'outside' Buddhism (Sathian 1965: 33; Suwit 2011: 4). But the boundary between Buddhism and magic is blurred, because the Buddha himself possessed supranormal power (*iddhi*) as well as potency. A Buddhist text states that 'a bodhisatva can introduce Mt. Sumeru into a grain of mustard and the water of the four oceans into a single pore of his own skin' (Benavides 2006: 295–7). Other non-canonical texts speak of the Buddha's psychic powers. He could fly into the sky, touch the Sun with his hand and make his body into many bodies. He could travel to other realms and converse with the deities there. He knew the thoughts of others and could recollect his own previous births (Reynolds 2005: 218). Yet, while he had attributed to him these extraordinary powers, he denied that he was a magician in any derogatory sense. Given the shaman's ability to travel to other worlds, he might also have denied that he was a shaman. Indeed, a secular definition of awakening or enlightenment is that it recognises the attainment of supreme psychic knowledge. The supernatural powers of the Buddha and his disciple Maudgalyāyana are pervasive in the early literature because such powers facilitated conversion to the Buddha's teachings.

The altered state of consciousness attained by shamans is the polar opposite of the mental awareness that is the goal of a Theravada Buddhist monk. The meditation techniques mentioned in the early scriptures focus on clarity and understanding the nature of existence. Other kinds of psychic states, such as trance and possession, which have become more popular with the emergence of global Buddhist movements, are at odds with many teachings of the Buddha, yet these practices are commonly found in many Buddhist societies today, including Thailand. Spirit mediums and their clients often conduct business in or near monastery compounds; monks or former monks may serve as vessels for the spirit to visit. While the Buddha rejected a magical or shamanic identity for himself, even a religion that tolerates magic and magical practices conducted by monks or ex-monks maintains a distinction between legitimate and non-legitimate encounters with the supernatural. The monastic ideal is withdrawal from the world and worldly ways; magic embraces the world and provides instruments to control it.

In the Buddha's time, ordinary monks were dissuaded from speaking about the special powers they might have acquired and what they might be used for. The *Vinaya*, the book of monastic discipline in the Buddhist canon, specifically disapproves of magic, including love magic, curses, astrology and alchemy, by characterising these as 'animal-like knowledge'. There is more than a tinge of elitism in this thinking, so it comes as no surprise that the Thai edition of the *Vinaya* in wide use today was edited by an aristocratic arbiter of Buddhist practice and thought, Prince Vajrayana, the eminent ecclesiastic brother of King Chulalongkorn who spent his entire adult life in the monkhood (Vajirananavarorasa 1973: 120–1). Yet this 'animal-like knowledge' is what laypeople crave as the savage mentality of the species rises to the surface when challenged by personal crises or natural disasters that call for desperate measures. Lay preoccupations and needs extend beyond the merely spiritual and must be acknowledged and met with the application of *saiyasat*.

Monks recite two kinds of invocation, *paritta* and *rakkha*, for protection; *dharani* is a synonym of these terms. The *paritta* recitations—a distinct genre of Buddhist literature found in the Pali tradition—keep a person safe from evil spells, weapons such as knives and guns, betrayal, fire and poison. The monks in these recitations are preaching to the spirits to warn them and to convert them to the way of the Buddha. A regular practice wherever Theravadin Buddhism has been established, *paritta* recitations are effective because of the sounds uttered in the chanting, and less so for the meaning of words, which often has nothing to do with a role in ritual (McDaniel 2004). Audience interest and concentration can be partial if not minimal, with much murmuring and sleeping throughout the proceedings (Tambiah 1970: 195). The performance of the recitation is the key to its effectiveness rather than its reception and internalisation by the listener.

The use of these texts dates from the earliest *sutta*, chronicles and commentaries in the Buddha's time, with lists of *paritta* titles to be found in the *Questions of Milinda* (*Milinda-pañha*), a composite text that dates from the middle of the second century BCE to the fifth century CE. Burma, Siam and Sri Lanka have parallel *paritta* traditions (Skilling 1992: 116–17, 120). The recital of *paritta* produces mental wellbeing in those who hear it, as well as the power of love and a virtuous state of mind. Popular belief holds that reciting the texts is not just rewarding for mental strength, but also efficacious in curing illness and keeping spirits at bay. The texts in the *rakkha* genre—pan-Indian as well as pan-Buddhist—are recited in the Mahayana tradition to invoke protection against disease, disaster and malignant spirits, and to avert misfortune of all kinds. Spirits—the embittered, hungry or cruelly murdered dead— may need to be appeased, and spirits dwelling in forests or rivers who have had their realms disturbed by human activity need to be placated. One type of spell, *mantra*, is recited specifically for worldly or mundane ends, such as warding off calamity or to promote physical wellbeing and welfare. In Sri Lanka, some of the Buddha's sermons were transformed in Mahayana Buddhism into these magical formulas (Saddhatissa 1991: 127; Skilling 1992: 110). The *mantras*, which are not found in the canon of the Theravadins, have both intelligible and unintelligible elements— phrases that are not arbitrary but are necessary for the efficacy of the *mantra*. The widespread use of these *mantras* in Theravada practice has led to a rethinking of what constitutes Theravada belief and practice (Skilling et al. 2012).

Rakkha can be written on paper or cloth and deposited in stupas, tied to banners carried by soldiers in battle or rolled up, encased and worn as *takrut* amulets (Skilling 1992: 167). These items provide bodily protection for the individual who has invested the time and money for the protective properties of the object once it has been charged by the religious specialist. Men who go to war, hunters in the jungles and forests and people in life-threatening occupations want the benefits of these protective devices. In the absence of an amulet, a *mantra* honouring a famous Buddhist saint such as Upagupta may be recited to thwart harm. Meditation practice also has protective power. Forest-dwelling monks in northeastern Thailand help villagers overcome their fears of spirits or ghosts by teaching meditation that gives the villagers confidence in their own spiritual powers (Kamala 1997: 209). Tattoos on young men, etched by monks who have the requisite skill and knowledge, also have protective and beneficial effects (Terwiel 2012: 77–88).

Auspiciousness and uncertainty

The manufacture of amulets evolved slowly in Thailand and was revolutionised in the mid-nineteenth century by the introduction of photography and coin-minting technology. During the twentieth century, the Buddhist amulet became a popular magical device for protection, not only for soldiers and police, but also for many others. The unsettled times after World War II, when crime and banditry posed security problems for the government, saw a boost in the popularity of amulets, and a literature began to develop around the phenomenon as specialists classified and ranked the objects for their sacredness and powers. An army major general proposed a league of five to identify the most sacred Buddhist amulets of the Thai nation and elevate them to the top rank. Beginning in the late 1980s and through the 1990s, Thailand's economic boom and prosperity saw religious movements transform amulet trading, marketing and publishing into an industry in its own right. The makeshift stalls in markets moved to shopping malls, where traders display their wares in boutique shops. Brisk business takes place in cyberspace as well, and newspapers run amulet columns for aficionados (Jackson 1999; Chalong 2013: 181–3, 191–2, 203–4).

Amulets of all kinds are popular for their value as commodities, for their characteristics and powers that help people and for their artistic qualities and their beauty. One Saturday in September 2012, I wandered through the Tha Prachan amulet market along the Chao Phraya River near Thammasat University. The regionalisation of Buddhist saints is a recent phenomenon and some stalls were selling trade magazines specialising in amulets that originated in different parts of the country: Chiang Mai, Sukhothai, Kamphaeng Phet, Ayutthaya, Surat Thani. Customers in civilian clothes or in uniform made their way through the aisles, occasionally stopping at a stall to examine their prospective purchase with a small magnifying glass or jeweller's loupe—essential tools for the serious amulet buyer. The objects for sale were of mind-boggling variety, and not all of them were sacred. One shop sold small ceramic Chinese sages with a beard and walking stick, 'tiger' fangs packaged in see-through cases and metallic droplets bound in a corded net. Also on sale were Buddha images large and small, busts of famous monks, medallions of Buddhist saints, tiny adept's knives and magical cloths with esoteric symbols (*yantra*). While food sellers delivered drinks and small dishes of noodles or rice, customers were selling as well as buying, and solicited valuations of what they were offering before bargaining for an agreeable price. Brokers who handle the transactions are known as Sian Phra, *sian* being a Chinese word for saint. Once a Buddhist amulet is in hand, for a small fee, it can be inserted in a see-through case known in Thai as a *talap*, the word for 'coffin'. Some brokers conducted their business encased in airconditioned glass cubicles, rather like the precious objects passing through their hands, the comfortable surroundings a reflection of their customers' affluence as much as the quality of the products and services they offered.

The ritual that transforms a stone, a piece of cloth or a mineral into a compound (*phong*), which is then crafted into an auspicious or powerful object, must be performed at a designated time and place calculated according to astrological manuals. Planning or timing any activity—be it the purchase of a property, the date for a wedding or a coup or the time and place for a thief to break into a house or for the police to try to catch the thief—requires such a calculation. In his 1976 inventory, Khun Phan listed the information required to calculate an auspicious moment or conjuncture (*roek*): time, day, compass point and place (Phantharakratchadet 2007: 476–7). Families, dynasties, cities and towns as well as individuals have their own horoscopes (Cook 2002: 198). In the mid-1980s, the urgency to recalculate Nakhon Si Thammarat's horoscope triggered the search for the spirit of the Jatukham-Ramathep deity who would restore stability and good fortune to the town.

The methods for identifying conjunctures are provided by applied sciences of prognostication. These are semiotic sciences, ways of reading signs that show the way forward. In the West in the late seventeenth century, astrology found itself eclipsed by probability theory. Knowledge of probabilities in the outcome of an action is by definition incomplete, so we are in the realm of uncertainty and maybe we have to guess about what to do. In Latin languages, 'conjecture' is a term that originates in divination (Ginzburg 1989: 106, 205n.48). Uncertainty is a state of mind that arouses its own emotions when a big decision looms or routine is suddenly disrupted and we need guidance. When to proceed? Which way to go? The science of prognostication enables people to face the uncertainty and unpredictability of life, to deal with misfortune, injury or death and to anticipate an outcome, whether or not it is favourable. People look forward as well as backward. They make plans and decisions about the next day or the next week. They assess risks and opportunities in personal relationships, in business and in the workplace. They dream of success. They abhor failure and strive to discern the odds to avoid it. Astrology, an applied science, involves reading and interpreting birth signs and using the information to make appropriate decisions to render guesswork unnecessary and optimise outcomes.

The keyword in the applied science of astrology is 'auspicious' (Skt, *maṅgala*; Th., *mongkhon*), a concept found in Hinduism and Jainism. Some translations of this word are luck, fortune, happiness, prosperity, welfare, auspiciousness, good omen, lucky object, amulet and festival. *The Scripture about Auspicious Things* (Pali, *Maṅgalasutta*) in the Theravada Buddhist canon consists of only 12 verses, but it is one of the most influential texts in the Theravada world from Sri Lanka to Southeast Asia and is often recited during the protective rituals performed by monks to ward off misfortune. The introduction to the *Maṅgalasutta* explains that a long discussion took place among gods and humans about what *maṅgala* means—a discussion that connects with the audience by mentioning various types of good and bad omens. The subtext is that *The Scripture about Auspicious Things* recognises the diversity of local contexts and traditions in which Buddhism took root and adapted to local conditions. *The Scripture about Auspicious Things* also recognises what Hallisey calls the shadows of a harsh world of agricultural labour and hard work in the largely peasant societies where Theravada Buddhism has thrived for centuries (Hallisey 1995: 413–14). This Pali text on auspiciousness has received the most attention in Thai history for its genre, based on a commentary composed in Chiang Mai in 1535 CE. It is also identified in at least one manuscript as a *paritta*, a protective text (McDaniel 2008: 134, 166, 293n.12).

The annals of Southeast Asian history are full of examples of auspicious timing determined by horoscopes and omens, particularly in times of war, although most historians skip over these details to get to 'the facts'. The French historian Aurore Candier has broken through modern scepticism by demonstrating how Burmese prophecies affected the strategic thinking of Western imperialists as well as the Burmese court as the British pushed into Burma during the second half of the nineteenth century. In his dealings with the British, the reigning monarch, King Mindon (r. 1853–78), was empowered by auspicious forecasts based on prophecies, omens and rumours. By the same token, the king's capacity to influence events was adversely affected by inauspicious forecasts. The British exploited the fear stirred by the Burmese prophecies, omens and rumours and pressured the Burmese king to agree to their demands. Candier was able to illustrate how historical events and conjunctures identified by astrological forecasts are related by cause and effect (Candier 2011: 235, 256).

Astrological calculations that determine a time to conduct an important event are only one of the semiotic sciences of divination that show the way forward. Other sciences of prognostication include palmistry, deciphering facial features, the interpretation of moles and freckles, the interpretation of dreams and reading the landscape. In Thailand, the archive of information on what signs to read and how to read them is the manual tradition of *phrommachat* (lit. 'Brahma-born' or 'Brahmanic lineage'). The role played by Brahmans in Siamese statecraft and royal rituals such as coronations and the ploughing and swing ceremonies is well documented, but the popular use of *phrommachat* knowledge in the management of daily affairs by people in all social classes has received little attention in Western scholarship. An exception is a book by the occasionally astute Quaritch Wales on divination that seems to be based almost entirely on a *phrommachat* manual of 1885 that Wales located in the British Library (Wales 1983: x–xi). In addition to horoscopes and other semiotic sciences such as palmistry and interpreting anatomical marks, the *phrommachat* manuals contain information on the colour associated with each day of the week, the animal associated with each year in the 12-year cycle, the characteristics of the cardinal directions and the deities that preside over each point. The Hindu gods Shiva, Vishnu and Brahma are only a few of the deities whose actions have an impact on the terrestrial world.

The semiotic sciences and associated ritual practices, including tantric Buddhism or *saiyasat* that involved knowledge of the Vedas, were prevalent in both the elite and the subaltern classes in the early Bangkok period. By the first half of the twentieth century, according to one study, there were 683 manuals in the National Library of Thailand concerning *saiyasat*; some of the *phrommachat* manuscripts dated from the very beginning of the Bangkok period in the late eighteenth century (Patthamakon 1996: 23).

The encounter with the West and some of the more practical applications of Western science by the nobility and royal families around the middle of the nineteenth century had an impact on elite thinking. Members of the aristocracy became intrigued with clocked time, for example, which gradually changed conceptions of time by introducing mechanically measured time in contrast to auspicious/inauspicious time, which had governed the way people made decisions and ordered their lives.

By 1900, the manual knowledge of *phrommachat* had been transformed by the printing press. Entrepreneurial publishers who foresaw the popularity of a printed edition and invested in the venture made the book a commercial success. The royal library had declined to publish the material, regarding it as outside its brief, and gave the manuscripts to private firms. What had previously been a corpus of knowledge scattered in manuscript versions in royal libraries and monasteries throughout the country was gathered up and compiled in a single volume. One of the editions of this published compilation of *phrommachat* manuals, subtitled the 'People's Edition for Household Use and Self-Instruction', can be purchased in Thailand today; smaller editions can be found for sale in Bangkok and provincial bookstores (Thep 1978).

The 'People's Edition' is an unwieldy tome of nearly 700 pages that bears the traces of its previous history as a heterodox compendium of lists, charts, chants, diagrams, drawings, sample horoscopes and details about numerology. For the specialist, there is even arcane information about Thai dominoes. The book is given the stamp of authority in the front matter with photographs of the palace astrologer and other royal Brahmans. The content is clearly categorised, but overall the organisation is haphazard, as though the various sections were tossed into the air and floated randomly down to form a book. The compiler's inclusion of everything—tables, charts, lists and graphics—contrasts with older manuals in which the knowledge was rare and privileged and required a master teacher to explain.

In the premodern era, time was like a lord with the power to reward or punish depending on the auspiciousness of an event (Patthamakon 1996: 42). The common perception of the *phrommachat* manuals is that they come from an earlier time and are retained in the present day rather as one might hold on to a family heirloom. Yet the continued use of astrology and other sciences for reckoning when and where to undertake an activity indicates that this knowledge continues to be of contemporary use. Knowledge from the manuals in various forms is still highly regarded by cultivators in deciding when to plant and when to harvest (Farrelly et al. 2011: 244–6). For advice to the busy and overworked homemaker, a recent edition of the *phrommachat* manual contains tips on cleaning and home management, herbal medicine and mental and physical health; how to remove unpleasant odours from the refrigerator; how to clean a clothes iron of rust; and how to keep ants out of the pantry (Saksit n.d.). The *phrommachat* of old typically had detailed information on when to schedule the humdrum chores of everyday life. Pages and pages are devoted to horoscopes and how to counter the adverse influences of one's birth sign. Nowadays, young people navigating their way through the choppy waters of adolescent uncertainty or house buyers wondering whether they should purchase what seems to be overpriced real estate are keen observers of the numbers and other conjunctures of their birth signs that bode well or ill for their decisions. People trying to find their way in life rely on the cosmic choreography of the planets to help them decide. In the Thai student groups I have known through the years, there always seems to be one person in the cohort adept at reading horoscopes and able to advise their friends on what lies in store for them. The journalist Wassana Nanuam has written several books showing how the logic of astrological calculations has affected the thinking of politicians, military officers and national leaders by identifying auspicious locations and determining the timing of important events. On the basis of interviews with 'big-shot army officers' (*bik thahan*), Wassana (2009) explains how astrological information enters into decisions about promotions in the upper echelons of the army. Over a decade ago, soldier-politicians decided that a date filled with nines in the reign of the ninth king of the Bangkok dynasty was a good day for their coup. The numbers in the coup date, 19 September 2006, were auspicious: the nineteenth day of the ninth month of the ninth year in the decade of the Buddhist Era, BE 2449. The coup became known as the royal coup.

This numerology may figure in strategic thinking elsewhere in the region. The indefatigable Italian journalist Tiziano Terzani stated confidently that counterespionage agencies in China, Vietnam, India and South Korea have astrology units to anticipate what their adversaries as well as their allies will advise in given situations (Terzani 1998: 75). Similarly, in Indonesia and Cambodia, the police use the same astrology manuals as burglars to figure out when a crime is likely to be committed so they can prevent the act by apprehending the thieves in advance (Quinn 1975; Broadhurst et al. 2015: 58). Scheduling, planning and timing are all-important in war and strategy, personal as well as political. In cultures where a systemic numerology links time, nature and human affairs, it is not surprising that numbers should have such a hold on the imagination. Alphanumerics are said to have life within them (Uthai 1979: 4474). At cremations in Thailand, the dates of the ceremony as well as the birth and death dates of the deceased have auspicious portent. The sale of lottery tickets is brisk and the monastery precinct becomes a veritable casino.

Decoding the alphanumerics is a way of deciding whether or not a risk is worth taking, and one sure-fire way to reduce risk is by cheating. In the financial world, this can be done by trading on insider information to buy and sell financial products. In the casino, the roulette table can be rigged or the deck stacked. In the cockfights and buffalo fights in the Thai countryside, animals are drugged or bribes paid. Khun Phan was adept at hedging his risks and could stack the deck in his favour to catch a criminal. With such methods, he could render the risk acceptable if not negligible.

The risk of loss may be ignored in the pursuit of specific ends. Cultivators in agricultural societies do not always make choices for monetary gain but for goals such as demonstrating loyalty, pleasing someone or helping out a friend or relative (Ortiz 1980: 193). Scholars of risk distinguish between 'random situations in which the underlying probabilities are fully known' and uncertainty, referring to 'all other random situations, which knowledge of the probabilities is less than complete' (Clark 1990: 48). It is in the realm of uncertainty where the probabilities are less than complete that people introduce information into their decision-making that might be thought non-rational. Uncertainty can be worrying and cause anxiety and trepidation. One is hesitant to act. The information found in the manuals from the Brahman lineage is systemic and logical and, if applied successfully by a trusted diviner, reassuring. The moment of the conjuncture is calculated by the astrologer from the astral and planetary alignments and the numbers encoded in one's birth sign personalise the decision to be made and reduce uncertainty about its outcome (Baker and Pasuk 2013: 221–2). The conjuncture, which connects the numbers in an individual's horoscope to forces and dynamics outside the range of ordinary human perception, is at once cosmic and personal. In Thailand, the cosmic is never far from the mundane.

Horoscopes personalise decision-making in the direction of action that will be auspicious, and the possession of the right amulets is another avenue by which to maximise auspicious outcomes. Given the magnitude of the amulet trade, which the vernacular refers to as commercial Buddhism (*phutthaphanit*), the financial aspect of the buying and selling of auspicious objects cannot be ignored. It is estimated that, at the height of Jatukham-Ramathep fever after Khun Phan's death, Thailand's GDP rose by as much as 0.2 per cent as a result of this amulet alone. Annual turnover in the amulet industry in the early 2000s, including sales and amulet-related media revenue, could have been about THB15 billion (US$300 million) (Chalong 2013: 184). The late Dr Pattana Kitiarsa talked about commercial Buddhism in Thailand as the occult economy—a concept he discovered in the African work of Jean and John Comaroff. Pattana saw the occult economy as a populist reaction against 'a centralized and hegemonic Buddhism promoted by the Sangha and Thai state' (Pattana 2008: 132–8; 2012: 112). The theme of capitalism and commercialism shoving religion aside is often on the surface of this kind of analysis, and this view is shared by scholastic modernist monks critical of the market economy and its destructive materialism and consumerism—'the true evils', according to some Buddhist monks. At the height of Jatukham-Ramathep fever, one of these monks put the amulet in its place by ranking it lower than the Buddha. The guardian deities fused in the Jatukham-Ramathep are merely custodians of the Great Relic in Nakhon Si Thammarat; they are not worthy of receiving the same homage as that paid to the Buddha. The saving knowledge of the Buddha, the Dhamma, he argued, is superior to any powers attributed to an amulet named after guardian deities. The monk warned people about being duped by the promises of the Jatukham-Ramathep. Worshipping it could cause society to lose its way (Phromkhunnaphon 2007: 5)

People may be devout Buddhists, but they can be enticed by auspicious objects whose expensive purchase promises reward and, for that reason, the objects are considered efficacious. It is as common to hear the expression *phutthaphanit* from devout Buddhists as it is from nonbelievers and sceptics. The owner of an authentic, valuable and famous amulet is well aware that the auspicious object has a monetary value. While the sell/ buy transaction renders these objects a commodity, in the case of Buddha amulets (*phra khrueang*), the object is said in Thai language to be not sold and purchased but leased (*hai chao*). This terminology presumably purges the transaction of the worldliness associated with the grubby business of attaching monetary value to a sacred object. If the transaction occurs at a monastery, however, it is an act of merit-making. In the frame of commercial Buddhism, the objects have value as an asset class for those who trade in them. In this asset class, as with any asset class, some items retain their value or even appreciate in value over time, while the value of other items exhibits volatility, sometimes rising to heights undreamed of before crashing if supply greatly outstrips demand. As an example of how a marketing push through police ranks alone could flood the market, in the early months of 2007, police in Nakhon Si Thammarat were given an option to buy 10 'sets' of Jatukham-Ramathep amulets at THB1,000 (US$28) per set. They could keep their allocation, but provincial police are not that affluent, so they had an incentive to recoup their costs by onselling the sets. If each of 4,000 police officers in the province onsold their set of 10 at THB1,000 per set—a generous assumption given the volume of the objects coming on to the market—the transactions would have yielded THB40 million (about US$1.25 million at the time). With such oversupply in this model it is no wonder the bubble burst in the months following Khun Phan's cremation. The rural policeman who told me this story had a fistful of Jatukham-Ramathep amulets but appeared to pay the objects little heed and said he never wore them.[6]

The volatile, risky amulet investments are what financial advisers call alternative investments. Whether investment in an object is conservative, in the expectation of gradual appreciation over time, or aggressive-risky, by riding an inflationary spike, the asset can be liquidated when the owner wishes, provided a buyer can be found, to release funds for a house purchase, school fees or a family wedding, or the funds may be used to rescue a financially troubled business with a quick infusion of cash. A policeman I met with to discuss the amulet business, after assuring me that he never parted with his amulets, subsequently sold two amulets for US$31,500. 'He needed the money', I was told.[7] No tax is paid on these private transactions, which are useful in disguising profits. Politicians are said to launder money in this way.

6   Conversation with Police Sub-Lieutenant Somthop Chuphom, Cha-uat District, Nakhon Si Thammarat, 7 September 2012.

7   Thongchai Liitpornsawan, Personal communication, 13 September 2012.

Buddha amulets can also be status markers and, if famous and valuable, mark the social position of those who wear them. A former Thai prime minister alighted from his Mercedes one day and a first-edition cookie-sized Jatukham-Ramathep amulet happened to tumble out of his open-necked shirt. Another celebrity, the businessman Sondhi Limthongkul, who led the antigovernment rallies in 2005–06, appeared on camera with his first-edition Jatukham-Ramathep amulet to describe how he nearly died of his injuries when someone tried to assassinate him. The amulet saved him from a hail of bullets that riddled his automobile. Sondhi's miraculous survival made the amulet even more famous. Status also accrues through connoisseurship as collectors acquire the skills to distinguish the real from the fake and build collections that become valuable enough to bequeath to their heirs. The home that houses these heirlooms must be secured with strong locks and barred windows, and it is best not to make too public the existence of one's hard-won collection.

Police officers boast of famous amulets they own and love to have their photographs taken with them, as did Khun Phan and his fellow retiree when they commissioned their amulets in 1963. Members of the public, including policemen, organise the manufacture of amulets to raise funds for monastery buildings, schools and hospitals as well as to enhance their status as public-spirited citizens.

A fundraising campaign was instigated in the early 1950s by Police General Phao Siyanon for renovations to the sanctuary and classrooms at Wat Intharawihan, a monastery along the Chao Phraya River that dates from the mid-eighteenth century, before the founding of Bangkok. Police General Phao, then at the height of his powers, was both Minister of the Interior and national police chief. He solicited the assistance of civil servants and merchants to help him in the campaign and, in October and November 1952, 84,000 triangular and rectilinear amulets were minted and made available to the public for THB10 (US$0.47) each. The number 84,000 was auspicious; in the third century BCE, the Mauryan Emperor Ashoka constructed 84,000 stupas containing relics of the Buddha. The consecration of the amulets was attended by senior monks of national repute as well as the spirits of four deceased monks, including Somdet To, the maverick monk of Wat Rakhang in the early Bangkok period whose amulets were already pricey because of their magical powers and stable value (McDaniel 2011: 189–90). Police General Phao's amulet is known as 'Somdet Phao' (Ek 2010: 21–7). The Somdet Phao and the Somdet To amulets look very much alike, and one wonders whether the incautious or inexperienced merit-making consumer-collector might mistake one for the other. Perhaps no confusion was intended, and Phao just liked the look of the Somdet To and wished to emulate it and let his creation bask in its resemblance to the famous Other. Despite the grandiosity of the event in 1952, the Somdet Phao amulet fell short of Somdet To's monetary and magical value. After Phao's forced exile to Switzerland after Sarit's coup in 1957, the Somdet Phao's value diminished sharply. The amulet he commissioned had failed to protect its creator from adversity.

A deity conjured from ancient heritage

A few metres from the bronze statue of Khun Phan in front of the Nakhon Si Thammarat police station, a statue of the Jatukham-Ramathep deity is adorned with regalia and shaded by a faux-gilt nine-tiered parasol. The left leg is tucked to the side of the seated image in a posture awkward except for yoga practitioners; the right leg is upright and the right hand rests on the knee. The chest is muscular, rather like the 'six-pack' abdominals favoured by bodybuilders. The image is modern, and it is not a Buddha, nor is it exactly Hindu, as one Thai friend declared, telling me emphatically when I brought it to his attention that it was 'Indian' (*khaek*). Such an attribution is understandable. Some Jatukham-Ramathep images in Nakhon are black, as though to reference Hinduism or the Tamils in Nakhon's past. It is not even clear whether the deity is a Bodhisattva—a Buddha-to-be who remains in the world to teach the Dhamma. The deity in its present material form is newborn and came into this world a little over 30 years ago when an amulet was minted to fund a local shrine.

Plate 9 The Jatukham-Ramathep deity outside Nakhon Si Thammarat police station

Source: Craig Reynolds.

In 1985, a new provincial police chief arrived in Nakhon Si Thammarat. Police Colonel (later Lieutenant General) Sanphet Thammathikun was a native of the town and a no-nonsense officer who had spent much of his career posted to other provinces. He had received counterinsurgency training from the Americans and was an expert marksman, able to shoot mangoes out of a tree into the waiting arms of an assistant. He was known for his terrorising tactic of placing coffins around the district as a warning, and his job now was to curtail the communist insurgency and end public unrest in the district.[8] In fact, by the mid-1980s, the communist movement in Thailand was a spent force. An amnesty had been granted to those who had fled into the jungle and the arms of the party after the 1976 massacre at Thammasat University. Still, the communist spectre continued to be raised to justify high defence budgets and to buttress the authority of the security services. Local people soon made the new police chief aware of the need to construct a city pillar (*lak mueang*), the palladium of the town and the abode of the guardian spirit that watched over it. During the 1980s, the economy had diversified in the provinces. The central government was boosting regional identity and a national effort was under way to furnish each of the major centres in the country with a city pillar.

In the early religious systems of monsoon Asia, territorial stone-spirits assimilated ancestral cults to fuse place, deity and sovereignty (Mus 2011). The Jatukham-Ramathep deity exemplifies such an amalgam, as does the city pillar in Nakhon. While the Great Relic in the town's ancient monastery commemorated the city's triumphant past, it did not fulfil the functions of a city pillar, and the existing foundation stone (*hin lak*) to the north of the town was far too modest, according to urgently made assessments. Police Lieutenant General Sanphet had privileged knowledge of Nakhon Si Thammarat's horoscope. He knew of a curse on the city and wanted to reverse any misfortune that might befall it. Before construction of the new city pillar and its shrine could begin, however, the old horoscope was ritually burnt to remedy the curse and a new horoscope divined to revive the city's fortunes (Phuttharat 2007: 108–9).

A group of Chinese merchants led the new police chief to a Chinese shrine near Wat Nang Phraya to the east of the town, where a spirit medium was known to conjure lucky numbers for the lottery and other gambling ventures. Wat Nang Phaya (Map 3) was not an affluent monastery and the wat committee was always looking for resources to renovate it, so a spirit medium popular with people eager for tips on numbers was helpful to its budget. The monastery was named after Jao Mae Nang Phaya, the mother of the Jatukham-Ramathep deity—as yet unidentified in the material

---

8   Phirayu (2007: 24, 190–1); Conversation with provincial policeman, Nakhon Si Thammarat, 7 September 2012.

form that would soon reveal itself. A local community association known as The '28 Society, which had named itself after the year of its founding in the Buddhist Era 2528 (1985 CE), took charge of organising the séances and preparing offerings for the medium. Sanphet was at first sceptical of the medium, but after performing a few experiments to satisfy himself of its authenticity, he decided to heed its advice, and not only about spiritual matters. With crime and public disorder rife in town at the time, the spirit medium asked bluntly at one of the séances: 'Why do you let these bad characters go on living?' Soon after, a number of bad characters in the municipality were found dead and public opinion attributed the deaths to the spirit medium's challenge. Fatal encounters with the police in such circumstances are not unknown in the troubled annals of crime suppression in Thailand. Sanphet was known for his terrorising.

According to several versions of the Jatukham Ramathep's pedigree, the spirit medium drew an indistinct picture and gave instructions to ask the 'the guy with the whiskers' (*ai nuat*) to explain the drawing. The devotees immediately identified Khun Phan, the legendary policeman who had sported a handlebar moustache throughout his career. When Sanphet and his delegation arrived at Khun Phan's house to hear his interpretation of the puzzling picture, the older policeman was waiting for them as though he had foreknowledge of the visit. He was very excited to see the drawing and immediately identified the image as Jatukham-Ramathep, or Chandrabhanu, the monarch of the ancient Srivijayan kingdom. Police Lieutenant General Sanphet and his Chinese merchant colleagues returned to Wat Nang Phraya to report the news and, through the medium, the spirit of the Jatukham-Ramathep deity spoke up to identify itself, saying: 'I've been waiting for you for a thousand years! Now I'll tell you how to build the city pillar shrine' (Nan Tapi 2007: 11–17). The face of the Jatukham-Ramathep turned out to be a composite of the twin deities guarding the relic chamber under the Great Relic stupa (Chaiyaphong 2007: 64; Nan Tapi 2007: 29; Phuttharat 2007: 125).[9] The Jatukham-Ramathep twin deities are regarded as guardians of the town and their images are found elsewhere at Wat Mahathat (Brawn 2018: 151).

---

9   See Reynolds (2017: xv) for illustrations. The late Michael Wright decoded 'Jatukham-Ramathep' as two Buddhist guardian deities known in Ceylon: Kataragam (Th., Jatukham-Ramathep, Khattukham), son of Shiva; and Upulwan (Th., Ramthep, Ubonwan), Vishnu or Narai (*Matichon Weekly*, 26 April 2007: 67; 8 June 2007: 30). Justin McDaniel has also identified Kataragama as a Sinhalese deity (Personal communication, 11 August 2011). *Chatukham* also means 'city of the four quarters' (Phuttharat 2007: 104–5).

The deity's spirit is always present but needs material form—a vessel—to become manifest in this world. Once the Jatukham-Ramathep gave instructions through the spirit medium, construction of the city pillar could begin, and Jatukham-Ramathep amulets were minted to fund the construction of the shrine, which was formally consecrated in 2000 by the Crown Prince of Thailand (Chaiyaphong 2007: 59–78; Nawamin 2007: 43–5).[10] The initial edition of the amulet cost THB10–20, and was produced in 1985 by local people. Sales were painfully slow at first; amulets four and five centimetres in diameter were unpopular with some buyers because of their size (Kong Bannathikan Khaosot 2007: 82; Phirayu 2007: 136). In March 1987, the city pillar was finished and, in a rite performed for Hindu and Buddhist guardian deities, it was brought to life when its eyes were ritually opened (*poet net*) (Nawamin 2007: 56–7).

That the deity's biography exists in present memory is one thing; the history of its incarnations in sculpture and talismanic form is quite another. I have discovered no oral explanation and no authoritative written account to explain the image's iconography. The Jatukham-Ramathep image is a work of bricolage, an amalgam that quotes elements from Hindu and Buddhist precursors. To make identification of its constituent parts even more elusive, the image has changed over the three decades of its life and assumed different postures. Just how the artists and craftsmen decided on the disparate elements that went into its fabrication is difficult to say with confidence, and I can only explore the possibilities.

Small bronze sculptures and votive tablets of Hindu and Buddhist deities dating from Srivijayan times have been found in several mid south provinces—Phatthalung, Songkhla and Trang—as well as in the deep south, often in limestone caves that are difficult to access. Collectors of guano and birds' nests first discovered the tablets. The earliest, dating from the seventh century, comes from Phatthalung. A familiar deity on many tablets is Jambhala (Th., *thao chumphon*), a Bodhisattva popular with merchants and seafarers who is the Mahayana Buddhist counterpart of Kubera, the Hindu god of wealth and riches, who is identifiable by his protruding belly and corpulence, signifying wealth and abundance.

---

10   After Khun Phan's cremation, when the Jatukham-Ramathep amulet craze was at fever pitch, five pop-history books were published on the amulet, the construction of the new shrine for the city pillar and Nakhon's legendary history (Chaiyaphong 2007; Nan Tapi 2007; Nawamin 2007; Phuttharat 2007). Police Lieutenant General Sanphet's story is told at length in a lavishly illustrated book published by Sondhi Limthongkun (Phirayu 2007). These books have no footnotes or bibliographies, but they clearly draw on academic works as well as oral accounts. The books by Chaiyaphong (2007) and Nawamin (2007) have black Jatukham-Ramathep images on their covers.

The terracotta votive tablet of Jambhala from Trang has been identified as tenth century, 'Srivijaya' period, and is seated in the posture of royal ease (*rajalilāsana*), with one leg crossed in front and the other hanging over the edge of the throne (Pattaratorn 1997: 33, 36, 75).[11] The stamp is sharp and deep. This posture is common in many Jatukham-Ramathep images, in both amulet form and full-sized.

Sculptures and votive tablets depicting the Bodhisattva Avalokiteśvara have been found in many sites in the mid south, especially at Chaiya. An antecedent image that almost certainly inspired the Jatukham-Ramathep is an Avalokiteśvara from the eighth and ninth centuries— that is, late in the Anuradhapura period—now housed in the Colombo National Museum. Michael Wright's columns about the Jatukham-Ramathep phenomenon reproduce the Late Anuradhapura Avalokiteśvara, but whether the image has been inserted by the publisher or the columnist is not clear, and Wright does not say that it is an antecedent (Wright 2007b, 2007c). Yet in posture, sumptuous crown and royal attire, the resemblance with many Jatukham-Ramathep images is striking. Falling over the upper legs is the front section of the hip cloth (*dhoti*); the headdress is the Bodhisattva's matted hair piled up in a high chignon (*jatamukuta*).[12] Many of the Jatukham-Ramathep images are seated in this pose of relaxation (*lalitāsana*); sometimes the right hand is resting on the knee and sometimes it is raised. In the Anuradhapura image, the abdominal muscles are moulded slightly to emphasise the twisting torso.

Avalokiteśvara enjoyed great popularity in medieval Sri Lanka. The zenith of its fame was the eighth to the tenth centuries, and the saviour cult may have spread from India to Sri Lanka and Southeast Asia about the same time. For example, an eight-armed Avalokiteśvara—'the Bodhisattva of Compassion'—was found at Chaiyu, Surat Thani, dated late eighth to early ninth century (Guy 2014: 258–60). The Hindu Brahmanical tradition had made a lasting impact on Sinhalese Buddhism and the sculpting of Avalokiteśvara was open to iconographic influences of Shiva and Durga

---

11   I thank Dr Piriya Krairiksh for identifying Jambhala (Personal communication, 25 November 2014). Pattaratorn (1997: 36) suggests the posture of relaxation (*lalitasana*), but Paul Lavy (Personal communication, 14 July 2011) thinks the pose with one leg crossed in front is royal ease (*rajalilasana*). A small bronze, mid-ninth-century Kubera with protruding belly was found in Sathingpra District, Songkhla (Krom 2006: 55).

12   Again, I thank Dr Piriya Krairiksh for this identification (Personal communication, 25 November 2014). The terracotta Jambhala and the Avalokiteśvara in the Colombo museum are illustrated in Reynolds (2017: xv). The late Anuradhapura Avalokiteśvara appeared in Michael Wright's columns but without explanation (Wright 2007a, 2007b).

(Holt 1991: 79, 82, 112). A Sanskrit work on iconography ascribes to Avalokiteśvara signs of the most important Hindu gods: Shiva, Brahma, Vishnu, Durga, Skanda and Ganesha. By the end of the fourteenth century, the Bodhisattva was assimilated into the Theravada tradition and acknowledged in Ceylon as an important and powerful deity. The deity was known as 'the king of gods' and became associated with monarchical rule and dynastic legitimacy in the Kandyan kingdom. The Avalokiteśvara shrine there had a prominent role in the consecration of its monarchs (Nandana 2002: 56–9). The Jatukham-Ramathep—'the Monarch of the Southern Seas'—impersonates the Avalokiteśvara, the guardian and protector of sovereign space, as the title of one of the pop-history books proudly states (Nan Tapi 2007). Later in its history, the Avalokiteśvara (male), the compassionate saviour, became China Guanyin (female), a deity associated with the sea, which is still very popular in Thailand today (Guy 2014: 62). The merging of Buddhist and Hindu influences and iconography runs deep in the religious history of India, Sri Lanka and Southeast Asia—a reminder that it would be misleading to read the Jatukham-Ramathep as either wholly Buddhist or wholly Hindu.

Early in its history, the Jatukham-Ramathep appeared with a multiheaded serpent hovering over it (Nan Tapi 2007: 26). Sometimes the serpent has had seven heads; sometimes, as in the example from Krabi municipality (Plate 10), it has nine heads. On the base of the Krabi image, the demon Rahu is swallowing the Moon in a mythical representation of a lunar eclipse—an icon shown on many Jatukham-Ramathep amulets.

The Jatukham-Ramathep with the polycephalic hood evokes an event after the Enlightenment when the Buddha endured seven days of storms and heavy rains, and the serpent Mucalinda wound its coils around Shakyamuni to shelter him. The halo-like *naga* hood protecting a deity is also common in Hindu and Jain as well as Buddhist art (Gaston-Aubert 2010: 117–18). In Thai, this representation of the Buddha is called *nak prok* ('the protecting *naga*') and, like the Jambhala and the Avalokiteśvara, it appears early in the history of Buddhist art on the Malay Peninsula. Piriya Krairiksh dates a *nak prok* found in Krabi to the second half of the sixth century; *nak prok* votive tablets have also been found in Yala (Piriya 2012: 82–3). *Nak prok* Buddha images were also common in Khmer art during the Angkor period as the supreme deity in the reign of Jayavarman VII (r. 1181–1218), a devotee of Mahayana Buddhism. A non-Buddhist ancient sculpture of the *nak prok* genre that resembles the Jatukham-Ramathep is the Nagaraja from the Ajanta cave complex in

Maharashtra State. In this image, the ruler in regal garb is protected by the hoods of a multiheaded serpent. For many Buddhist devotees, this tangled pedigree of the Jatukham-Ramathep proves to them that the deity is not Buddhist, and the power of the amulet to create wealth is a distortion, even a perversion (*rueang wipparit*), of the Buddha's teachings (Wright 2007c).

Plate 10 The Jatukham-Ramathep deity, Krabi City Hall
Source: Craig Reynolds.

Plate 11 Jatukham-Ramathep image in a Nakhon Si Thammarat restaurant
Source: Craig Reynolds.

At a seafood restaurant in Nakhon, I came across an unusual Jatukham-Ramathep image of the *nak prok* type. Jatukham-Ramathep images, including a black one made of heavy timber, looked out from niches in the restaurant's private dining rooms, and a large collection of Buddha images and other objects, sacred and otherwise, was on display in the restaurant lobby.

There was a bust of King Bhumibol and busts of renowned monk teachers, a few Ganeshas and dancing Shivas, old manual presses for making Chinese noodles and flattening dried squid, some very dead stag coral resting in a waterless tank, a large tortoise shell, an adding machine from a bygone age and two Remington typewriters. I thought I had stepped into a flea market, although the only items on sale were small amulets for THB100 each. The brass image depicted in Plate 11, weighing 130 kilograms, was commissioned by a local Chinese amulet broker, a Sian Phra from Nakhon, and produced in nearby Surat Thani; the deity and its base were cast separately. About 100 copies were made and sold for THB100,000 each (US$3,125). Rather than coiled up to form a throne, the undulating serpent curls up from below and rises above the body posed in *lalitāsana*. The seven-headed hood shelters the image; the torso is deeply moulded like the 'six-pack' abdominals of the Jatukham-Ramathep in front of the Nakhon provincial police station. The restaurant proprietor, who assembled his collection at the height of Jatukham-Ramathep fever, explained that the Chinese amulet broker who ordered the image selected a European face.[13]

Images such as this one in the restaurant are what make it difficult to keep up with the morphing Jatukham-Ramathep over the 30 years of its existence. Most amulets are produced by particular monks and monasteries, but the Jatukham-Ramathep seems to have floated free of any copyright, making it even more difficult to track as it popped up all over the country. After a tour of the iron mine at Nam Phi in 2017, I visited Wat Pasak Rerai in Mueang District in Uttaradit Province, where a Jatukham-Ramathep was produced soon after Khun Phan's death. A former soldier—deafened by a mortar blast during his military service and wearing an oversized hearing aid in his left ear—told the story of how the amulet had been manufactured at the monastery in 2007. Prasit Phrommani, who had served as a village headman for 10 years until 2012 and was now an official on the monastery committee, explained that a senior monk in the province had blessed 1,000 amulets, which were then distributed through the monastery's network of devotees, who paid THB1,000 each. The funds were used for new buildings and renovations in the monastery compound. I bought two of the amulets and handed the money to an elderly monk.[14]

---

13   Restaurant owner, Personal communication, 6 December 2014.
14   Prasit Phrommani, Interview with the author, Wat Pasak Rerai, 10 November 2017.

Uttaradit is hundreds of kilometres north of Nakhon Si Thammarat, far from the Jatukham-Ramathep's origins and the religious history of the Malay Peninsula. The deity was first called into service to raise funds for the renovation of the city's pillar shrine—the spiritual heart of the town— and to restore Nakhon's prosperity and keep it from harm's way. After the military coup of September 2006 and the cremation in February 2007 of the Lion Lawman, devotion to the deity grew into a prosperity cult that was a financial phenomenon as much as a social and religious one. The power of the image, known as the Monarch of the Southern Seas, drew on Nakhon's heritage in community memory as an ancient coastal power to be reckoned with, as a principality that treasured its autonomy and as a religious centre that sent learned monks and Brahmans to the Siamese courts on the central plains. The deity's hold on the local imagination derives from its undecidable origins: the spirit medium it spoke through, the paired deities it embodied that continued to guard the town's great relic, the policeman with magical knowledge and a reputation for taking no prisoners who discovered its modern incarnation and a new horoscope that broke a curse and kickstarted Nakhon's fortunes with a new shrine for the city pillar.

Reflecting on the pedigree of the Jatukham-Ramathep deity, I am reminded of Stanley O'Connor's memorable phrase about 'the sedimentation of long memory' (Wannasarn 2013a: 272). For two millennia, the landscape of the mid south has been transformed by human imagination. Deities were fashioned out of stone and shrines were built for their shelter. What we now call works of art were living gods embodied in terracotta, stone and bronze. As a work of bricolage, the Jatukham-Ramathep deity is just such an object of worship, little different from the ancient sculptures and votive tablets that have been studied by art historians. These devotional objects were conjured from local lore and Southeast Asian, Indic and Lankan religious belief. Promises of quick wealth and good fortune in the auspicious moment of Khun Phan's cremation inflated the Jatukham-Ramathep's value, and the deity became another instantiation of modern cultural production infused with mythic significance.

In November 2005, just before the Yellow Shirts began their rallies to overthrow the elected government of Police Lieutenant Colonel Thaksin Shinawatra, a special edition of the Jatukham-Ramathep known as Take Back the Nation (*run ku chat*) was minted and consecrated. In June 2006, the king would have been on the throne for six decades and the Yellow Shirts whipped up enough fury and public unease in the following months to precipitate a coup in September of that year aimed at freeing the nation from the grip of Thaksin, the power-mad champion of capitalism, whom the crowds saw as a threat to the monarchy. The Jatukham-Ramathep deity had instructed the rally leader, Sondhi Limthongkul, to commence the demonstrations in February 2006 at the equestrian statue of the fifth Bangkok king. To curb violence, to keep the demonstrators safe from harm and to protect the lives of all patriotic Thais, the Jatukham-Ramathep deity further instructed—by what means we are not told—that batches of the powdery compound fused in the amulet should be placed underneath the stage's centre and at its four corners to mark out a sacred space. The righteousness of the Yellow Shirt campaign, thus endorsed by the supernatural, would bring certain victory in the political battle that was unfolding. Needless to say, hyping the protective qualities of the Jatukham-Ramathep by such theatrical shenanigans had the intended consequence of inflating the amulet's price (Phirayu 2007: Ch. 4). When Khun Phan passed away in July 2006, a month after the celebrations for the king's fifth-cycle anniversary on the throne, the amulet received its biggest boost in value.

Like Pallas Athena, on which the safety of ancient Athens depended, the Jatukham-Ramathep served as a palladium that protected the leaders of the Yellow Shirts as they issued their demands of the elected government. The deity conjured in the mid south was not just a lucky charm, nor was it merely a volatile commodity that could make a fortune in a single transaction if the purchase was timed correctly. It had begun its modern incarnation as a guardian deity watching over the reliquary at the Wat Mahathat reliquary in Nakhon Si Thammarat, and it could now be assigned the duty of keeping safe a patch of the Earth's surface during a political battle that was shaking the Thai state.

6

Invulnerability and protecting the sovereign body

Video content for this chapter is available online:
press.anu.edu.au/publications/series/asian-studies/
power-protection-and-magic-thailand#media

Khun Phan's dealings with bureaucrats in the capital, his police contacts in other provinces and his encounter with villagers and officials in many parts of the country yield a story that transcends the local or the regional. The social world of place, religion, policing and banditry he inhabited as he moved from post to post and town to town breaks down the distinctions between local, regional and national that bedevil the entrenched categories that fragment writing about Thailand's past. The narrative of Khun Phan's life tells the story of a country boy who succeeded wherever he was posted and who made a name for himself in the police force—an institution that has dominated Thai political culture since World War II.

Yet Khun Phan's deeds in the field are not what commend the policeman's story for consideration to better understand law and order in the Thai countryside in the first half of the twentieth century. Rather, it is invulnerability, both personal and institutional, that preoccupied him from his adolescent years through his career in the police force as he planned and executed his operations in the pursuit of outlaws. For Khun Phan's personal protection, the therapies and dietary regimens in the *saiyasat* repertoire kept his body healthy and free from disease. His daily supplications and ritual bath aimed to deflect or neutralise whatever might befall him in the course of his duties if he breached religious tenets against taking human life, and he did breach those tenets on many occasions. From his first serious encounter with the outlaw Suea Sang, whom he killed in 1930, Khun Phan was made aware of his own vulnerability and the precarity of police life.

The anthropologist Andrew Turton once proposed that ideas and practices of invulnerability were forms of knowledge that served as strategic moves employed by the weak, the powerless and the disenfranchised. These ideas of invulnerability coexist with powers of bilocation, metamorphosis, becoming very small, hiding, invisibility, masking, disguising, anonymity and pseudonymity. Such strategic moves enable the person employing them to elude or resist authority. Turton—adopting and adapting models of power relations from Louis Althusser, Antonio Gramsci, Maurice Bloch and British Marxist social scientists—went on to suggest that intimidation and surveillance were instrumental in the exercise of power, while their opposites, invulnerability and invisibility, were valuable to underground leaders and subaltern insurgents who worry established authority with their threats of popular mobilisation and uprising (Turton 1991: 164, 176). While the context of Turton's discussion hardly corresponds with the southern policeman's operations in the Thai countryside, his insight is a stepping-stone to further inquiry into how these binaries function.

As Khun Phan's story demonstrates, and as Turton's discussion implicitly acknowledges, invulnerability and invisibility are available not only to the weak but also to state institutions. Turton illustrates powers of invulnerability combined with powers of invisibility, disguise, escape, personal charm and the ability to render one's foes immobile by pointing to a character in the Thai epic poem *Khun Chang Khun Phaen*. This character, Khun Phaen—not to be confused with Khun Phan, the southern policeman—is no ordinary foot soldier but a senior military commander in the service of the king. Considering the period of the epic poem, which is mostly the eighteenth and nineteenth centuries, we can speak not of the state and its institutions but of a kingdom, a king and military officers, all of whom were at the apex of the social and political hierarchy. The character Khun Phaen in the poem was not among the weak and the powerless, but an officer in that hierarchy, yet the nimble strategies to which he resorted were no different from those available to the subaltern classes.

Police officers in Khun Phan's time knew these strategies well. Khun Phan himself occasionally worked incognito, as did Luang Adul, the national police chief during World War II who wore civilian clothes during his night patrols to appear non-threatening and to conceal his official identity. Khun Phan once disguised himself as a railway worker in Phatthalung to ferret out thieves. On another occasion, the southern policeman, disguised as a Chinese hawker shouldering baskets of chickens at the ends of a carrying pole, was spotted by an alert villager returning from his garden, who shouted to his son: 'There, there goes Khun Phan!'[1] The villager may have erred in his identification—perhaps it was someone who resembled the policeman—but that is the point of disguise. Khun Phan could be anywhere and everywhere in the mode of all-seeing police who, when it suits them, choose not to be seen. Maintaining law and order involves the optic of rule.

Government does its work not only by legislating, providing services and maintaining law and order using its monopoly over the use of violent force, but also by watching, recording and knowing where everything is located. Nowadays the optic necessary to government is centralised thanks to digital technology and is diffused through society in handheld electronic devices—a development that worries citizens everywhere. In premodern Siam, the optic of monarchical rule operated—apart from tax collectors, spies and other informants—through ceremony and royal progress. The king and his entourage would occasionally venture out of the royal base into the nearby countryside. He would be able to see for himself, to the extent he was curious, the benefits and munificence of his rule; equally important, he could be seen by at least some of his subjects. In the 1950s, early in the reign of the ninth Bangkok monarch when the elite was still reeling from the tragic 1946 death of the king's brother in the royal bed chamber, King Bhumibol visited many provinces in the kingdom and subsequently built palaces in the north, the northeast and the south. Over the many decades of his reign, he travelled widely around the country with a camera and maps in hand. This activist monarch, who was constrained by the Thai constitution to reign only but not to rule, reinvented the royal progress to bind himself to his subjects using photography and cartography—tell-tale instruments of the optic of rule.

---

1   Akhom Dechathongkham (1949–2016), Personal communication, 22 September 2009; and Akhom (2001: 209).

He also took his sacral duties seriously and availed himself of the iconography of the sacred image that allowed him to be, miraculously, omnipresent. Over three days in late August 1965, a royal Buddha image was cast at Wat Bowonniwet in Bangkok, the royal monastery where Prince Mongkut had been abbot and where King Bhumibol had been ordained. The image was similar in its iconography and morphology to one cast in Kanchanaburi in 1963 to commemorate a visit by the king when he turned 36, his third-cycle birthday and an occasion to be celebrated in a special way. Kanchanaburi was the birth province of Phra Nyanasamvara, who was to serve as the king's spiritual adviser and who became supreme patriarch in his later years, until his death in 2013. All Buddha images are copies of a previous image—reminders of the Buddha—but the copies are never exact, as they are subject to the constraints of different materials (bronze, terracotta, timber, crystal, stucco), to the different skills of sculptors and to the tastes of patrons who commission the images. The 1965 royal Buddha image was different from the 1963 Buddha in one important respect. On its base was inscribed 'nation, religion, and monarchy'—words that conveyed a political message.

The timing was not happenstance, for earlier in August 1965 an armed conflict between the army and the CPT erupted, which the communists declared later to be the onset of a people's war against the Thai Government (Morrell and Chai-anan 1981: 81–2). The Second Indochina War that would draw the United States into a bloody conflict in Vietnam, Cambodia and Laos was just beginning and, from air bases in Thailand, which served as a loyal US ally in the prosecution of the anticommunist campaigns in the region, American warplanes would take off to carpet-bomb targets in the neighbouring countries. The 'political message' of the amulet, in the words of Natthaphon Yurungrueangsak (2012: 108–11) in his history of Thailand through Buddha images and amulets, pointed to an existential crisis for the Thai state. Anticommunist legislation had been framed to defend the monarchy and Buddhism as well as the sovereign nation-state, and the sacredness of the image bearing this political message turned the anticommunist struggle into a holy war.

A year after the armed conflict with the CPT, yet another royal Buddha image was cast, in April 1966, which was nearly identical to the Wat Bowonniwet image. To the base of this image, known as the Phra Nawaratbophit, was affixed a small amulet, Phra Somdet Chitralada—the Buddha seated in meditation, designed by the king's own hand and known popularly as the Might of the Kingdom amulet (*phra khrueang kamlang phaendin*). The compound from which the amulet was stamped contained dried flowers from garlands that the citizenry had offered in homage to the Emerald Buddha in Bangkok when the king attended to change the image's seasonal robes, ashes from burned incense and candle wax from royal monasteries and lichen from sacred sites all over the country. Bits of every province in the land were embedded in the amulet, transforming the tiny object into a ritual map of the kingdom, the geo-body scaled down and compressed into a miniature.

To celebrate the king's talents and creative works, the amulet also contained paint from his canvases and resins and colours from his sailboat, for he was a keen sailor and had built many vessels with his own hands. Strands of the king's hair collected after it was cut were also fused into the compounded material (Chaidiaw and Chaiya 1998: 33–49; Natthaphon 2012: 108–9). The Might of the Kingdom amulet containing parts of the king's body and the fruits of his labours moulded into the base of the Phra Nawaratbophit image and ritually empowered was no mere representation or symbol of the king. The corporeal king and his person now dwelt within the object. From 1965 to 1970, limited editions of the tiny Might of the Kingdom amulet were produced and distributed to reward government officials, soldiers and police for their public service and loyalty to the Crown (Chaidiaw and Chaiya 1998: 1–116). Paying homage to this amulet was equivalent to paying homage to the king.

The Phra Nawaratbophit Buddha image was charged with a special mission. Small copies with the Might of the Kingdom amulet at its base were cast and distributed to each provincial capital in the kingdom, and protocols were prescribed for its public display. The dimensions of the portable image were small (40 centimetres high and 23 centimetres wide), enabling it to be carried by hand and thus easily transported. The image was to preside over ceremonies where its presence would not conflict with protocols for other Buddha images, and it was to be brought out whenever the king visited or stayed in the province. Local authorities had discretion to display the image for festivals and ceremonies. The first province to receive one of the portable images was Nong Khai, on the Mekong River bordering Laos, marking the frontline of the Indochina conflict unfolding to the east (Nop 2002: 34–5; Natthaphon 2012: 112–13).

The Phra Nawaratbophit image with the amulet at its base aimed to bind the monarch to his subjects, but another, quite different, version of its origins explains its inception. It had been a custom from ancient times, so it was said, that when the king visited one of the satellite states guarding the frontiers of the kingdom, he would present the local lord with a royal sword, a weapon that took the place of the king's 'eyes and ears' as he watched over his domain. The local ruler would use this weapon to punish or subdue enemies who threatened his own domain. When the local ruler was replaced, this royal sword would be returned to the king, who might or might not confer it on the successor. In March 1964, King Bhumibol determined that times had changed and royal swords in the hands of provincial governors were no longer required to defend the country and maintain order. Criminal law would now be used to subjugate rebels and insurgents. The king conceived the Phra Nawaratbophit as a replacement for the royal sword—a Buddha image that would seal his relationship with his subjects. Materials taken from every province were fused in the image, so prostration to pay respect to this Buddha image was tantamount to paying homage to all the sacred sites in the country (Nop 2002: 31–4).

The explanations of how the Phra Nawaratbophit image came to be cast at a time when the Thai state was embarking on a war with what it deemed to be an alien ideology seem light-years from the social life and environmental niche of the southern policeman's beloved Songkhla lakes. The Red Sword he had acquired from the noble family in Uttaradit was retired with him at the very moment the ninth Bangkok king and his advisers decided that this item of the royal regalia—an emblem of royal punishment and subjugation—needed to be replaced with the image of the Buddha challenged by Mara, the incarnation of evil. In response, the Buddha lowers his right hand and points downward, calling the Earth to witness that he is, indeed, the Buddha. The king wanted to modernise the symbolism of the royal sword traditionally given to local lords to punish wrongdoers and defend the kingdom by replacing it with a sacred image that was engaged in existential defence, a serene Buddha defying an enemy that was said to be threatening every corner of the realm.

Khun Phan retired in the mid-1960s at the time the king commissioned these images, and the Red Sword he had carried was wrapped in its cloth for the last time. He had desired the sword as soon as he was introduced to it and cherished it for the rest of his life—a weapon for punishment and for defence to accompany the 'Little Raja' title conferred on him by Muslims in Malaya after he carried out a successful mission in the late 1930s. The title, the sword and his Malay *kris* emboldened him. He sensed that his authority would be enhanced if he embraced the weapons of supralocal, sovereign rule, convincing him that he would not, and could not, be defeated. He had modern firearms, martial arts he used with deadly effect and he possessed talismans and rituals that could frighten an adversary or spook a lawbreaker who dared to venture into the province he protected.

Aspects of Khun Phan's life, such as his lifelong quest for *saiyasat* knowledge and his observance of its regimens, hark back to an earlier age in Thailand. The writ of central government stopped at the edge of the village and people relied on local forms of security unregulated by institutional constraints. The *saiyasat* magic that he cultivated belongs to an underdeveloped rural sector that no longer exists in an age when villagers have mobile phones and access to the internet. The countryside had been absorbed into a royal state rejuvenated by a young, still untested monarch and his advisers. The scope for a single rural policeman to exercise his magical powers, intimidation and surveillance narrowed as authority and power moved gradually from the periphery to the centre.

National history has little place, perhaps no place, in its narrative for such a figure. The southern policeman is too small and his reputation too darkened by violence. He can be a hero to local people but not a hero in the national story. Readers wanting to understand a complex past yearn for big paradigms or large-scale tragedies such as the humiliation of an indigenous ruler by Western colonial powers, rather than the bruising encounters between the police and outlaws in the remote Thai countryside in the first half of the twentieth century. Khun Phan's willingness to trade life for life, as he did when he set free Suea Dam after the outlaw surrendered one of his men to certain death, does not fit into big-paradigm history. That incident barely makes it into the historical record, partly because the evidence to corroborate it is slim and partly because the sacrifice of such a man's life is not ennobling. The episode fits neither the grand narrative of tragedy nor the grand narrative of romance. A social history built around a biographical study of a provincial policeman whose accomplices disrespected human remains by leaving the corpses of men they had killed for days in the tropical sun is a microhistory for which it is awkward to find a place in national history.

Khun Phan's record of arresting lawbreakers, and sometimes killing them with his police team when they refused to surrender and preferred to fight to the death, stands out in the annals of Thai police history. Some of his actions were brutish and shocking by any measure, yet in the police culture at the time they were worthy of only moderate disciplinary action. His ruthless methods were popular in communities beset by violence and crime. At the same time, he epitomises the emotional significance that attaches to the police, who stir in the Thai citizenry anxiety and fear, notwithstanding the fraternisation and rapport that draw citizens to police in the communities they serve and that make possible peaceable policing. The aura of apprehension surrounding the police runs like an iridescent thread through the life and times of Khun Phan.

Details of Khun Phan's police operations that illustrate his willingness to use the power to punish are unsettling and, as I read through the accounts, I thought about what the Australian historian Greg Denning once said about the need for history of the Aboriginal people. 'For me', said Denning,

> the dead and the living need history. The dead need history for the voice it gives them. The living need history, not to be made to feel guilty for a past they are not responsible for or cannot change. The living need a history disturbing enough to change the present. (Denning 1998: 4–5)

Denning's sentiments do not apply to the southern policeman in all respects. In the last decades of his life, Khun Phan had so much to say about himself that has found its way into books and into community memory that he hardly needs another biographer to give him voice. It is the last sentence in Denning's comment that fits the policeman's case. The disturbing history that Khun Phan made needs to be kept alive in present knowledge.

Appendix: Biographies of Khun Phan

In the wake of Khun Phan's death in 2006, biographers rushed to produce accounts of his life, and several appeared in 2007 after his cremation in February of that year. Owing to Khun Phan's role in identifying the Jatukham-Ramathep deity (described in Chapter 5), the value of the amulet spiked between his death in July 2006 and his cremation, and books about the deity never fail to include him in the story.

In 1983, the policeman began to give interviews about his career and, while the stories he told to various authors overlap with one another, the biographies have different emphases and, in a few cases, unique details. His recalling of his provincial postings and outlaw captures conveys a ring of truth, although numerous retellings of the stories have burnished the accounts to the point where they are difficult to corroborate for lack of external evidence. His fluent storytelling suggests that he had a remarkable memory and he had told the stories many times (see Samphan 1996 below).

Anat Anantaphak. 2006. *Khunphatharakratchadet jomkhamangwet daen sayam phu sang khong khlang jatukhamramthep* [*Khun Phuntharakratachadet: Siam's Vedic master of Siam who created the magic Jatukham-Ramathep*]. Bangkok: Warati Midia.

Anat lists at the end of his book the biographies he used, including Samphan (1996) and Wira (2001). This small book has copious illustrations that appear in other biographies except for a rare photograph in which Khun Phan is shown performing a sword dance, on 4 August 1987, to celebrate the consecration of the city pillar shrine in Nakhon Si Thammarat.

Chalong Jeyakhom (comp.). 2007. *Pho lo to to khun phantharakratchadet* [*Police Major General Khun Phantharakratchadet*]. Kanchanaburi: Fa Sayam.

Chalong, born in Phatthalung in 1966 and raised in Bangkok, was a Buddhist novice and monk for 10 years. A law graduate of Ramkhamhaeng University, he first met Khun Phan in 1986 and spoke with him over 15 days. In my conversation with Chalong, on 31 January 2012, he referred to Wat Khao Or as 'an academy for men' at which some of the outlaws had been disciples. He agreed with me that Khun Phan was 'a Brahman in his practices'. This book contains little new information and skips around chronologically, but it is written in a lively style. A Thai colleague thought it the best of the biographies of the policeman she had read. According to internal evidence, it was published in 2007, the year of Khun Phan's cremation.

Chanthip Phantharakratchadet. 2007. 'Wicha khong khun phan [Khun Phan's knowledge]', in Chintapati (2007: 133–6).

Chanthip (b. 1952), the second eldest of Khun Phan's surviving sons, inherited the knowledge his father acquired from the master teachers at Wat Khao Or and from other teachers during his long career. In these pages of the cremation biography, he classifies this 'Vedic' knowledge into four parts and lists the teachers who taught his father and their fields of expertise.

Chanthip and his older brother, Nasan, went through Khao Or's ritual of initiation, including immersion in the prophylactic herbal bath (p. 135). Chanthip attended the Sirisinlapa Muslim kindergarten; the family home at the time was near the Muslim market. In his primary and secondary years, he attended the AMC Christian School because it was in the neighbourhood, and on weekends he went to a Buddhist school. From a young age, he accompanied his father everywhere. A physically fit man with a ready sense of humour when I spoke with him in September 2012, Chanthip had aspired to be a policeman but struggled with the studies required and baulked at paying a bribe to join the force.

'Kon Hoi' [Chanthip Phantharakratchadet]. 2007. 'Phonngan nai thana nai tamruat [Accomplishments as a police officer]', in Chintapati (2007: 84–132).

Chanthip Phantharakratchadet here relates highlights of his father's life, including many of the outlaw episodes. Chanthip spoke with several of Khun Phan's biographers, including Samphan Kongsamut, in 2001 (Samphan 2007: 368–92).

Okha Buri [Supharuek Khachonklin]. 2007. *Thot rahat khun phantharakratchadet mue prap khamang wet* [*Unlocking the Secrets of Khun Phantharakratchadet: The lawman with the Vedic magic*]. Bangkok: Utthayan Khwamru.

The author, whose real name is Supharuek Khachonklin, is a native of Phichit in north-central Thailand, where Khun Phan was posted from 1943 to 1945 during the Japanese occupation after he closed the Ivory Bamboo Casino in Surat Thani. The Yom and Nan rivers flow through the province, and Supharuek's pen name means 'River Town'. A prolific writer with degrees in education management and Thai studies, 'Okha Buri' offers episodes of and insights into the policeman's life unavailable in other biographies, including Khun Phan's friendship with a couple of Chinese brothers from Hainan who provided him with local knowledge and resources for his crime suppression in Phichit. Supharuek heard many Khun Phan tales from Ko Yueang, the elder of the Chinese brothers; Ko Yang, the younger brother, was the author's paternal grandfather (p. 32). While stationed in Phichit, Khun Phan acquired the Red Sword that he kept to the end of his days from the noble family in Uttaradit.

Phantharakratchadet, Khun. n.d. Prawat phi phroi pantharak [The life of 'elder sister' Phroi Phantharak]. Photocopy of typescript, 30 pp.

This cremation eulogy by Khun Phan, of uncertain date, for one of his relatives sets out the southern policeman's family tree without dates. A history of the relations between Nakhon Si Thammarat and Kedah as well as between Nakhon Si Thammarat and Ayutthaya in the seventeenth and eighteenth centuries is also included. I extracted a few nuggets from this fascinating document, which I think is based on oral history, but the dates do not jibe with modern scholarship.

Phantharakratchadet, Khun. 1986. Recording of interview with Chatthip Nartsupha held at the National Archives of Thailand. Personal copy.

This interview with Khun Phan, conducted by Professor Chatthip Nartsupha during a meal, is barely audible in places through the clatter of dishware and background conversation. Chatthip, an economic historian, solicited information from the policeman for a book he was co-authoring on the southern Thai economy (Chatthip and Phunsak 1997). He was interested not in Khun Phan's exploits capturing bandits, but in the economic life of southern peoples, so rather than interrogating Khun Phan about crime and banditry, Chatthip asked about the price of bananas and pineapples and the cost of boat transportation through the Songkhla lakes.

Praphon Rueangnarong. 1983. 'Prasopkan nai phon tamruat tri khun phantharakratchadet [Experiences of Police Major General Khun Phantarakratchadet]', *Warasan rutsamilae* [*Rutsamilae Journal*] 7(1) (September–December): 60–6.

Published by Songklanakarin University in Patani, where Praphon was a lecturer, *Rutsamilae Journal* specialised in the life and culture of people in the country's four southern provinces. This interview is one of the first Khun Phan gave and covers his early life and exploits in Phatthalung, Narathiwat and provinces in the central plains. The author, known eponymously as Rutsamilae, is identified by Wira (2001: 19) and Okha (2007: 239–49). Another excerpt of Praphon's interview with Khun Phan was published as 'Khui kap naiphon tamruat tri khunphantarak ratchdet [In conversation with Police Major General Khunphantarak Ratchadet]' in *Sinlapa Watthanatham* (5[2][December 1983]: 14–18). The accounts in these interviews are corroborated to an extent in Samphan Kongsamut's books, but the details do not jibe in all respects.

Praphon, a native of Trang, was born in 1942. His father was an agricultural official whose duties took him to many southern provinces, and Praphon lived in Surat Thani, Trang and Narathiwat. A man of letters from an early age, who attended teachers' college in Songkhla, he has worked in publication and marketing. A short memoir is in Ajin et al. (2009: 245–304).

Ran Niranam [Samphan Kongsamut]. 2007. *Jom witthaya yut phutthakkhom khao or saolin haeng muang phatthalung* [*The Khao Or Masters of the Science of Struggle and Buddhist Incantations: The Shaolin of Phatthalung*]. Bangkok: Wasi Khri-echan.

Niranam means 'anonymous', raising the question of why the author of this book about Wat Khao Or and Khun Phan, its most famous disciple, wished to keep his identity private. The author eventually revealed himself to be Samphan Kongsamut, a writer and publisher now based in Bangkok and the most prolific of Khun Phan's biographers. Samphan comes from Ko Samui, an island in the Gulf of Thailand, and his family had connections with Khao Or through his maternal great-grandfather, who had acquired the *saiyasat* knowledge taught at the cave monastery.

Samphan is a disciple of Buddhadasa Bhikkhu (1906–93), a revered Thai monk and Buddhist philosopher of international repute who came from Chaiya in Surat Thani. Many of the beliefs and practices of the monks at the cave monastery that mixed Buddhism and Brahmanism were outside the ken of Buddhadasa's Buddhism, and Samphan did not want to use his real name out of respect for the philosopher's reformist teachings and reinterpretations of Buddhist texts. Although Ran's book is repetitive and disjointed in places, it has rare data on the Khao Or medicinal therapies and the monastery's lineage of master teachers that are unavailable in other documents. Samphan published an informative memoir in Ajin et al. (2009: 161–243).

Samphan Kongsamut. 1996. *Rayo kaji pho lo to to khun phantharakratchadet dap daeng* [*'Little Raja': Police Major General Khun Phantharakratchadet and the red sword*]. Bangkok: Thammachat Press.

The title 'Little Raja' was bestowed by Muslim people in the deep south to honour Khun Phan's capture in 1938 of a Malay separatist in Narathiwat. In the reprint of *Little Raja* (2016), Samphan added a paragraph noting Khun Phan's death in July 2006 and his cremation in February 2007, and identified himself as Ran Niranam (2007). In *Little Raja* and his other books, Samphan concentrates on Khun Phan's exploits pursuing and capturing bandits; some material in this book is not to be found in his larger biography of Khun Phan (Samphan 2007 [2001]). Samphan began interviewing Khun Phan in March 1992 for a series of articles on the Thai mafia for a crime magazine. Much to Samphan's dissatisfaction—to say the least—instalments in the magazine were pirated and published anonymously under the title *Khon tai nang niaw* [*The Man with the Tough Hide*] (p. 11). Interviewing Khun Phan was easy. He spoke in complete sentences with such fluency it was as though he had a tape running in his head, and Samphan had little to do except transcribe the policeman's words.

Samphan Kongsamut. 2007. *Pho lo to khun phantharakratchadet: Sing moe prap sip thit* [*Police Major General Khun Phantarakratchadet: Lion lawman of the ten directions*]. Bangkok: Wasi Khri-echan.

This edition of Samphan's most comprehensive biography was published after Khun Phan's death and contains an interview with Khun Phan's younger son, Chanthip, who has continued his father's interest in *saiyasat*. The last of the four appendices is Khun Phan's essay 'Saiyasat beliefs of the southern Thai people' (Phantharakratchadet 2007). The 2001 edition of this book has six appendices, including several excerpts from Wira (2001).

Wira Saengphet. 2001. *Phumpanya kanprappram khong pho lo to to khun phantharakratchadet* [*The Local Wisdom of Khun Phantharakratchadet for Maintaining Law and Order*]. Bangkok: Thailand Research Fund.

This book, with footnotes and full academic citations, was reworked from an MA thesis supervised by Professor Paritta Chalermpow-Koanantakool and the late Professor Suthiwong Pongpaiboon, among others. Based on extensive research and interviews with Khun Phan and local people, the book includes a detailed local map and a list of the men fatally shot as a result of operations by the southern policeman and his team. Wira places Khun Phan in the culture, society and history of the mid south and shows how he exploited local knowledge and belief systems to develop his skills as a lawman. When I spoke with Wira in 2008, he was teaching in a Songkhla district school.

Bibliography

Agamben, Giorgio. 2000. 'Sovereign police', in Giorgio Agamben, *Means Without End: Notes on politics*, Vincenzo Binetti and Cesare Casarino (trans.), pp. 102–7. Theory out of Bounds Volume 20. Minneapolis: University of Minnesota Press.

Ajin Janthararamphon, Arun Wetsuwan, Samphan Kongsamut and Praphon Rueangnarong. 2009. *Si mit nam muek* [*Four Friends in the Print World*]. Bangkok: Wali Kri-echan.

Akhom Dechathongkham. 2000. *Hua chueak wua chon* [*Tethered Heads, Fighting Bulls*]. Bangkok: Thailand Research Fund.

Akhom Dechathongkham. 2001. *Phuk yot* [*Sticking Together*]. Nakhon Si Thammarat: Rajabhat University of Nakhon Si Thammarat.

Anan Ariwong, ed. 2008. *Photchananukrom phasa thin tai* [*Dictionary of the Southern Thai Language*]. Nakhon Si Thammarat: Institute of Southern Thai Studies, Rajabhat University.

Anat Ananthaphak. 2006. *Khun Phantharakratchadet chom khamangwet daen sayam phu sang khong khlang Jatukham-Ramathep* [*Khun Phantharakratchadet: The master of Vedic magic in Siam and the creator of miraculous objects Jatukham-Ramathep*]. Bangkok: Waralmldla.

Anderson, Benedict. 2014. 'Studies of the Thai State: The state of Thai studies', in Benedict Anderson, *Exploration and Irony in Studies of Siam over Forty Years*, pp. 15–45. Ithaca, NY: Southeast Asia Program, Cornell University.

Anuson phon tor or phao siyanon wan thoeng kae anitchakam khrop 10 pi 21 phroetsachikayon 2513 [*In Memory of Police General Phao Siyanond on the Tenth Anniversary of His Death, 21 November 1970*]. Privately printed.

Anusonsitthikam, Luang [Bua na Nakhon]. 1962. 'Phongsawadan muang nakhon si thammarat [Chronicle of Nakhon Si Thammarat]', in *Ruam rueang mueang nakhon si thammarat* [*Collected Articles on Nakhon Si Thammarat*], pp. 64–77. Bangkok: Cremation volume for Chao Phraya Bodintharadechanuchit (Yaem na Nakhon).

Baker, Chris and Pasuk Phongpaichit. 1996. *Thailand's Boom*. Chiang Mai: Silkworm Books.

Baker, Chris and Pasuk Phongpaichit. 2005. *A History of Thailand*. Cambridge: Cambridge University Press.

Baker, Chris and Pasuk Phongpaichit. 2009. *Thaksin*. Chiang Mai: Silkworm Books.

Baker, Chris and Pasuk Phongpaichit, trans. and eds. 2010. *The Tale of Khun Chang Khun Phaen: Siam's folk epic of love, war, and tragedy*. Chiang Mai: Silkworm Books.

Baker, Chris and Pasuk Phongpaichit. 2013. 'Protection and power in Siam: From *Khun Chang Khun Phaen* to the Buddha amulet', *Southeast Asian Studies* 2(2)(August): 215–42.

Baker, Chris and Pasuk Phongpaichit. 2017. *A History of Ayutthaya: Siam in the early modern world*. Cambridge: Cambridge University Press. doi.org/10.1017/9781108120197.

Baker, Chris and Pasuk Phongpaichit. 2018. '*Yuan Phai*: The mysteries of a 15th century military epic', in *The Renaissance Princess Lectures: In Honour of Her Royal Highness Princess Maha Chakri Sirindhorn on her fifth cycle anniversary*, pp. 133–51. Bangkok: The Siam Society.

Ball, Desmond. 2013. *Tor Chor Dor: Thailand's border patrol police. Volume 1: History, organisation, equipment, and personnel*. Bangkok: White Lotus.

Battye, Noel Alfred. 1974. The military, government and society in Siam, 1868–1910: Politics and military reform during the reign of King Chulalongkorn. PhD thesis, Cornell University, Ithaca, NY.

Benavides, Gustavo. 2006. 'Magic', in Robert A. Segal (ed.), *Blackwell Companion to the Study of Religion*, pp. 295–308. Oxford: Blackwell Publishing.

Bloembergen, Marieke. 2011. 'The perfect policeman: Colonial policing, modernity, and conscience on Sumatra's west coast in the early 1930s', *Indonesia* 91(April): 165–91. doi.org/10.5728/indonesia.91.0165.

Bradley, Dan Beach. 1971 [1873]. *Dictionary of the Siamese Language*. Reprint. Bangkok: Khurusaphalatphrao.

Bradley, Francis. 2013. 'Siam's conquest of Patani and the end of *mandala* relations, 1786–1838', in Patrick Jory (ed.), *Ghosts of the Past in Southern Thailand: Essays on the history and historiography of Patani*, pp. 149–60. Singapore, NUS Press. doi.org/10.2307/j.ctv1qv31q.13.

Brawn, Kelly Meister. 2018. The networks of a Thai Buddhist monastery: Communities, material culture, and contemporary practice at Wat Phra Mahathat Woramahawian, Nakhon Si Thammarat, Thailand. PhD dissertation, Divinity School, University of Chicago, Chicago.

Broadhurst, Roderic, Thierry Bouhours and Brigitte Bouhours. 2015. *Violence and the Civilizing Process in Cambodia*. Cambridge: Cambridge University Press. doi.org/10.1017/CBO9781316271339.

Brummelhuis, Han ten. 1987. *Merchant, Courtier and Diplomat: A history of the contacts between the Netherlands and Thailand*. Lochem: Uitgeversmaatschappij De Tijdstroom BV.

Bunnag, Tej. 1977. *The Provincial Administration of Siam, 1892–1915*. Kuala Lumpur: Oxford University Press.

Buranasinlapa Adunladecharat. 1970. *Anuson nai ngan phraratchakan phloengsop phon tamruat ek adun adunladetcharat* [*Cremation Volume for Police General Adun Adunladetcharat*]. Bangkok: Buranasinlapa Adunladetcharat.

Candier, Aurore. 2011. 'Conjuncture and reform in the late Konbaung period: How prophecies, omens and rumors motivated political action from 1866 to 1869', *Journal of Burma Studies* 15(2)(December): 231–62. doi.org/10.1353/jbs.2011.0008.

Chaidiaw Phatthanasuwan and Chaiya Phatthanasuwan. 1998. *Phra kamlang phaendin* [*Might of the Kingdom Amulet*]. Bangkok: Amarin Printing.

Chaiyan Rajchagool. 1994. *The Rise and Fall of the Thai Absolute Monarchy: Foundations of the modern Thai state from feudalism to peripheral capitalism*. Bangkok: White Lotus.

Chaiyaphong Chiwachoen. 2007. *Jatukham-Ramathep patihan haeng barami su prakottakan sattha jak mahachon* [*Jatukham-Ramathep: The miracles of its charismatic powers affirm people's beliefs in it*]. Nonthaburi: Thiwlip Press.

Chaiyawut Piyakun. 1996. *Khati khamchuea lae phithikam thang saiyasat khong wat khao or amphoe khuankhanun jangwat phatthalung* [*The magical beliefs and practices of Wat Khao Or, Khuankhanun District, Phatthalung*]. Research Paper, mimeograph. Songkhla: Southern Studies Institute, Thaksin University.

Chaiyong Patiphimphakhom, comp. 1980. *Athibodi tamruat samai nueng* [*A Police Chief Once-Upon-A-Time*]. Bangkok: Phrae Phitthaya.

Chali Naparasmi. 2007. *Rueang khao or: Mahawitthayalai phram haeng suwannaphum* [*On Khao Or: Suwannaphum's Brahmanic university*]. Academic Paper No. 446, [Photocopy of typescript], Chawang, Nakhon Si Thammarat.

Chalong Jeyakhom. 2007. *Phon to to khun phantharakratchadet* [*Police Major General Khun Phantharakratchadet*]. Kanchanaburi: Rom Fa Sayam.

Chalong Soontravanich. 2005. 'Small arms, romance, and crime and violence in post–WWII Thai society', *Tonan Ajia Kenkyu* [*Southeast Asian Studies*] 43(1) (June): 26–46.

Chalong Soontravanich. 2013. 'The regionalization of local Buddhist saints: Amulets, crime and violence in post–World War II Thai society', *Sojourn* 28(2)(July): 179–215. doi.org/10.1355/sj28-2a.

Chandler, David P. 2008. *A History of Cambodia*. 4th edn. Boulder, CO: Westview Press.

Chanida Chitbundid. 2007. *Khrongkan an nueang ma jak phraratchadamri: Kansathapana phraratchamnat nam nai phrabat somdet phrachao yu hua* [*Royal Projects: The making of King Bhumibol's royal hegemony*]. Bangkok: The Foundation for the Promotion of the Social Sciences and Humanities Textbooks Project, Thammasat University.

Chanthip Phantharakratchadet. 2007. 'Wicha khong khun phan [Khun Phan's knowledge]', in Chintapati Thapthimthong, *Anuson nai ngan phraratchathan phloeng sop phon tamruat tri khun phantharakratchadet to mo tho cho na men chuakhrao wat mahathatworawian nakhon si thammarat wanpharuehatsabodi thi 22 kumphaphan* [*Celebration of the Royal Cremation of Police Major General Khun Phantharakratchadet at the Temporary Meru at Wat Mahathat Nakhon Si Thammarat on 22 February*], pp. 133–6. Nakhon Si Thammarat: Chintapati Thapthimthong.

Charan Chanthalakhana and Pakapun Skunman, eds. 2000. *Wua chon kap khon tai* [*Bull Fighting and Southern People*]. Bangkok: Buffalo and Beef Production Research and Development Centre, Suwanvajokkasikij Animal Research and Development Institute, Kasetsart University.

Charnvit Kasetsiri. 2015. *Studies in Thai and Southeast Asian History*. Bangkok: The Foundation for the Promotion of Social Science and Humanities Textbooks Project and Toyota Thailand Foundation.

Chatthip Nartsupha. 1999. *The Thai Village Economy in the Past*. Chris Baker and Pasuk Phongpaichit (trans.). Chiang Mai: Silkworm Books.

Chatthip Nartsupha and Phunsak Chanikornpradit. 1997. *Setthakit muban phaktai fang tawanok nai adit* [*The Southern Thai Village Economy on the East Coast in the Past*]. Bangkok: Sangsan Publications.

Cheesman, Nicholas. 2015. *Opposing the Rule of Law: How Myanmar's courts make law and order*. Cambridge: Cambridge University Press. doi.org/10.1017/ CBO9781316014936.

Che Man, W.K. 1990. *Muslim Separatism: The Moros of southern Philippines and the Malays of southern Thailand*. Singapore: Oxford University Press.

Chintapati Thapthimthong. 2007. *Anuson nai ngan phraratchathan phloeng sop phon tamruat tri khun phantharakratchadet to mo tho cho na men chuakhrao wat mahathatworawian nakhon si thammarat wanpharuehatsabodi thi 22 kumphaphan* [*Celebration of the Royal Cremation of Police Major General Khun Phantharakratchadet at the Temporary Meru at Wat Mahathat Nakhon Si Thammarat on 22 February*]. Nakhon Si Thammarat: Chintapati Thapthimthong.

Chit Wiphasatthawat. 1960. *Phao saraphap burut lek haeng esia* [*Phao, the Iron Man of Asia Tells All*]. Bangkok: Phrae Phitthaya.

Cholthira Satyawadhna. 2013. 'Nora: A living cultural survival of southern Thailand', in Pasuk Phongpaichit and Chris Baker (eds), *Essays on Thailand's Economy and Society for Professor Chatthip Nartsupha at 72*, pp. 23–50. Bangkok: Sangsan Press.

Clark, Colin W. 1990. 'Uncertainty in economics', in Elizabeth Cashdan (ed.), *Risk and Uncertainty in Tribal and Peasant Economics*, pp. 47–64. Boulder, CO: Westview Press.

Clayton, Anthony and David Killingray. 1989. *Khaki and Blue: Military and police in British colonial Africa*. Monographs in International Studies, Africa Series Number 51. Athens, OH: Center for International Studies, Ohio University.

Cohen, Erik. 2012. 'Contesting discourses of blood in the "Red Shirts" protests in Bangkok', *Journal of Southeast Asian Studies* 43(2)(June): 216–33. doi.org/ 10.1017/S0022463412000033.

Collins, Steven. 2014. 'Postscript: What kind of Buddhism is that?', in Bénédicte Brac de la Perrière, Guillaume Rozenberg and Alicia Turner (eds), *Champions of Buddhism: Weikza cults in contemporary Burma*, pp. 216–27. Singapore: NUS Press. doi.org/10.2307/j.ctv1qv364.16.

Cook, Nerida. 2002. 'Thai identity in the astrological tradition', in Craig J. Reynolds (ed.), *National Identity and its Defenders: Thailand today*, pp. 189–211. Chiang Mai: Silkworm Books.

Corfield, Justin, ed. 1993. *Rama III and the Siamese Expedition to Kedah in 1839: The dispatches of Luang Udomsombat*. Cyril Skinner (trans.). Melbourne: Centre of Southeast Asian Studies, Monash University.

Crawfurd, John. 1967 [1820]. *Journal of an Embassy from the Governor-General of India to the Courts of Siam and Cochin China*. Oxford in Asia Historical Reprints. Kuala Lumpur. Oxford University Press.

Crosby, Kate. 2000. 'Tantric Theravada: A bibliographic essay on the writings of Francois Bizot and others on the Yogavacara tradition', *Contemporary Buddhism* 1(2): 141–98. doi.org/10.1080/14639940008573729.

Crosby, Kate. 2014. 'Preface', in Bénédicte Brac de la Perrière, Guillaume Rozenberg and Alicia Turner (eds), *Champions of Buddhism: Weikza cults in contemporary Burma*, pp. xxi–xxvii. Singapore: NUS Press.

Cushman, Jennifer. 1991. *Family and State: The formation of a Sino-Thai tin-mining dynasty, 1797–1932*. Craig J. Reynolds (ed.). Singapore: Oxford University Press.

Daeng Kaosaen. 2006. *Lek lai mi jing [Fluid Iron Exists!]*. Nonthaburi: Butsarakham Publishing.

Damrong Rajanubhab. 1963. *Nithan borannakhadi [Tales of Old. Part 11]*. Bangkok: Bannakit.

Davids, T.W. Rhys and William Stede. 1966. *The Pali Text Society's Pali–English Dictionary*. London: Luzac & Company.

Davisakd Puaksom. 2007. *Kanphaet samai mai nai sangkhom thai chuea rok rangkai lae rat wetchakam [Modern Medicine in Thai Society: Germs, the body, and the medicalised state]*. Bangkok: Chulalongkorn University Press.

Davisakd Puaksom. 2008. 'Of a lesser brilliance: Patani historiography in contention', in Michael J. Montesano and Patrick Jory (eds), *Thai South and Malay North: Ethnic interactions on a plural peninsula*, pp. 71–88. Singapore: NUS Press.

de la Perrière, Bénédicte Brac, Guillaume Rozenberg and Alicia Turner, eds. 2014. *Champions of Buddhism: Weikza cults in contemporary Burma*. Singapore: NUS Press. doi.org/10.2307/j.ctv1qv364.

Denning, Greg. 1998. 'Past imperfect', *The Australian Review of Books* 3(3) (April): 4–5.

Dixon, Chris and Michael J.G. Parnwell. 1991. 'Thailand: The legacy of non-colonial development in South-East Asia', in Chris Dixon and Michael J. Heffernan (eds), *Colonialism and Development in the Contemporary World*, pp. 204–25. London: Mansell Publishing Limited.

Donner, Wolf. 1978. *The Five Faces of Thailand: An economic geography*. Brisbane: University of Queensland Press.

Ek Angsanan, comp. 2010. *Phra tamruat sang* [*Buddha Images Created by Police*]. Bangkok: Matichon.

Exell, F.K. 1963. *Siamese Tapestry*. London: The Travel Book Club.

Farrelly, Nicholas, Craig J. Reynolds and Andrew Walker. 2011. 'Practical and auspicious: Thai handbook knowledge for agriculture and the environment', *Asian Studies Review* 35(June): 244–6.

Gaston-Aubert, Jean-Pierre. 2010. 'Naga-Buddha images of the Dvaravati period: A possible link between Dvaravati and Angkor', *Journal of the Siam Society* 98: 116–50.

Gesick, Lorraine. 1995. *In the Land of Lady White Blood: Southern Thailand and the meaning of history*. Ithaca, NY: Southeast Asia Program, Cornell University.

Gilmore, David D. 1990. *Manhood in the Making: Cultural concepts of masculinity*. New Haven, CT: Yale University Press.

Ginzburg, Carlo. 1989. 'Clues: Roots of an evidential paradigm', in Carlo Ginzburg, *Clues, Myths, and the Historical Method*, John and Anne C. Tedeschi (trans.), pp. 96–125. Baltimore: The Johns Hopkins University Press.

Gobbett, D.J and C.S. Hutchison. 1973. *Geology of the Malay Peninsula, West Malaysia and Singapore*. New York: Wiley Interscience.

Gramsci, Antonio. 1983 [1971]. *Selections from the Prison Notebooks of Antonio Gramsci*. Quinten Hoare and Geoffrey Nowell Smith (eds and trans.). 7th edn. New York: International Publishers.

Griffiths, Percival. 1971. *To Guard My People: The history of the Indian police*. London: Ernest Benn Limited.

Gupta, Avijit. 2005. *The Physical Geography of Southeast Asia*. Oxford: Oxford University Press.

Guy, John. 2011. 'Tamil merchants and the Hindu-Buddhist diaspora in early Southeast Asia', in Pierre-Ives Manguin, A. Mani and Geoff Wade (eds), *Early Interactions between South and Southeast Asia: Reflections on cross-cultural exchange*, pp. 243–62. Singapore: Institute of Southeast Asian Studies. doi.org/10.1355/9789814311175-014.

Guy, John, ed. 2014. *Lost Kingdoms: Hindu–Buddhist sculpture of early Southeast Asia*. New York and Bangkok: The Metropolitan Museum of Art and River Books.

Haanstead, Eric James. 2008. Constructing order through chaos: A state ethnography of the Thai police. PhD dissertation, University of Wisconsin-Madison, Madison.

Haberkorn, Tyrell. 2013. 'Getting away with murder in Thailand: State violence and impunity in Phatthalung', in N. Ganesan and Sung Chull Kim (eds), *State Violence in East Asia*, pp. 185–208. Lexington, KY: University Press of Kentucky.

Haberkorn, Tyrell. 2018. *In Plain Sight: Impunity and human rights in Thailand*. Madison: University of Wisconsin Press.

Haiman, John. 2011. *Cambodian Khmer*. Amsterdam: John Benjamin's Publishing Company.

Hallisey, Charles. 1995. 'Auspicious things', in Donald S. Lopez (ed.), *Buddhism in Practice*, pp. 412–26. Princeton, NJ: Princeton University Press.

Handley, Paul. 2006. *The King Never Smiles*. New Haven, CT: Yale University Press.

Hewison, Kevin and Maniemai Thongyu. 2000. 'Developing provincial capitalism: A profile of the economic and political roles of a new generation in Khon Kaen, Thailand', in Ruth McVey (ed.), *Money and Power in Provincial Thailand*. Copenhagen and Singapore: Nordic Institute of Asian Studies and Institute of Southeast Asian Studies.

Holt, John Clifford. 1991. *Buddha in the Crown: Avalokitesvara in the Buddhist traditions of Sri Lanka*. New York: Oxford University Press.

Hong Lysa. 2003. 'Extraterritoriality in Bangkok in the reign of King Chulalongkorn, 1868–1910: The cacophonies of semi-colonial cosmopolitanism', *Itinerario* 27(2): 125–43. doi.org/10.1017/S0165115300020568.

Hong Lysa. 2007. 'Subject Siam: Family, law, and colonial modernity in Thailand by Tamara Loos', *Journal of Southeast Asian Studies* 38(1): 188–9. doi.org/10.1017/S0022463406330998.

Iijima, Akiko. 2008. 'The "international court system" in the colonial history of Siam', *Taiwan Journal of Southeast Asian Studies* 5(1): 31–64.

Ileto, Reynaldo C. 1999. 'Religion and anticolonial movements', in Nicholas Tarling (ed.), *The Cambridge History of Southeast Asia. Volume 2. Part 1*, pp. 193–244. Cambridge: Cambridge University Press.

Ivarsson, Soren. 2016. 'La gendarmerie royale du Siam et ses officiers Danois, instruments du contrôle d'un territoire et de ses habitants, 1897–1926 [The Royal Siam Gendarmerie and its Danish officers: Instruments of the control of a territory and its inhabitants, 1897–1926]', in Arnaud-Dominique Houte and Jean-Noel Luc (eds), *Les gendarmeries dans le monde* [*The Gendarmeries in the World*]. Paris: Presses de l'Université Paris-Sorbonne.

Jackson, Peter A. 1999. 'Royal spirits, Chinese gods, and magic monks: Thailand's boom-time religions of prosperity', *South East Asia Research* 7(3): 245–320. doi.org/10.1177/0967828X9900700302.

Jackson, Peter A. 2010. 'Virtual divinity: A 21st-century discourse of the Thai royal influence', in Søren Ivarsson and Lotte Isager (eds), *Saying the Unsayable: Monarchy and democracy in Thailand*, pp. 29–60. Copenhagen: NIAS Press.

Jaturawit. 2008. *Patihan khruang rang tang daen* [*Miraculous Talismans of Foreign Lands*]. Bangkok: Biphlat Phaplitching.

Jauregui, Beatrice. 2016. *Provisional Authority: Police, order, and security in India*. Chicago: University of Chicago Press. doi.org/10.7208/chicago/9780226403847.001.0001.

Jenner, Philip N. 2009. *A Dictionary of Angkorean Khmer*. Canberra: Research School of Pacific and Asian Studies, The Australian National University.

Johnston, David B. 1980. 'Bandit, *nakleng*, and peasant in rural Thai society', in Constance M. Wilson and Richard W. Smith (eds), *Contributions to Asian Studies. Volume 15. Royalty and Commoners: Essays in Thai administrative, economic, and social history*, pp. 90–101. Leiden: E.J. Brill.

Jory, Patrick. 2011. 'Thai historical writing', in Axel Schneider and D.R. Woolf (eds), *The Oxford History of Historical Writing. Volume 5: Historical writing since 1945*, pp. 539–58. Oxford: Oxford University Press.

Jory, Patrick, ed. 2013. *Ghosts of the Past in Southern Thailand: Essays on the history and historiography of Patani*. Singapore: NUS Press. doi.org/10.2307/j.ctv1qv31q.

Jory, Patrick. 2015. 'Republicanism in Thai history', in Maurizio Peleggi (ed.), *A Sarong for Clio: Essays on the intellectual and cultural history of Thailand*, pp. 97–117. Ithaca, NY: Southeast Asia Program, Cornell University. doi.org/10.7591/9781501725937-007.

Jory, Patrick. 2016. *Thailand's Theory of Monarchy: The Vessantara Jataka and the idea of the perfect man*. Albany, NY: State University of New York Press.

Kadir Che Man, Wan. 1990. *Muslim Separatism: The Moros of southern Philippines and the Malays of southern Thailand*. Singapore: Oxford University Press.

Kamala Tiyavanich. 1997. *Forest Recollections: Wandering monks in twentieth-century Thailand*. Honolulu: University of Hawai`i Press.

Kantorowicz, Ernst H. 1970. *The King's Two Bodies: A study in mediaeval political theology*. 3rd edn. Princeton, NJ: Princeton University Press.

Kapferer, Bruce. 2002. 'Introduction: Outside all reason—Magic sorcery and epistemology in anthropology', *Social Analysis* 46(3)(Fall): 1–30. doi.org/10.3167/015597702782409310.

Kasem Jandam. 2008. *Prawattisat thongthin nakhon sithammarat [A Local History of Nakhon Si Thammarat]*. Nakhon Si Thammarat: Nakhon Si Thammarat Provincial Administration.

Katz, Brigit. 2018. 'Thailand drops charges against historian who questioned the facts around historic 16th-century duel', *Smithsonian.com*, 19 January. Available from: www.smithsonianmag.com/smart-news/thailand-drops-charges-against-historian-facts-duel-180967881/.

Kaufman, Scott. 2013. *Project Plowshare: The peaceful use of nuclear explosives in Cold War America*. Ithaca, NY: Cornell University Press. doi.org/10.7591/cornell/9780801451256.001.0001.

Kessler, Clive S. 1977. 'Conflict and sovereignty in Kelantanese Malay spirit seances', in Vincent Crapanzano and Vivian Garrison (eds), *Case Studies in Spirit Possession*, pp. 295–331. New York: John Wiley & Sons.

Kheng, Cheah Boon. 1988. *The Peasant Robbers of Kedah, 1900–1929: Historical and folk perceptions*. Singapore: Oxford University Press.

Khrongkan Chapho Kit Phu Banthat. 2001. *Bon senthang phu banthat tamnan kan tor su duai kamlang awut khong prachachon phatthalung trang satun* [*On Phu Banthat Way: A history of the armed struggle of the Phatthalung, Trang and Satun peoples*]. Bangkok: Khrongkan Chapho Kit Phu Banthat.

Khunjomphonlan, nai roi tamruat tri, comp. 1922–24. *Samut khamsang tamruat nakhonban* [*Metropolitan Police Field Manual*]. Bangkok: Thai News Press.

Kiernan, Kevin. 1988. 'Mangroves, mountains and munching molluscs: The evolution of a tropical coastline', *Helictite* 26(1): 16–31.

Klam Kriangkrai. 2008. *Mettamahaniyom* [*Powerful Attractions and Charms*]. Bangkok: Phuan Chaoban.

Kobkua Suwannathat-Pian. 1988. *Thai–Malay Relations: Traditional intra-regional relations from the seventeenth to the early twentieth centuries*. Singapore: Oxford University Press.

Kobkua Suwannathat-Pian. 2013. 'Historical identity, nation, and history-writing: The Malay Muslims of southern Thailand, 1940s–1980s', in Patrick Jory (ed.), *Ghosts of the Past in Southern Thailand: Essays on the history and historiography of Patani*, pp. 228–54. Singapore: NUS Press. doi.org/10.2307/j.ctv1qv31q.16.

Kong Bannathikan. 1997. 'Buk tham suea poet tamnan jon thai [Entering the tigers' cave to reveal Thai bandit history]', *Sinlapa Watthanatham* [*Art & Culture*] 18(7)(May): 83–7.

Kong Bannathikan Khaosot. 2007. *Cho chatukham-khun phan chatuphon chatuphithi thang chatuthit* [*Going Deep into the Chatukham and Khun Phan: Four boons and four rites for the four quarters*]. 3rd edn. Bangkok: Matichon.

Krom Sinlapakorn. 2002. 'Phongsawadan mueang phatthalung [The Phatthalung chronicle]', in *Prachum phongsadan chabap kanchanaphisek* [*Collected Chronicles Golden Anniversary Edition*], pp. 217–55. Bangkok: Literature and History Division, Department of Fine Arts.

Krom Sinlapakorn. 2006. *Boran watthu nai phiphitthaphansathan haengchat songkhla* [*Ancient Artefacts from the National Museum in Songkhla*]. Bangkok: Department of Fine Arts, Ministry of Culture.

Lim, Samson. 2012. 'Detective fiction, the police and secrecy in early twentieth-century Siam', *South East Asia Research* 20(1)(March): 83–102. doi.org/10.5367/sear.2012.0089.

Lim, Samson. 2016. *Siam's New Detectives: Visualizing crime and conspiracy in modern Thailand.* Honolulu: University of Hawai'i Press. doi.org/10.21313/hawaii/9780824855253.001.0001.

Little, Stephen. 1999. *Spirit Stones of China.* Chicago: The Art Institute of Chicago and University of California Press.

Lom Phengkeo. 1994. 'Chum jon dawnsai rung dawnsai lae dam huaphrae [The Dawn Sai outlaw gang: Rung Dawnsai and Dam Huaphrae]', *Warasan thaksin khadi* 4(1)(June–September): 40–53.

Loos, Tamara. 2006. *Subject Siam: Family, law, and colonial modernity in Thailand.* Ithaca, NY: Cornell University Press.

Low, James. 2007. *Low's Mission to Southern Siam 1824.* Anthony Ferguson (ed.). Bangkok: White Lotus.

McCargo, Duncan. 2005. 'Network monarchy and legitimacy crises in Thailand', *The Pacific Review* 18(4)(December): 499–519. doi.org/10.1080/09512740500338937.

McCargo, Duncan. 2009. *Tearing Apart the Land: Islam and legitimacy in southern Thailand.* Singapore: NUS Press.

McCoy, Alfred W., Cathleen B. Read and Leonard P. Adams II. 1972. *The Politics of Heroin in Southeast Asia.* New York: Harper & Row.

McDaniel, Justin Thomas. 2004. 'Paritta and Raksa texts', in Robert E. Buswell (ed.), *Encyclopedia of Buddhism. Volume 2*, pp. 634–5. New York: Macmillan Reference.

McDaniel, Justin Thomas. 2008. *Gathering Leaves and Lifting Words: Histories of Buddhist monastic education in Laos and Thailand.* Seattle: University of Washington Press.

McDaniel, Justin Thomas. 2011. *The Lovelorn Ghost and the Magical Monk: Practicing Buddhism in modern Thailand.* New York: Columbia University Press. doi.org/10.7312/mcda15376.

McDaniel, Justin Thomas. 2013. 'This Hindu holy man is a Thai Buddhist', *South East Asia Research* 21(2): 191–209. doi.org/10.5367/sear.2013.0151.

MacDonald, Alexander. 1949. *Bangkok Editor.* New York: Macmillan.

McVey, Ruth, ed. 2000. *Money and Power in Provincial Thailand.* Copenhagen and Singapore: Nordic Institute of Asian Studies and Institute of Southeast Asian Studies.

Maier, Hendrik M.J. 1988. *In the Center of Authority: The Malay hikayat merong mahawangsa*. Ithaca, NY: Southeast Asia Program, Cornell University.

Malinowski, Bronislaw. 1974 [1948]. *Magic, Science and Religion and Other Essays*. Reprint. London: Souvenir Press.

Mana Khunweechuay. 2003. Chum jon haeng lum nam thalesap songkhla phor sor 2437-2465 [Bandit gangs of the Songkhla lakes basin]. MA thesis, Department of History, Silpakorn University, Thailand.

Mana Khunweechuay. 2017. 'Sangkhom lum thalesap songkhla nai phawa rai khue pae phap sathon jak raingan phra saritphotjanakon ro so 113 [Lawless social conditions in the Songkhla lakes basin as depicted in the 1895 report of Phra Saritphotjanakon]', in Walailak University, *Khatthakam atchyakam lae phawa nok kotmai nai phak tai khong thai Ekkasan prakop prachum wichakan radap chat khrueakhai prawattisat manutwitthaya lae sangkhom witthaya phak tai khrang thi 3 [Murder, Crime, and Lawlessness in Southern Thailand: Proceedings, Third National Academic Conference, History, Humanities, and Social Sciences Network]*, pp. 38–56. Nakhon Si Thammarat: Walailak University.

Manat Ophakun. 1997. 'Suphanburi pen mueang jon mueang khon du jing rue? [Is Suphanburi really an outlaw town, a town of fierce people?]', *Sinlapa Watthanatham [Art & Culture]* 18(7)(May): 90–101.

Manguin, Pierre-Ives. 2014. 'Early coastal states of Southeast Asia: Funan and Srivijaya', in John Guy (ed.), *Lost Kingdoms: Hindu–Buddhist sculpture of early Southeast Asia*, pp. 114–15. New York and Bangkok: The Metropolitan Museum of Art and River Books.

Mansurnoor, Iik Arifin. 2013. 'Locating traditional, Islamic, and modern historiography in Patani-Jawi identity', in Patrick Jory (ed.), *Ghosts of the Past in Southern Thailand: Essays on the history and historiography of Patani*, pp. 255–76. Singapore: NUS Press. doi.org/10.2307/j.ctv1qv31q.17.

Matichon. 2014a. 'Buk tham suea nai tamnan [Entering the legendary bandit caves]', *Matichon*, 21 November.

Matichon. 2014b. 'Luang Pho Suea Dam', *Matichon*, 30 November: 13–14.

Matichon. 2015. 'Tamnan suea bai robin hut lum jaophraya [The legend of Suea Bai, the Robin Hood of the Chaophraya basin]', *Matichon*, 26 May.

Mauss, Marcel. 2010 [1972]. *A General Theory of Magic*. Robert Brain (trans.). Reprint. London: Routledge.

Monruethai Chaiwiset. 2002. *Prawattisat sangkhom waduai suam lae khruangsukkhaphan nai prathet thai* [*A Social History of Toilets and Sanitary Ware in Thailand, 1897–1997*]. Bangkok: Sinlapa Watthanatham.

Montesano, Michael J. and Patrick Jory, eds. 2008. *Thai South and Malay North: Ethnic interactions on a plural peninsula*. Singapore: NUS Press.

Morrell, David and Chai-anan Samudavanija. 1981. *Political Conflict in Thailand: Reform, reaction, revolution*. Cambridge, MA: Oelgeschlager, Gunn & Hain.

Mulholland, Jean. 1987. *Medicine, Magic and Evil Spirits*. Canberra: Faculty of Asian Studies, The Australian National University.

Munro-Hay, Stuart. 2001. *Nakhon Sri Thammarat: The archeology, history and legends of a southern Thai town*. Bangkok: White Lotus.

Mus, Paul. 2011. *India Seen from the East: Indian and indigenous cults in Champa*. I.W. Mabbett (trans.). I.W. Mabbett and D.P. Chandler (eds). Melbourne: Monash University Press.

Nan Tapi [pseud.]. 2007. *Rajan haeng thale tai Jatukham-Ramathep* [*Monarch of the Southern Seas*]. Bangkok: Komen-ek Publishing Nan Tapi.

Nandana Chutiwongs. 2002. *The Iconography of Avalokitesvara in Mainland South East Asia*. New Delhi: Indira Gandhi National Centre for the Arts and Aryan Books International.

Natthaphon Yurungrueangsak. 2012. *Prawattisat phan phra khrueang khati khwamchuea lae phutthaphaanit* [*History through Buddhist Amulets: Beliefs and commercial Buddhism*]. Bangkok: Silpakorn University, Sanam Jan Palace.

Nawamin [pseud]. 2007. *Patihan ong Jatukham-Ramathep* [*Miracles of the Jatukham-Ramathep Deity*]. Bangkok: My Bangkok Publishing House.

Nidhi Eoseewong. 1995. *Chat thai mueang thai baeprian lae anusawari* [*The Thai Nation, the Thai Lands: Textbooks and monuments*]. Bangkok: Matichon.

Nidhi Eoseewong. 2005. *Pen and Sail: Literature and history in early Bangkok*. Chris Baker and Ben Anderson (eds). Chiang Mai: Silkworm Books.

Nidhi Eoseewong. 2012. 'The culture of the army', in Michael J. Montesano, Pavin Chachavalpongpun and Aekapol Chongvilaivan (eds), *Bangkok May 2010: Perspectives on a divided Thailand*, pp. 10–14. Singapore: Institute of Southeast Asian Studies. doi.org/10.1355/9789814345347-003.

Nishizaki, Yoshinori. 2011. *Political Authority and Provincial Identity in Thailand: The making of Banharn-buri*. Ithaca, NY: Southeast Asia Program, Cornell University.

Nop Thaphrajan. 2002. *Phraratchasattha* [*The King's Religious Convictions*]. Bangkok: Nopphawan Press.

Nordholt, Henk Schulte and Margreet van Till. 1991. 'The jago in the shadow: Crime and "order" in the colonial state in Java', *Review of Indonesian and Malaysian Affairs* 25(1)(Winter): 74–91.

Nordholt, Henk Schulte and Margreet van Till. 1999. 'Colonial criminals in Java, 1870–1910', in Vincente L. Rafael (ed.), *Figures of Criminality in Indonesia, the Philippines, and Colonial Vietnam*, pp. 47–69. Ithaca, NY: Southeast Asia Program, Cornell University. doi.org/10.7591/9781501718878-004.

Nostitz, Nick. 2010. 'Bangkok or bust, part I', *New Mandala*, 25 March. Available from: www.newmandala.org/bangkok-or-bust-part-1/.

Ockey, James. 2000. 'The rise of local power in Thailand: Provincial crime, elections and the bureaucracy', in Ruth McVey (ed.), *Money and Power in Provincial Thailand*. Copenhagen and Singapore: Nordic Institute of Asian Studies and Institute of Southeast Asian Studies.

Ockey, James. 2004. *Making Democracy: Leadership, class, gender, and political participation in Thailand*. Honolulu: University of Hawai`i Press.

Ockey, James. 2008. 'Elections and political integration in the lower south of Thailand', in Michael J. Montesano and Patrick Jory (eds), *Thai South and Malay North: Ethnic interactions on a plural peninsula*, pp. 124–54. Singapore: NUS Press.

O'Connor, Stanley J. 1972. *Hindu Gods of Peninsular Siam*. Ascona, Switzerland: Artibus Asiae Publishers. doi.org/10.2307/1522663.

O'Connor, Stanley J. 1985. 'Metallurgy and immortality at Candi Sukuh, central Java', *Indonesia* 39(April): 53–70. doi.org/10.2307/3350986.

O'Connor, Stanley J. 1986a. 'An early Brahmanical sculpture at Songkhla', in *The Archaeology of Peninsular Siam*, pp. 104–10. Bangkok: Siam Society.

O'Connor, Stanley J. 1986b. 'Some early Siva lingas in Nakhon Si Thammarat', in *The Archaeology of Peninsular Siam*, pp. 159–63. Bangkok: Siam Society.

O'Connor, Stanley J. 1986c. 'Tambralinga and the Khmer empire', in *The Archaeology of Peninsular Siam*, pp. 135–49. Bangkok: Siam Society.

Okha Buri [Supharuek Khachonklin]. 2007. *Thot rahat khun phantharakratchadet mue prap khamang wet* [*Unlocking the Secrets of Khun Phantarakratchadet: The lawman with the Vedic magic*]. Bangkok: Utthayan Khwamru.

Ortiz, Sutti. 1980. 'Forecasts, decisions, and the farmer's response to uncertain environments', in Peggy F. Barlett (ed.), *Agricultural Decision Making: Anthropological contributions to rural development*, pp. 172–202. London: Academic Press. doi.org/10.1016/B978-0-12-078882-8.50013-1.

Pallegoix, Jean Baptiste. 1972. *Dictionarium linguae thai sive siamensis interpretatione latina, gallica et anglica illustratum*. Reprint. Farnborough, UK: Gregg International.

Pasuk Phongpaichit and Chris Baker, eds. 2009. *Thaksin*. Rev. edn. Chiang Mai: Silkworm Books.

Pasuk Phongpaichit and Chris Baker, eds. 2013. *Essays on Thailand's Economy and Society for Professor Chatthip Nartsupha at 72*. Bangkok: Sangsan Press.

Patravadi Phuchadaphirom. 2006. *Watthanatham banthoeng nai chat thai kanplianplaeng khong watthanatham khwambanthoeng nai sangkhom krungthep pho so 2491-2500 1948* [*Entertainment Culture of Thai People: Change in entertainment culture in Bangkok society, 1948 to 1957*]. Bangkok: Matichon.

Pattana Kitiarsa. 2008. 'Buddha Phanit: Thailand's prosperity, religion and its commodifying tactics', in Pattana Kitiarsa (ed.), *Religious Commodifications in Asia: Marketing gods*. London: Routledge. doi.org/10.4324/9780203937877.

Pattana Kitiarsa. 2012. *Mediums, Monks, and Amulets: Thai popular Buddhism today*. Chiang Mai: Silkworm Books.

Pattaratorn Chirapravati. 1997. *Votive Tablets in Thailand: Origin, styles, and uses*. Kuala Lumpur: Oxford University Press.

Patthamakon Bunlasathaphon. 1996. Khwamru nai tamra phrommachat [Knowledge in Brahmanical manuals]. MA thesis, Department of History, Chiang Mai University, Chiang Mai.

Peerasak Chaidaisuk. 2008. *Chatsuea wai lai* [*A Tiger Never Changes its Stripes*]. Bangkok: Matichon.

Peleggi, Maurizio. 2013. 'From Buddhist icons to national antiquities: Cultural nationalism and colonial knowledge in the making of Thailand's history of art', *Modern Asian Studies* 47(5): 1520–48. doi.org/10.1017/S0026749X12000224.

Peleggi, Maurizio. 2017. *Monastery, Monument, Museum: Sites and artifacts of Thai cultural memory*. Honolulu: University of Hawai`i Press. doi.org/10.21313/hawaii/9780824866068.001.0001.

Phanida Sanguansriwanit. 1997. '"Jon" nai ngan wannakam ["Outlaws" in literary art]', *Sinlapa Watthanatham* [*Art & Culture*] 18(7)(May): 110–12.

Phantharakratchadet, Khun. 2007. 'Khwamchuea thang saiyasat khong chao paktai [Saiyasat beliefs of the southern Thai people], *Suwitcha* [10 September 1976]', in Samphan Kongsamut, *Pho lo to khun phantharakratchadet: Sing moe prap sip thit* [*Police Major General Khun Phantarakratchadet: The lion-lawman of the ten directions*], pp. 469–92. Bangkok: Wasi Khri-echan.

Phantharakratchadet, Khun. n.d. Prawat phiphroi phantharak [The life of 'elder sister' Phroi Phantharak]. Photocopy of typescript, 30 pp.

Phatthamakon Bunlasathaphon. 1996. Khwam ru nai tamra phrommachat [Knowledge in Brahmanical manuals]. MA thesis, Department of History, Chiang Mai University, Chiang Mai.

Phinit Intharathut. 1976. 'Nithan tamruat ton thi 1 nithan tamruat ton thi 2 [Police tales: Parts 1 and 2]', in Prayut Sitthiphan (comp.), *Phramahakasat kap prawatisat tamruat sayam* [*Kings and History of the Police*]. Rungrot Thepphalip (ed.). Bangkok: Wacharin Press.

Phirayu Diprasoet, comp. 2007. *Jatukham-Ramathep khwamjing lae khwamlap thi mai mi khrai ru* [*The Jatukham-Ramathep: Truths and unknown secrets*]. Bangkok: Ban Phra-athit Publishing.

Phromkhunnaphon, Phra. 2007. *Khati Jatukham-Ramathep* [*The Jatukham-Ramathep Cult*]. Bangkok: Wanlada Press.

Phut Buranasomphop. 1981. *13 pi kap burut lek haeng esia* [*13 Years with the Iron Man of Asia*]. Bangkok: Praphansan.

Phuttharat. 2007. *Jatukham-Ramathep thep ong mai mueang Nakhon si thammarat* [*Jatukham-Ramathep: Nakhon Si Thammarat's new deity*]. Bangkok: Si-etyukhechan [C-Education Public Company].

Pinyo Srichumlong. 1994. *Khun phrai* [*Khun Phrai*]. 2nd edn. Bangkok: Bang Luang.

Piriya Krairiksh. 1980. *Art in Peninsular Thailand Prior to the Fourteenth Century AD*. Bangkok: Fine Arts Department.

Piriya Krairiksh. 2012. *The Roots of Thai Art*. Narisa Chakrabongse (trans.). Bangkok: River Books.

Pisit Charoenwongsa. 2013. 'Ninth century seaborne trade in peninsular Thailand', in John N. Miskic and Goh Geok Yian (eds), *Ancient Harbours in Southeast Asia: The archaeology of early harbours and evidence of inter-regional trade*, pp. 149–54. Bangkok: SEAMEO SPAFA.

Porphant Ouyyanont. 2017. *A Regional Economic History of Thailand*. Singapore: Chulalongkorn Press and ISEAS Yusof Ishak Institute.

Powers, John. 2009. *A Bull of a Man: Images of masculinity, sex, and the body in Indian Buddhism*. Cambridge, MA: Harvard University Press. doi.org/10.4159/9780674054431.

Pramuan Manirote. 1994. 'Jon phatthalung korani tamnan jon haeng tambon dawn sai [Phatthalung outlaws: Outlaw legends of Dawnsai sub-district]', *Thaksin Khadi* 4(1)(June–September): 54–105.

Pramuan Manirote. 2017. 'Nai wara 100 pi khong rao lao len: "Jon phatthalung" nai rueang lao khong lum thalesap [100 years of our storytellings: The "Phatthalung outlaws" in tales of the lakes basin]', in Walailak University, *Khatthakam atchyakam lae phawa nok kotmai nai phak tai khong thai Ekkasan prakop prachum wichakan radap chat khrueakhai prawattisat manutwitthaya lae sangkhom witthaya phak tai khrang thi 3* [*Murder, Crime, and Lawlessness in Southern Thailand. Proceedings: Third National Academic Conference, History, Humanities, and Social Sciences Network*], pp. 105–18. Nakhon Si Thammarat: Walailak University.

Praphon Rueangnarong. 1983. 'Khui kap naiphon tamruat tri khunphantarak ratchdet [In conversation with Police Major General Khunphantarak Ratchadet]', *Sinlapa Watthanatham* [*Art & Culture*] 5(2)(December): 14–18.

Prayut Sitthiphan, comp. 1976. *Phramahakasat kap prawatisat tamruat sayam* [*Kings and History of the Police*]. Rungrot Thepphalip (ed.). Bangkok: Wacharin Press.

Preecha Noonsuk. 1982. *Lakthan thang borankhadi nai phak tai khong prathetthai thi kieokap anachak siwichai* [*Archaeological Evidence from Southern Thailand about the Kingdom of Srivijaya*]. Nakhon Si Thammarat: Southern Cultural Centre, Nakhon Si Thammarat Teachers College.

Preedee Hongsaton. 2015. Wela wang: Technologies, markets, and morals in Thai leisure culture, 1830s – 1932. PhD dissertation, The Australian National University, Canberra.

Quinn, George. 1975. 'The Javanese science of burglary', *Review of Indonesian and Malayan Affairs* 9(1): 33–54.

Ran Niranam [Samphan Kongsamut]. 2007. *Jom witthaya yut phutthakkhom khao or saolin haeng mueang phatthalung* [*The Khao Or Masters of the Science of Struggle and Buddhist Incantations: The Shaolin of Phatthalung*]. Bangkok: Wasi Khri-echan.

Ratchakawi, Phra lae khana. 2000. *Prawat wat ratchathiwatwihan* [*History of Wat Ratchathiwatwihan*]. Bangkok: Wat Ratchathiwatwihan.

Reynolds, Craig J. 1994. *Thai Radical Discourse: The real face of Thai feudalism today*. Reprint. Ithaca, NY: Southeast Asia Program, Cornell University.

Reynolds, Craig J. 1997. 'Review of Justin Corfield (ed.), "Rama III and the Siamese expedition to Kedah in 1939: The dispatches of Luang Udomsombat"', *Asian Studies Review* 21(2–3): 265–7.

Reynolds, Craig J. 2005. 'Power', in Donald S. Lopez (ed.), *Critical Terms for the Study of Buddhism*, pp. 211–28. Chicago: University of Chicago Press.

Reynolds, Craig J. 2009. 'Review of Southern Thai Encyclopedia', *New Mandala*, 8 July. Available from: www.newmandala.org/book-review/review-of-southern-thai-encyclopedia/.

Reynolds, Craig J. 2010. 'Review of Sgt. Phian', *New Mandala*, 20 August. Available from: www.newmandala.org/book-review/review-of-sgt-phian/.

Reynolds, Craig J. 2011. 'Rural male leadership, religion and the environment in Thailand's mid-south, 1920s–1960s', *Journal of Southeast Asian Studies* 42(1) (February): 39–57. doi.org/10.1017/S0022463410000536.

Reynolds, Craig J. 2013. 'Chatthip Nartsupha, his critics, and more criticism', in Pasuk Phongpaichit and Chris Baker (eds), *Essays on Thailand's Economy and Society for Professor Chatthip Nartsupha at 72*, pp. 1–22. Bangkok: Sangsan Press.

Reynolds, Craig J. 2014. 'Homosociality in modern Thai political culture', *Journal of Southeast Asian Studies* 45(2): 258–77.

Reynolds, Craig J. 2015. 'Applied sciences for hedging risk and anticipating outcomes in police work', *Thammasat Journal of History* 2(1)(June): 13–51.

Reynolds, Craig J. 2016. 'Magic and Buddhism', in John Powers (ed.), *The Buddhist World*, pp. 338–50. London: Routledge.

Reynolds, Craig J. 2017. 'A deity conjured from the mid-south's ancient heritage', in Wannasarn Noonsuk (ed.), *Isthmus: Essays on history of peninsular Siam and maritime Southeast Asia in memory of Dr Preecha Noonsuk*, pp. 125–48. Nakhon Si Thammarat: Cultural Council of Nakhon Si Thammarat Province.

Reynolds, Craig J. and Hong Lysa. 1983. 'Marxism in Thai historical studies', *Journal of Asian Studies* 43(1)(November): 77–104. doi.org/10.2307/2054618.

Reynolds, E. Bruce. 2004. *Thailand's Secret War: OSS, SOE and the Free Thai underground during World War II*. Cambridge: Cambridge University Press. doi.org/10.1017/CBO9780511497360.

Rozenberg, Guillaume. 2015. *The Immortals: Faces of the incredible in Buddhist Burma*. Ward Keeler (trans.). Honolulu: University of Hawai`i Press. doi.org/10.21313/hawaii/9780824840952.001.0001.

Ruth, Richard. 2012. 'Dressed for war', in Julius Batista (ed.), *The Spirit of Things: Materiality and religious diversity in Southeast Asia*, pp. 129–46. Ithaca, NY: Southeast Asia Program, Cornell University.

Saddhatissa, Hammawala. 1991. 'The significance of *paritta* and its application in the Theravada tradition', in David J. Kalupahana (ed.), *Buddhist Thought and Ritual*, pp. 125–38. New York: Paragon House.

Saichol Satyanurak. 2013. *Phraya Anumanratchathon prat samanchon phu niramit khwampen thai* [*Phaya Anuman Rajadhon: The commoner-philosopher and creator of 'Thainess'*]. Bangkok: Matichon.

Saichol Satyanurak. 2014. *10 panyachon sayam* [*Ten Siamese Intellectuals*]. Bangkok: Openbooks.

Saksit Sitthinan. n.d. *Tamra phrommachat chabap phrommalikhit chiwitkhun* [*The Phrommachat Manual: Brahma's instructions for the good life*]. Bangkok: Liang Siang Press.

Samphan Kongsamut. 1996. *Rayo kaji pho lo to to khun phantharakratchadet dap daeng* [*'Little Raja': Police Major General Khun Phantharakratchadet and the red sword*]. Bangkok: Thammachat Press.

Samphan Kongsamut. 2007. *Pho lo to khun phantharakratchadet: Sing moe prap sip thit* [*Police Major General Khun Phantarakratchadet: Lion lawman of the ten directions*]. Bangkok: Wasi Khri-echan.

Sangop Songmueang. 1994. '*Sut narai* [The Narai strategy]', *Warasan thaksin khadi* 4(1)(June–September): 30–9.

Sanphet Thammathikun. 1995. *Tampharaling siwichai anajak thi thuk lum* [*Tambralinga-Siwichai: The forgotten kingdom*]. Bangkok: Matichon.

Sathaban Thai Khadi Sueksa. 2011. *Withi satsatra pritsana sattha lae akhom haeng awut thai* [*The Evolution of Bladed Weapons: Intricate complexities of the magic and beliefs associated with Thai weapons*]. Bangkok: Thai Research Institute, Thammasat University.

Sathian Koset [Phya Anuman Rajadhon]. 1965. 'Satsana priapthiap [Comparative religion]', in Khropkrua Nang Samutmanirat, *Anuson nang samutmanirat* [*In Memory of Nang Samutmanirat*], 9 December. Bangkok: Sutthisan Press.

Shweder, Richard A. 1977. 'Likeness and likelihood in everyday thought: Magical thinking in judgments about personality', *Current Anthropology* 18(4)(December): 637–58. doi.org/10.1086/201974.

Shweder, Richard A. 1984. 'Anthropology's romantic rebellion against the enlightenment, or there's more to thinking than reason and evidence', in Richard A. Shweder and Robert A. LeVine (eds), *Culture Theory: Essays on mind, self, and emotion*, pp. 27–66. Cambridge: Cambridge University Press.

Sitthiphon Siphong, Thawiphon Jankeo and Chuliphon Thawisi. 2017. 'Jon lak wua khwai atchayakam rue withi chaoban [Cattle rustling: Crime or a way of life for villagers]?', in Walailak University, *Khatthakam atchyakam lae phawa nok kotmai nai phak tai khong thai Ekkasan prakop prachum wichakan radap chat khrueakhai prawattisat manutwitthaya lae sangkhom witthaya phak tai khrang thi 3 [Murder, Crime, and Lawlessness in Southern Thailand: Proceedings, Third National Academic Conference, History, Humanities, and Social Sciences Network]*, pp. 125–32. Nakhon Si Thammarat: Walailak University.

Sitthithep Eaksittipong. 2012. *Kabot jin jon bon thanon phlapphlachai* [*A Rebellion of the Chinese Poor on Phlupphlaichai Road*]. Bangkok: Matichon.

Skilling, Peter. 1992. 'The *Raksa* literature of the *Sravakayana*', *Journal of the Pāli Text Society* 16(NS): 109–82.

Skilling, Peter. 1997. 'The advent of Theravada Buddhism to mainland Southeast Asia', *Journal of the International Association of Buddhist Studies* 20(1): 93–107.

Skilling, Peter, Jason A. Carbine, Claudio Cicuzza and Santi Pakdeekham, eds. 2012. *How Theravada is Theravada? Exploring Buddhist identities*. Chiang Mai: Silkworm Books.

Skinner, Quentin. 1999. 'Hobbes and the purely artificial person of the state', *Journal of Political Philosophy* 7(1). 1–29. doi.org/10.1111/1467-9760.00063.

Skinner, Quentin. 2007. 'Transcript of Quentin Skinner on Hobbes on the state', *Philosophy Bites*, [Podcast], 21 October. Available from: nigelwarburton. typepad.com/philosophy_bites/2007/10/transcript-of-q.html.

Skinner, Quentin. 2016. Hobbes's Leviathan frontispiece: Some new observations, Address to The Warburg Institute, 14 June, London. Available from: www.youtube.com/watch?v=FlPf7IvOlx0.

Sombat Chantornvong. 2000. 'Local godfathers in Thai politics', in Ruth McVey (ed.), *Money and Power in Provincial Thailand*, pp. 53–73. Copenhagen and Singapore: Nordic Institute of Asian Studies and Institute of Southeast Asian Studies.

Sombat Sawangkhawat. 2011. *Yon tamnan wetwong muai thai jak adit thoeng patjuban* [*Looking into the History of the Thai Boxing World from Past to Present*]. Bangkok: Kaoraek Press.

Somsak Jeemteerasakul. 2001. *Prawattisat thi phueng sang ruam botkhwam kiao kap korani 14 tula lae 6* [*History Invented Just Yesterday: Collected articles, on 14 and 6 October*]. Bangkok: Samnakphim hok tula ramluk.

Stengs, Irene. 1998. 'Collectible amulets: The triple fetishes of modern Thai men', *Etnofoor* 12(1): 55–76.

Strate, Shane. 2015. *The Lost Territories: Thailand's history of national humiliation*. Honolulu: University of Hawai`i Press. doi.org/10.21313/hawaii/9780824838911.001.0001.

Streckfuss, David. 2010. 'The intricacies of lese-majesty: A comparative study of imperial Germany and modern Thailand', in Søren Ivarsson and Lotte Isager (eds), *Saying the Unsayable: Monarchy and democracy in Thailand*, pp. 105–44. Copenhagen: NIAS Press.

Streckfuss, David. 2011. *Truth on Trial in Thailand: Defamation, treason, and lèse-majesté*. Abingdon, UK: Routledge. doi.org/10.4324/9780203847541.

Sujit Wongthes. 1987. *Jek pon lao* [*Chinese Mixed with Lao*]. Bangkok: Samnakphim Sinlapa Watthanakham.

Sujit Wongthes. 2000. *Siwichai nai sayam* [*Srivijaya in Siam*]. Bangkok: Matichon.

Suthiwong Phongphaibun. 1999. 'Kloe [Friends]', in *Saranukrom watthanatham thai phak tai* [*Encyclopaedia of Southern Thai Culture*], Vol. 1, p. 468. Bangkok: Thanakhan Thai Phanit Munnithi Saranukrom Watthanatham Thai.

Suthiwong Phongphaibun. 1999. '*Krit* [*Kris*]', in *Saranukrom watthanatham thai phak tai* [*Encyclopaedia of Southern Thai Culture*], Vol. 8, pp. 112–39. Bangkok: Thanakhan Thai Phanit Munnithi Saranukrom Watthanatham Thai.

Suthiwong Phongphaibun. 2008. 'Afterword', in Michael J. Montesano and Patrick Jory (eds), *Thai South and Malay North: Ethnic interactions on a plural peninsula*. Singapore: NUS Press.

Suwan Suwannawecho. 1996. *Prawattisat lae wiwatthanakan khong tamruat thai* [*History and Evolution of the Thai Police Force*]. Bangkok: Police Publishing.

Suwit Khanthawit. 2011. *Heng phraiwan sut yot paramajan saiyasat kharawat ha paendin mueang sayam* [*Heng Praiwan: The supreme saiyasat lay master through five Siamese reigns*]. Nonthaburi: Thana Press.

Suwit Maprasong. 2017. 'Yasang sang son sang tai jarit kanlongthan khong thongthin nai chumchon choeng hao banthat phatthalung trang kon pho so 2500 [Poison to admonish and to cause death: Traditional punishment in the local Mt Banthat community of Phatthalung and Trang before 1957]', in Walailak University, *Khatthakam atchyakam lae phawa nok kotmai nai phak tai khong thai Ekkasan prakop prachum witchakun radap chat khrueakhai prawattisat manutwitthaya lae sangkhom witthaya phak tai khrang thi 3* [*Murder, Crime, and Lawlessness in Southern Thailand: Proceedings, Third National Academic Conference, History, Humanities, and Social Sciences Network*], pp. 140–51. Nakhon Si Thammarat: Walailak University.

Svendsen, Lars. 2008. *A Philosophy of Fear*. London: Reaktion Books.

Tambiah, Stanley Jeyaraja. 1970. *Buddhism and the Spirit Cults of Northeast Thailand*. Cambridge: Cambridge University Press.

Teo Kok Seong. 2008. 'Chinese–Malay–Thai interactions and the making of Kelantan Peranakan Chinese ethnicity', in Michael J. Montesano and Patrick Jory (eds), *Thai South and Malay North: Ethnic interactions on a plural peninsula*, pp. 214–30. Singapore: NUS Press.

Terwiel, Barend Jan. 2012. *Monks and Magic: Revisiting a classic study of religious ceremonies in Thailand*. 4th rev. edn. Copenhagen: NIAS Press.

Terzani, Tiziano. 1998. *A Fortune-Teller Told Me: Earthbound travels in the Far East*. London: Flamingo.

Textor, Robert B. 1973. *Roster of the Gods*. New Haven, CT: Human Relations Area Files.

Thammanit Chamnan. 2010. *Tamnan suea plon: khun jon lmueang tai* [*Stories of 'Tiger' Raiders: Bandits of the south*]. Bangkok: Thai Khwalitibuk.

Thammathat Phanit. 2000 [1960]. *Prawattisat thai samai siwichai* [*Thai History: The Srivijaya period*]. Reprint. Bangkok: Arun Witthaya.

Thatchai Yotphichai, ed. 2013. *Phraprawat somdet phra ariyawongsakhatayan (sa pussathewo) somdet phrasangkharat somdet phrasangkharat phra-ong thi 9 haeng krung rattanakosin watratchapraditsathimahasimaram* [*Biography of Somdet Phra Ariyasawongsakhatayan (Sa Pussathewo), the Ninth Supreme Patriarch of the Bangkok Period, of Wat Ratchapradit*]. Bangkok: Wat Ratchapradit.

Thep Sarikkhabut. 1978. *Tamra phrommachat chabap rat prajamban du duai ton eng* [*The Phrommachat Manual: People's edition for household use and self-instruction*]. Bangkok: Luk So Thammaphakdi Press.

Thongchai Winichakul. 1995. 'The changing landscape of the past: New histories in Thailand since 1973', *Journal of Southeast Asian Studies* 26(1)(March): 99–120. doi.org/10.1017/S0022463400010511.

Thongchai Winichakul. 2001. 'Prawattisat thai baep rachachatniyom [Royal nationalist Thai history]', *Sinlapa Watthanatham* [*Art & Culture*] 23(1) (November): 56–65.

Thongchai Winichakul. 2008. 'Nationalism and the radical intelligentsia in Thailand', *Third World Quarterly* 29(3): 575–91. doi.org/10.1080/0143659 0801931520.

Thongchai Winichakul. 2011. 'Siam's colonial conditions and the birth of Thai history', in Volker Grabowsky (ed.), *Southeast Asian Historiography: Unravelling the myths*, pp. 21–43. Bangkok: River Books.

Thongchai Winichakul. 2016. *Chomna rachachatniyom wa duai prawattisat thai* [*The Real Face of Royal Nationalism as it Affects Thai History*]. Nonburi: Fa Diawkan.

Thotsaphon Jangphanitchakun. 2012. *Leklai lae that kai sit* [*Fluid Iron and Magical Matter*]. Bangkok: Khomma Publishing.

Turton, Andrew. 1991. 'Invulnerability and local knowledge', in Manas Chitakasem and Andrew Turton (eds), *Thai Constructions of Knowledge*, pp. 155–82. London: School of Oriental and African Studies, University of London.

Uthai Sinthusan. 1979. *Saranukrom thai* [*Thai Encyclopaedia*]. Bangkok: Bamrungnukunlakit Press.

Vajirananavarorasa, Prince. 1973. *The Entrance to the Vinaya Vinayamukha. Volume 2*. Bangkok: Mahamakut Rajavidhyalaya Press.

Van Vliet, Jeremias. 2005. *Van Vliet's Siam*. Chris Baker, Dhiravat na Pombejra, Alfon van der Kraan and David K. Wyatt (eds). Chiang Mai: Silkworm Books.

W. Jinpradit. 1996. *Jutmungmai khong chaichatri* [*Expectations of a Warrior*]. Bangkok: Ho Samutklang 09.

Wade, Geoff. 2013. 'The Patani region in Chinese texts of the 6th to the 19th centuries', in Patrick Jory (ed.), *Ghosts of the Past in Southern Thailand: Essays on the history and historiography of Patani*, pp. 58–63. Singapore: NUS Press.

Walailak University. 2017. *Khatthakam atchyakam lae phawa nok kotmai nai phak tai khong thai Ekkasan prakop prachum wichakan radap chat khrueakhai prawattisat manutwitthaya lae sangkhom witthaya phak tai khrang thi 3* [*Murder, Crime, and Lawlessness in Southern Thailand. Proceedings: Third National Academic Conference, History, Humanities, and Social Sciences Network*]. Nakhon Si Thammarat: Walailak University.

Wales, H.G. Quaritch. 1983. *Divination in Thailand: The hopes and fears of a Southeast Asian people*. London: Curzon.

Walker, Dennis. 2013. 'The formation of the Islamo-Patanian nation: Ideological structuring by nationalist historians', in Patrick Jory (ed.), *Ghosts of the Past in Southern Thailand: Essays on the history and historiography of Patani*, pp. 185–227. Singapore: NUS Press. doi.org/10.2307/j.ctv1qv31q.15.

Wanlaya, comp. 1999. *Thaksin chinnawat ta du dao thao tit din* [*Thaksin Shinnawatra: Starry eyed and earth-bound*]. Bangkok: Matichon.

Wannasarn Noonsuk. 2013a. 'Kingdom on the beach ridge: A landscape archaeology of Tambralinga in peninsular Siam', *Asian Perspectives* 52(2): 268–99. doi.org/10.1353/asi.2013.0016.

Wannasarn Noonsuk. 2013b. 'The political landscape of the Tambralinga kingdom', *Tai Culture: Interdisciplinary Tai Studies Series* 23: 146–59.

Wannasarn Noonsuk. 2014. 'New evidence of early Brahmanical vestiges in Pattani Province', in Nicolas Revire and Stephen A. Murphy (eds), *Before Siam: Essays in art and archaeology*, pp. 174–85. Bangkok: River Books and the Siam Society.

Wassana Nanuam. 2009. *Lap luang phrang phak phitsadan* [*Secrets, Trickery, and Camouflage: Improbable phenomena*]. Bangkok: Post Books.

Weed, Albert. 1970. *Police and the Modernization Process: Thailand*. Princeton, NJ: Woodrow Wilson School of Public and International Affairs.

Wet Worawit [Chalong Jeyakhom]. n.d. *Khao or witthayalai saiwet haeng sayam* [*Khao Or: Siam's academy of Vedic knowledge*]. Bangkok: Rom Fa Sayam.

Whyte, B.R. 2010. *The Railway Atlas of Thailand, Laos and Cambodia*. Bangkok: White Lotus.

Wira Saengphet. 2001. *Phumpanya kanprappram khong pho lo to to khun phantharakratchadet* [*The Local Wisdom of Khun Phan for Maintaining Law and Order*]. Bangkok: Thailand Research Fund.

Wirayut Pisamli. 2014. *Krungthep yam ratri* [*Bangkok at Night*]. Bangkok: Matichon.

Wirayut Sisuwannakit. 2006. Kanphakphon yon jai baep tawantok khong chonchan nam sayam pho so 2445-2475 [Western-style leisure pursuits of the Siamese elite]. MA thesis, Chulalongkorn University, Bangkok.

Wisit Siphibun. 2008. *Phalang neramit* [*Laws of Attraction*]. 6th edn. Bangkok: Fisik Sentoe.

Wiwat Phanthawutikhanon. 2000. 'Review of Akhom Thongkham 2000', *Sarakhadi* (16): 189.

Wiwat Suthiwiphakorn, ed. 2007. *Lesap rao* [*Our Lakes*]. Songkhla: Songkhla Ratchaphat University and Prince of Songkla University.

Wolters, O.W. 1958. 'Tambralinga', *Bulletin of the School of Oriental and African Studies* 21(3): 587–607. doi.org/10.1017/S0041977X00060195.

Wolters, O.W. 2008. 'Restudying some Chinese writings on Sriwijaya', in Craig J. Reynolds (ed.), *Early Southeast Asia: Selected essays*. Ithaca, NY: Southeast Asia Program, Cornell University.

Wong Yee Tuan. 2008. 'Penang's big five families and southern Siam during the nineteenth century', in Michael J. Montesano and Patrick Jory (eds), *Thai South and Malay North: Ethnic interactions on a plural peninsula*, pp. 201–13. Singapore: NUS Press.

Woodward, Hiram W. 2003. *Art and Architecture of Thailand from Prehistoric Times through the Thirteenth Century*. Leiden: Brill.

Woolley, G.C. 1947. 'The Malay *keris*: Its origin and development', *Journal of the Malayan Branch of the Royal Asiatic Society* 20(2): 60–103.

Worayut Phonprasoet. 2017. 'Nakleng phranakhon kap kandoenthang su phak tak: boribot chiwit lae kanlopni khong nakleng krungthep [Nakleng from the capital and their travels to the south: The context, lives and flight of Bangkok nakleng]', in Walailak University, *Khatthakam atchyakam lae phawa nok kotmai nai phak tai khong thai Ekkasan prakop prachum wichakan radap chat khrueakhai prawattisat manutwitthaya lae sangkhom witthaya phak tai khrang thi 3* [*Murder, Crime, and Lawlessness in Southern Thailand: Proceedings, Third National Academic Conference, History, Humanities, and Social Sciences Network*], pp. 74–87. Nakhon Si Thammarat: Walailak University.

Wright, Michael. 2007a. 'Farang mong thai [A Farang observes the Thai]', *Matichon Sutsapda* 1394(4–10 May): 67.

Wright, Michael. 2007b. 'Farang mong thai [A Farang observes the Thai]', *Matichon Sutsapda* 1399(8–14 June): 30.

Wright, Michael. 2007c. 'Farang mong thai [A Farang observes the Thai]', *Matichon Sutsapda* 1407(3–9 August): 67.

Wyatt, David K. 1984. *Thailand: A short history.* New Haven, CT: Yale University Press.